Transformative Dimensions of Adult Learning

Jack Mezirow

✌ Transformative
Dimensions of Adult Learning

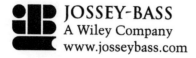
JOSSEY-BASS
A Wiley Company
www.josseybass.com

Published by

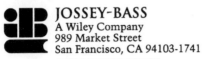

JOSSEY-BASS
A Wiley Company
989 Market Street
San Francisco, CA 94103-1741

www.josseybass.com

Jossey-Bass books and products are available through most bookstores. To contact Jossey-Bass directly, call (888) 378-2537, fax to (800) 605-2665, or visit our website at www.josseybass.com.

Substantial discounts on bulk quantities of Jossey-Bass books are available to corporations, professional associations, and other organizations. For details and discount information, contact the special sales department at Jossey-Bass.

We at Jossey-Bass strive to use the most environmentally sensitive paper stocks available to us. Our publications are printed on acid-free recycled stock whenever possible, and our paper always meets or exceeds minimum GPO and EPA requirements.

JACKET DESIGN BY WILLI BAUM
JACKET ART BASED ON ART BY QUINCY

Library of Congress Cataloging-in-Publication Data
Mezirow, Jack, date.
    Transformative dimensions of adult learning / Jack Mezirow.
       p.   cm. — (The Jossey-Bass higher and adult education series)
    Includes bibliographical references (p.   ) and index.
    ISBN 1-55542-339-6
    1. Adult learning.   2. Transfer of training.   3. Adult education.
  I. Title. II. Series.
LC5225.L42M53   1991
374—dc20   90-24155

FIRST EDITION
HB Printing   10 9

The Jossey-Bass
Higher and Adult Education Series

Consulting Editor
Adult and Continuing Education

Alan B. Knox
University of Wisconsin, Madison

35 70 ⊭

108949

✍ Contents

ᥬᥩ Preface

A disturbing fault line separates theories of adult learning from the practice of those who try to help adults learn. Psychologists interested in adult learning often find themselves trapped within the framework of particular theories and paradigms, such as the behaviorist or psychoanalytic; they seldom communicate with each other, let alone with educators. Philosophers, linguists, sociologists, and political scientists also have legitimate interests in adult learning, but each group has a different frame of reference and a different vocabulary for interpreting the phenomenon. Few efforts have been made to develop a synthesis of the different theories that educators of adults can use.

As a result, adult educators—instructors, counselors, trainers, tutors, social workers, and others—have had to fly by the seat of their pants. Those unfamiliar with the literature of adult education tend to use the approaches that they themselves have experienced in universities or public schools—practices that are often dysfunctional with adults and are incompatible with the prevailing consensus among writers in the field of adult education. These writers share a professional orientation, a "theory-in-practice," based upon common experience. However, that experience has often been predicated upon behaviorist assumptions simply because the behaviorist approach has so many features amenable to bureaucratic control, such as accountability, measurability, and focus on anticipated behavioral outcomes. Other adult educators may attempt to embrace the appealing but fuzzy and sometimes contradictory assumptions of humanist psychology. Neither of these sets of assumptions provides a sound basis that can help adult educators work toward the broad social and political goals envisioned by many of the leaders in the field.

A missing dimension in these psychological theories is *meaning*—how it is construed, validated, and reformulated—and the social conditions that influence the ways in which adults make meaning of their experience. There is need for a learning theory that can explain how adult learners make sense or meaning of their experiences, the nature of the structures that influence the way they construe experience, the dynamics involved in modifying meanings, and the way the structures of meaning themselves undergo changes when learners find them to be dysfunctional. These understandings must be explained in the context of adult development and social goals. A learning theory centered on meaning, addressed to educators of adults, could provide a firm foundation for a philosophy of adult education from which appropriate practices of goal setting, needs assessment, program development, instruction, and research could be derived. *Transformative Dimensions of Adult Learning* attempts to provide such a theory and explain its relevance to adult education.

The Bases of Transformation Theory

George Kelly (1963, pp. 10–12) observed that since the same event may be construed simultaneously by people from various disciplines and we have no universal system of constructs, each of our constructs or theories has its own limited "range of convenience." What is reasonably true within a limited range of experience is not necessarily as true outside it. Scholars in different disciplines view the same concepts from different perspectives and employ different vocabularies in articulating them. Transformation theory, as presented here, is constrained not only by my personal limitations but also by the fact that it has been formulated by an adult educator for other adult educators.

Transformation theory seeks to elucidate universal conditions and rules that are implicit in linguistic competence or human development. Specifically, it seeks to explain the way adult learning is structured and to determine by what processes the frames of reference through which we view and interpret our experience (meaning perspectives) are changed or transformed. In this reconstructive approach it follows Chomsky, Piaget, Kohlberg, and most other psychologists who theorize about adult development; sociologists such as Habermas, who theorizes about the social and linguistic conditions required for communicative action; and philosophers such as Bateson and Cell, who directly address learning theory.

My approach to transformation theory, as elaborated in this book, has as its current context the insurgence of constructivism, critical theory, and deconstructivism in social theory and in all of the social sciences, law, literature, and art. Transformation theory also grows out of the cognitive revolution in psychology and psychotherapy instigated by scores of studies that have found that it is not so much what happens to people but how they interpret and explain what happens to them that determines their actions, their hopes, their contentment and emotional well-being, and their performance.

Philip Candy (1989, p. 98) has identified the following assumptions of constructivist thought:

- People participate in the construction of reality.
- Construction occurs within a context that influences people.
- Construction is a constant activity that focuses on change and novelty rather than fixed conditions.
- Commonly accepted categories or understandings are socially constructed, not derived from observation.
- Given forms of understanding depend on the vicissitudes of social processes, not on the empirical validity of the perspective.
- Forms of negotiated understanding are integrally connected with other human activities.

- The "subjects" of research should be considered as "knowing" beings.
- Locus of control resides within the subjects themselves, and complex behavior is constructed purposefully.
- Human beings can attend to complex communications and organize complexity rapidly.
- Human interactions are based on intricate social roles, the rules governing which are often implicit.

   Specific constructivist assumptions underlying transformation theory include a conviction that meaning exists within ourselves rather than in external forms such as books and that the personal meanings that we attribute to our experience are acquired and validated through human interaction and communication. Our actions toward things are based on the meanings that the things have for us. These meanings are handled in and modified through an interpretive process that we use in dealing with the things we encounter. As far as any particular individual is concerned, the nature of a thing or event consists of the meaning that that individual gives to it. This does not negate the existence of a world external to us but only asserts that what we make of that world is entirely a function of our past personal experiences. Conception determines perception, and we can know reality only by acting on it. Inasmuch as this viewpoint presupposes that meaning is interpretation, and since information, ideas, and contexts change, our present interpretations of reality are always subject to revision or replacement.
   Transformation theory does not derive from a systematic extension of an existing intellectual theory or tradition such as behaviorism, neo-Marxism, positivism, or psychological humanism. Although I have taken ideas from the work of Jurgen Habermas, for example, I do not write from the perspective of the Frankfurt School with which he is associated, nor have I attempted to interpret systematically what Habermas or any other single theorist has to say about adult learning. I have adopted some of Habermas's ideas, such as his distinction be-

tween instrumental and communicative learning and his description of the ideal conditions for rational discourse, but I have freely changed others; for example, I have extended the process of emancipatory learning to include the instrumental learning domain (see Chapter Three).

This book incorporates ideas from a wide range of writers in the fields of philosophy, psychology (developmental, cognitive, counseling, and psychoanalytic), sociology, neurobiology, linguistics, religion, and education, as well as, of course, presenting my own thoughts about the dynamics of making meaning, reflection, and transformative learning. I would like the ideas presented here to be understood in relationship to one another and to our common experience rather than assessed for their fidelity to a particular intellectual tradition, theory, or discipline.

Overview of the Contents

Chapter One presents an overview of an emerging transformation theory of adult learning, compares it with other theories of adult learning, and describes the dynamics of the processes (both prelinguistic and linguistic) through which we make meaning of our experience. Chapter Two examines the way our meaning perspectives or habits of expectation serve as perceptual and cognitive codes to structure the way we perceive, think, feel, and act on our experience.

The nature of intentional learning (as opposed to tacit or unintentional learning, which is covered in Chapter One) is explained in Chapter Three. This chapter includes a brief summary of Habermas's theory of communicative action, which provides the social theoretical context for transformation theory. The chapter also differentiates between learning to control and manipulate the environment (instrumental learning), learning to understand the meaning of what is being communicated (communicative learning), and learning to understand oneself and one's perspectives (emancipatory or reflective learning).

Chapter Four explains the concept of reflection and shows how reflection can change or transform both meaning schemes (specific attitudes and beliefs) and meaning perspectives (sets of meaning schemes). Chapter Five describes several kinds of distortions in meaning perspectives (including epistemic, sociolinguistic, and psychological distortions) that can limit our ability to make meaning of our experiences.

Chapter Six describes the role of perspective transformation in adult development, summarizes several authors' overviews of perspective transformation and its dynamics, and cites studies of perspective transformation that were done in a variety of settings and focus on both individuals and groups. Chapter Seven concludes the book by discussing philosophical, ethical, social, and methodological issues in adult education that are raised by transformation theory and suggesting possible ways to resolve these issues.

Background and Influences

This book is the result of my continuing interest in perspective transformation over the past decade. Four events have particularly influenced this long-standing involvement. The first was a crisis or "disorienting dilemma" that I encountered in my own career.

I spent much of my earlier professional life as an adult educator engaged in fostering democratic social action through community development and adult literacy programs in the United States and abroad. Having had the good fortune to serve as a consultant in many Third World countries, to train professionals in community development, and to write extensively on this topic, I invested much of my sense of identity in my self-image as a social action educator.

In the early 1970s, however, I encountered the writings of Paulo Freire and Ivan Illich, which unequivocally challenged the validity of my relatively unsophisticated premises concerning adult education for social action and consequently the validity of the roles I had played in programs designed to foster this kind of learning. The critical dimension missing from my work had been my lack of awareness both of the centrality of conscientization in the learning process (Freire defines *conscientization* as the process by which adults "achieve a deepening awareness of both the sociocultural reality which shapes their lives and . . . their capacity to transform that reality through action upon it" [1970b, p. 27]) and of the importance of entrenched power in the community development process I had attempted to foster. This realization precipitated an absorbing process of transformative learning — learning that changed my meaning perspectives or basic ways of looking at the world — that lasted for several years.

About the same time, Edee, my wife, decided to return to college to complete her undergraduate education after several years away from formal schooling. Interested as I was in attempting to understand both her and adult learning, I found her dramatically transformative experience, which led to a new career and life-style, both fascinating and enlightening. Her experience influenced my decision to undertake an ambitious national study of women returning to college and the work force (Mezirow, 1975; described briefly in Chapter Six of this book), out of which evolved my earliest concept of perspective transformation.

The final valuable and formative influence was an opportunity to spend part of a sabbatical leave working with psychiatrist Roger Gould as he was attempting to develop ways to adapt some of the approaches of psychotherapy to an educational format, using workbooks that he prepared, in a workshop setting. Studying the way that adult learners who were engaged in difficult life transitions could help themselves overcome childhood learning impediments through a transformative learning experience added a psychological dimension to my theorizing. This seemed a natural extension of Freire's process of conscientization, which involves learning about social assumptions, as well as a corroboration of the finding, from our study of women returning to college, that learning difficulties grow out of distorted concepts about formation and use of knowledge.

In short, this book is both a vehicle and an artifact of a richly rewarding long-term learning experience. By publishing it I hope to evoke critical discourse that will either validate my unconventional ideas or help me determine what changes in them are necessary. I have attempted to synthesize my thoughts, building upon previous writings, and to situate my ideas within the literature produced by others who have had something to say about this topic. My goal is to work with others to formulate a theory of adult learning that will be useful to professionals engaged in helping adults learn.

Acknowledgments

I want to thank Jerold Apps, David Deshler, and John Dirkx for their perceptive, critical, and helpful reviews of the manuscript; M. Carolyn Clark, Susan Collard, Mechthild Hart, Michael Law, and Arthur Wilson for their constructive criticism of my earlier writings; and others who have sent me materials and references relevant to my interests. The encouragement of Lynn Luckow of Jossey-Bass was an important influence on my decision to write a book on adult learning theory. Lisa Yount was an outstanding copyeditor. She challenged concepts, redrafted obscure passages, reordered content, and helped eliminate unnecessary jargon. Finally, I am deeply indebted to Edee Mezirow. Without her transformative experience, insight, tolerance, humor, and empathic support, this book could not have been written.

New York   Jack Mezirow
February 1991

ᗈ The Author

Jack Mezirow is chairman of the Department of
Higher and Adult Education and professor of Adult and Continuing Education at Teachers College, Columbia University.
He received his B.A. (1945) and M.A. (1946) degrees from
University of Minnesota in social sciences and education, respectively, and his Ed.D. degree (1955) from University of California, Los Angeles, in adult education. He is editor of a companion
volume, *Fostering Critical Reflection in Adulthood: A Guide to Transformative and Emancipatory Learning* (1990) and coauthor of *Last
Gamble on Education* (1975, with G. G. Darkenwald and A. B.
Knox), which received the 1980 Imogene Okes Award for Outstanding Research in Adult Education.

Transformative
Dimensions of Adult Learning

1

✍ Making Meaning: The Dynamics of Learning

As adult learners, we are caught in our own histories. However good we are at making sense of our experiences, we all have to start with what we have been given and operate within horizons set by ways of seeing and understanding that we have acquired through prior learning. This formative learning occurs in childhood both through socialization (informal or tacit learning of norms from parents, friends, and mentors that allows us to fit into society) and through our schooling. Although we are encouraged to become increasingly self-directed in our learning as we grow older, the learning provided by our particular culture and by the idiosyncratic requirements of parents or parent surrogates is the learning that is rewarded. Approved ways of seeing and understanding, shaped by our language, culture, and personal experience, collaborate to set limits to our future learning.

The Cultural Context of Learning

Bowers (1984, pp. 35–44) summarizes findings from the sociology of knowledge regarding socialization with the following five propositions:

Proposition I: Social reality is shared, sustained, and continuously negotiated through communication.

1

Proposition II: Through socialization the individual's subjective self is built up in a biographically unique way. It serves as a set of interpretational rules for making sense of everyday life.

Proposition III: Much of the social world of everyday life is learned and experienced by the individual as the natural, even inevitable order of reality. This attitude toward the everyday world is taken for granted.

Proposition IV: The individual's self-concept is constituted through interaction with significant others. The individual requires not only socially shared knowledge but an understanding of who he or she is in relation to that knowledge.

Proposition V: Human consciousness is characterized by intentionality: it is the intentionality of consciousness that assures that socialization is not deterministic.

Socialization involves inherent inequality. Parents and mentors, who have an identity investment in their own interpretations and values, define a child's reality, including such fundamentals as ways of recognizing social threat, relating to authority, reacting to rejection and failure, being competitive, role playing, and using time responsibly.

As Bowers noted, socialization involves internalizing the definitions, assumptions, and arbitrary typifications taken for granted and communicated by significant others. The image of an autonomous individual free from oppression thus is illusory, although the individual's unique social biography, perspectives, and awareness of different interpretive schemes assure that he or she is never entirely the victim of determinism. In view of the nature of socialization, the familiar and simplistic dichotomy between oppression and freedom loses its credibility. We can never be totally free from our past. Bowers redefines autonomy as "a process of making explicit the message system" that enables us to reformulate a constraining frame of reference (p. 39).

Contradictions generated by rapid, dramatic change and a diversity of beliefs, values, and social practices are a hallmark of modern society. Adults in such a society face an urgent need to keep from being overwhelmed by change. Formerly accepted sources of authority and the early learning provided by socialization and schooling no longer suffice for them. Rather than merely adapting to changing circumstances by more diligently applying old ways of knowing, they discover a need to acquire new perspectives in order to gain a more complete understanding of changing events and a higher degree of control over their lives. The formative learning of childhood becomes transformative learning in adulthood. Unfortunately, the significance of transformative adult learning and the nature of its dynamics have not as yet been fully recognized by the learning theorists and practitioners charged with facilitating adult learning.

Bowers posits a transitional phase in the process of modernization in which the breakdown of traditional forms of authority in a culture makes possible the negotiation of new meanings and the creation of new forms of authority through a more democratic and educative process. It is in these "liminal spaces" in thought and social practice, where the individual is between established patterns of thought and behavior, that new definitions and new concepts of authority can be negotiated. The existence of this uncertain, transitional state gives discourse a powerful new role: those who can name "what is" in new ways and can convince others of their naming acquire power.

In order to be free we must be able to "name" our reality, to know it divorced from what has been taken for granted, to speak with our own voice. Thus it becomes crucial that the individual learn to negotiate meanings, purposes, and values critically, reflectively, and rationally instead of passively accepting the social realities defined by others. Transformation theory provides a description of the dynamics of the way adults learn to do this.

Culture can encourage or discourage transformative thought. Modernization creates an imperative need for the transformations in learning that become possible as the result of developmental changes in adults' ability to become more critically reflective of presuppositions. (This theme will be elaborated in Chapter Three.) Transformation theory contributes a needed and emancipatory dimension to socialization theory.

Overview of Transformation Theory

This book attempts to redress an apparent oversight in adult learning theory that has resulted from a failure to recognize the central roles played by an individual's acquired frame of reference, through which meaning is construed and all learning takes place, and by the transformation of these habits of expectation during the learning process. The following brief overview presents the central concepts involved in transformation theory. Each is elaborated later in this chapter and throughout the book.

The approach here differentiates between symbolic models or exemplars (Lady Liberty, a siren, a clock ticking, Camelot, Gary Cooper in *High Noon,* standing alone on a deserted street bravely awaiting his menacing fate), which we project imaginatively onto our sense impressions to construe meaning, and our habits of expectation, which frame and organize these symbols into systems. Sets of habitual expectation or "meaning perspectives" (created by ideologies, learning styles, neurotic self-deceptions) constitute codes that govern the activities of perceiving, comprehending, and remembering. The symbols that we project onto our sense perceptions are filtered through meaning perspectives. The resulting "loaded" perception is objectified through speech. Language is a system of ideal objects in the form of signs; it has no direct relationship to the objects and events of the external world. Meaning is an interpretation, and to make meaning is to construe or interpret experience — in other words, to give it coherence. Meaning is construed both prelinguistically, through cues and symbolic models, and through language. These two ways of construing meaning are interactive processes involving two dimensions of awareness, the presentational and the propositional.

The idea that uncritically assimilated habits of expectation or meaning perspectives serve as schemes and as perceptual and interpretive codes in the construal of meaning constitutes the central dynamic and fundamental postulate of a constructivist transformation theory of adult learning. These meaning schemes and meaning perspectives constitute our "boundary structures" for perceiving and comprehending new data. Experience strengthens our personal meaning system by refocusing or extending our expectations about how things are supposed to be. We allow our meaning system to diminish our awareness of how things really are in order to avoid anxiety, creating a zone of blocked attention and self-deception. Overcoming limited, distorted, and arbitrarily selective modes of perception and cognition through reflection on assumptions that formerly have been accepted uncritically is central to development in adulthood.

A crucial dimension of adult learning involves the process of justifying or validating communicated ideas and the presuppositions of prior learning. Uncritically assimilated presuppositions may distort our ways of knowing, involving epistemic assumptions; our ways of believing, involving social norms, cultural or language codes, and social ideologies; and our ways of feeling, involving repressed parental prohibitions from childhood that control adult feelings and behavior through anxiety. It is within this process of consensually determining the conditions under which an expressed idea is true or valid that problematic meaning schemes (specific knowledge, beliefs, value judgments, or feelings involved in making an interpretation) are confirmed or negated and meaning perspectives (rule systems governing perception and cognition) are significantly restructured.

The familiar hypothesis testing and deductive logic of the natural sciences often is asserted to be the analog of human problem solving. Transformation theory sees this logic as relevant to instrumental learning (learning to manipulate physical objects or other people) but less applicable to understanding the meaning of what is being communicated. In the realm of communication a different logic of problem solving pertains, one in which metaphoric analogy replaces hypotheses and each step dictates the next. Transformative learning involves reflective assessment of premises, a process predicated upon still another logic, one of movement through cognitive structures by identifying and judging presuppositions.

Meaning schemes, made up of specific knowledge, beliefs, value judgments, and feelings that constitute interpretations of experience, become more differentiated and integrated or transformed by reflection on the content or process of problem solving in progressively wider contexts. Habits of expectation or meaning schemes and perspectives are transformed through reflection on the assumptions that underlie problem solving. Reflection involves validity testing, which can be an integral element in taking thoughtful action or can involve a hiatus in the action process during which a retroactive critique of the content, process, or premises of problem solving takes place. Reflection on content or process may result in the elaboration, creation, or transformation of meaning schemes. Reflection on assumptions involves a critique of these premises that may result in the transformation of both meaning perspective and the experience being interpreted.

Reflective learning involves assessment or reassessment of assumptions. Reflective learning becomes transformative whenever assumptions or premises are found to be distorting, inauthentic, or otherwise invalid. Transformative learning results in new or transformed meaning schemes or, when reflection focuses on premises, transformed meaning perspectives. To the extent that adult education strives to foster reflective learning, its goal becomes one of either confirmation or transformation of ways of interpreting experience.

Transformation theory views memory as an inherent function of perception and cognition, an active process of recognizing again and reinterpreting a previously learned experience in a new context. The dialectic involved may result in the creation of new meaning schemes when old ones prove inadequate. Remembering depends upon how well the original experience was integrated into past learning and on how frequently the memory has been called upon. When an experience appears incompatible with the way meaning is structured or provokes anxiety, integration is less likely and recall probably will be distorted.

Remembering appears to involve recognizing an object or event that previously had meaning and either strengthened or transformed an existing meaning perspective or a specific meaning scheme or schemes. We remember symbolic models that are organized by our habits of expectation into frames with which we make interpretations of sense perceptions. We forget, not when associative bonds are attenuated or the brain's capacity for information storage is exceeded, but when the event is no longer recognizable, its context has changed, or our habits of expectation have been transformed. Rather than positing a decrement of learning or memory performance as an adult ages, therefore, transformation theory holds that age involves changes reflecting qualitatively different dimensions of context awareness, focus, goal awareness, critical reflectivity, and greater integration of the cognitive dimensions of learning.

Adult development is seen as an adult's progressively enhanced capacity to validate prior learning through reflective discourse and to act upon the resulting insights. Anything that moves the individual toward a more inclusive, differentiated, permeable (open to other points of view), and integrated meaning perspective, the validity of which has been established through rational discourse, aids an adult's development.

The ideal conditions for free, full participation in reflective discourse, as defined by Jurgen Habermas, are also the ideal conditions for adult learning. They imply a set of social and political goals grounded in the nature of human communication. Habermas's theory of communicative action (1987, 1984) provides the social theoretical context for the transformation theory of learning, and his writings are very helpful in understanding transformation theory.

Other Theories of Adult Learning

Transformation theory provides a perspective different from those of the currently predominant approaches to adult education, which emphasize either the functioning of stimulus-response associations or the encoding, storage, and retrieval of information. Because these theories have not been centrally concerned with the structure and process of construal, validity testing, and reorganization of meaning, they have limited usefulness as a foundation for professionals who wish to facilitate significant learning in adults. Some of these theories are classified by Hultsch and Pentz (1980) into what they see as three historical shifts in basic research in psychology on adult learning and memory. The following descriptions are based on their classification.

Associative Bond Theory. The associative approach was dominant until the late 1950s. According to this theory, learning involves the formation of stimulus-response bonds that define the contents of memory. Activity is the result of external stimulation. Changes in learning and memory are quantitative rather than qualitative. Increases in the number and repetition of stimulus-response associations result in retention. Problem solving and affective behavior can be reduced to simple phenomena governed by specific cause-effect relationships.

Remembering involves making previously acquired responses under appropriate stimulus conditions. Forgetting involves the weakening of associative bonds through interference or decay. The aged are more susceptible to interference than younger people and are likely to show an irreversible decrement of learning and memory.

Development consists of behavior change, and later behaviors can be predicted from earlier ones. Research focuses on the analysis of behavioral/situational elements and the discovery of cause-effect relationships.

Information Processing Theory. The information processing model of adult learning has been dominant since the early 1960s. This theory sees memory traces as located in three types of storage structures: sensory, short-term, and long-term stores. Material is transferred from one storage structure to another by such "control operations" as attention, rehearsal, and organization.

Sensory memory is described as visual or auditory copies of stimuli. These stored representations decay if not further processed. Attending to information in the sensory store transfers this information to the short-term memory store, in which information items are coded for features of sight and sound. The short-term store has limited capacity, and items in it often are displaced by other information and lost. Items can be kept in the short-term store for a longer time by rehearsal or transferred to the long-term store by processing through linguistic signs. The long-term memory store has unlimited capacity. Retrieval of an item from this store depends on the organization or elaboration of the material. Qualitative changes in memory are produced by processes that transfer material from one storage structure to another. Some of these processes are controlled by the individual.

Information processing theory holds that what we learn and recall is not a set of stimulus-response associations but an active totality that we organize through the various processing mechanisms. According to this theory, age differences in sensory and short-term storage capacity are minimal, but there are age-related decrements in the active processing involved in learning and memory. These decrements can be modified by manipulating such variables as the organization of learning materials and instructions.

Development is seen as structural change, both qualitative and quantitative. Later states cannot be predicted from previous states. Research focuses on specifying age and other factors that affect memory encoding, storage, and retrieval processes.

Contextual Theories. Recently, a "contextual" approach to learning and memory has emerged. This approach sees experience as events that have a meaning as a whole. The quality of events is a product of transactions between the organism and its context, or the totality of events that the organism has experienced. The essence of experience is seen as continuous activity and change. What is learned and remembered depends on the various contexts of the event — psychological, social, cultural, physical — and the context within which evidence of remembering and learning is requested.

In contextual theories, learning and memory are by-products of the transaction between individual and context. Understanding lies in the interfaces between psychological, linguistic, problem-solving, social, and cultural processes. Remembering is a reconstruction of past events. Its success depends on how well the materials have been articulated and integrated with past experience during the process of acquisition, which in turn depends upon the total set of experiences to which the event belongs. Memory also depends on events that follow acquisition. Events are continually constructed and reconstructed as an individual's context changes.

Memory is intimately related to perception and learning, which involve the integration of novel information with past experience. Past experience provides boundary conditions for integrating and differentiating information and for determining the meaning of an event. A schema is one formulation of such boundary conditions; it is an organized representation of an event that may serve as a prototype, norm, or context. The relation of new information to past experience allows the learner to go beyond the information given.

Remembering involves the recreation of previous events. It is enhanced if the events have been integrated well with previous knowledge and distracting events have not intervened. Remembering may be reproductive, constructive, or reconstructive and can involve a copy of an experience, the construct of the meaning of a new experience, or the reconstrual of a meaning previously assigned to an experience.

Research moves outward from the event into broader contexts, and inquiry is directed toward identifying and describing these transitions in context. Contextual theories focus on the nature of the events one experiences. Transformation theory is more closely allied to these theories than to the other theories of adult education described in this section.

Meaning as Interpretation

Our need to understand our experiences is perhaps our most distinctively human attribute. We *have* to understand them in order to know how to act effectively. "Only when things about us have meaning for us, only when they signify consequences that can be reached by using them in certain ways, is any such thing as intentional, deliberate control of them possible" (Dewey, 1933, p. 19).

Learning means using a meaning that we have already made to guide the way we think, act, or feel about what we are currently experiencing. Meaning is making sense of or giving coherence to our experiences. *Meaning is an interpretation.*

Learning as Making Meaning. Making meaning is central to what learning is all about. The learning process may be understood as the extension of our ability to make explicit, schematize (make an association within a frame of reference), appropriate (accept an interpretation as our own), remember (call upon an earlier interpretation), validate (establish the truth, justification, appropriateness, or authenticity of what is asserted), and act upon (decide, change an attitude toward, modify a perspective on, or perform) some aspect of our engagement with the environment, other persons, or ourselves. Learning always involves making a new experience explicit and schematizing, appropriating, and acting upon it. We seek validation when, in the process of interpreting an experience, we find reason to question the truth, appropriateness, or authenticity of either a newly expressed or implied idea or one acquired through prior learning. It is important to recognize how crucial the validation of knowledge is to the learning process in adults.

Learning is a dialectical process of interpretation in which we interact with objects and events, guided by an old set of expectations. Normally, when we learn something, we attribute an old meaning to a new experience. In other words, we use our established expectations to explicate and construe what we perceive to be the nature of a facet of experience that hitherto has lacked clarity or has been misinterpreted. In transformative learning, however, we reinterpret an old experience (or a new one) from a new set of expectations, thus giving a new meaning and perspective to the old experience.

When we confront an aspect of an encounter that we do not understand, our expectations from prior learning serve as habits of selective perception that govern, first, how we delimit the experience and, second, how we select those elements of it that past experience tells us may be relevant to understanding. We have to sort through our past experience, that is, the alternative interpretations currently available to us, in order to assess what is relevant. Thus the way our prior experience is organized and the way we interpret its relevance become central to making a new interpretation.

Defining Learning. Learning may be understood as the process of using a prior interpretation to construe a new or a revised interpretation of the meaning of one's experience in order to guide future action.

We use our revised interpretations to guide future action. Action here includes making a decision, making an association, revising a point of view, reframing or solving a problem, modifying an attitude, or producing a change in behavior. Action in transformation theory is not only behavior, the effect of a cause, but rather "praxis," the creative implementation of a purpose.

Remembering is central to learning because we learn with our old interpretations. Any new or revised interpretation also must be remembered for subsequent use in making extrapolations, analyses, syntheses, generalizations, or judgments. If an interpretation is not remembered, it implies thinking but not learning. Interpretation here means offering a meaning of something. Interpretation can also mean drawing inferences from or explaining something.

An interpretation is a meaningful construal of experience. We will explain in a later section how, in perception, construal occurs outside of our local awareness and without the use of language categories. By contrast, comprehension is a process of making an experience coherent by using categories acquired through language. An interpretation is meaningful in either case because the learner finds points of relevance in it to which he or she can relate.

Thinking and learning are overlapping terms. Thinking here refers to the immediate, conscious psychological processes of associating, differentiating, imagining, and inferring. Interpretations may be the result of intentional thought, but often they also incorporate culturally assimilated or "tacit" learning. Learning involves using thought processes to make or revise an interpretation in a new context, applying the knowledge resulting from prior thought and/or prior tacit learning to construe meaning in a new encounter.

Even in the case of psychomotor learning, it is difficult to imagine how someone could acquire the intention to learn to ride a bike, juggle, or ski without having some tentative concept (interpretation) of how these things are done. Learning a motor skill means guiding our action with an interpretation of how to do something that becomes modified with experience. What we learn is a revised or refined interpretation of how to perform, using our body more effectively to achieve mastery of the skill.

From our first infantile discovery of a link between crying and being fed, our interpretations give meaning to our experiences. We unintentionally and unreflectively learn to reinforce responses because they have significance and meaning for us. Emotions are interpretations of the meaning of feeling. Feelings and impulses become transformed into emotions as we learn how to interpret what they mean in relation to others and to ourselves.

Following activity theory in Soviet psychology, transformation theory asserts that, like attention, memory, and thinking, learning is best understood as an activity resulting from social interaction that involves goals, actions, and conditions under which goal-directed actions are carried out, all of which must be taken into account (Wertsch, 1979). To explain an activity such as learning, we must also analyze its origins, development, and consequences.

The Contexts of Learning. It is important to understand that learning always involves the following five primary interacting contexts:

1. The frame of reference or meaning perspective in which the learning is embedded

2. The conditions of communication: language mastery; the codes that delimit categories, constructs, and labels; and the ways in which problematic assertions are validated
3. The line of action in which learning occurs
4. The self-image of the learner
5. The situation encountered, that is, the external circumstances within which an interpretation is made and remembered.

The line of action has to do with implementing the purpose and intentionality of the learner and involves the exercise of his or her conative power. Conation involves both desire and volition, the intensity with which one wants to do something. It is conditioned by the tacit learning that occurs in the process of socialization. Behavioral intentions involve conative, cognitive, and affective dimensions. Intuition — the ability to have immediate, direct knowledge without the use of language or reason — also plays a key role. Movement toward a goal tends to set one up to make the next move in the same direction. Herbert Blumer (1969), a leading interpreter of George Herbert Mead, was among the first American social scientists to underscore clearly the crucial role that the line of action plays in any social interaction. Although seldom explicitly acknowledged, line of action is a central influence on perception, remembering, problem solving, and learning.

The fourth context of learning, that of self-image, is easily overlooked. Grendlin (1978–79) reminds us of the Heideggerian concept of *Befindlichkeit,* a "felt sense" of self — how we feel, how things are going, how we see our situation. The meaning of this felt sense is implicit; that is, it is never equal to specific cognitive units. We explain our felt sense by interpreting it and reflecting on our interpretation, using it as a criterion for assessing the correctness of our interpretation of our situation. Knowledge of our felt sense is conscious. Heidegger wrote, "Understandability is always already articulated even before it is appropriately interpreted. Speech is the articulation of understandability" (Boyd and Myers, 1988, p. 62). This reference is to the domain of "presentational construal" (p. 32). It is important here to highlight the fact that this prelinguistic domain affects and, in a sense, monitors our efforts to apply linguistic concepts to our experience. The process by which this happens is intuition.

Reflection. Reflection serves a purpose, and purposes serve as organizing principles that give coherence and order to activities. Clearly, reflection is different depending on whether the learner's purpose is task-oriented problem solving, understanding what someone else means, or understanding the self.

Most significant statements made by adults involve a continuing sequence of judgments regarding what is important, just, relevant, worthwhile, truthful, authentic, or the like; the reason for something; or the best action to take. These judgments are based upon assumptions, and these assumptions are open to question. Reflection upon assumptions thus becomes crucially important in learning to understand meaning.

Reflection is not the same as introspection, when this latter term refers to simply becoming aware of the fact that we are perceiving, thinking, feeling, or acting in a certain way. Much, perhaps most, of the time we think and learn nonreflectively. All reflection involves a critique. As I will show in Chapter Four, there are distinct advantages in seeing reflection as the intentional reassessment of prior learning to reestablish its validity by identifying and correcting distortions in its content, process, or premises. What I have referred to in earlier writings as *critical reflectivity* focuses on the latter of these considerations, a critique of the premises or presuppositions upon which habits of expectation are predicated.

Perception: Prereflective Learning

Learning is not solely the function of language. Perception or prereflective learning is the learning that occurs prior to the use of language to form categories. It involves our ability to differentiate space, time, direction, dimensions, sequence, entity, focus, states, moods, feelings, and the punctuation (identifying the beginnings and ends) of events. This ability becomes modified with experience. The character of this prelinguistic dimension of learning has been most fully elaborated in the writings of Jung. Boyd and Myers (1988; see also Boyd, 1989; Boyd, Kondrat, and Rannells, 1989) have delineated the relevance of Jung's ideas for transformative learning (see Chapter Six). Our "executive" sense of agency—the capacity of the self to make decisions independent of socially imposed expectations, assessments, or conditions—is located in this prelinguistic domain.

We have to draw upon our past knowledge to make interpretations that help us choose the dimensions of a new experience to which we will attend. We also draw upon prior learning so that we may associate the new experience with related ideas. This tacit process of reviewing and making interpretations based on prior experience to delimit the slice of new experience to which we will attend is what we refer to as perception. Typification refers to the nonreflective review and selection of constructs from prior learning that we use to construe the meaning of a new experience. Zaner (1981) holds that there can be no apprehension of what is actual as actual without its being apprehended as one among other possibilities.

If we are to explicate or spell out a hitherto unclear patch of experience, or even if we are to perceive it in the first place as something relevant to our interest—and our interest is decisive here—we must take some dimensions or aspects of the experience into consideration and disregard or exclude others. The philosopher Percy has argued that every conscious perception is an act of recognition in that it involves the identification of an experience (object, event, act, or emotion) by matching the experience against the internalized background of an appropriate symbol. The apprehension of a gestalt is different from grasping it symbolically. Being conscious of something being something is not usually a cognitive act involving symbols or signs. "It is not enough to say that one is conscious of something," Percy says. "One is also conscious of something being something" (Geertz, 1973, p. 215).

We effortlessly and unreflectively identify familiar objects through this process. An unfamiliar object makes us aware that one term of the match—an applicable symbolic model for interpreting the object's meaning and rendering it familiar — is missing. As Percy says,

> If I see an object at some distance and do not quite recognize it, I may see it, actually see it, as a succession of different things, each rejected by the criterion of fit as I come closer, until one is positively certified. A patch of sunlight in a field I may actually see as a rabbit — a seeing which goes much further than the guess that it may be a rabbit; no, the perceptual gestalt is so construed actually stamped by the essence of rabbitness: I could have sworn it was a rabbit. On coming closer, the sunlight pattern changes enough so that the rabbit-cast is disallowed. The rabbit vanishes and I make another cast: it is a paper bag, and so on. But most significant of all, even the last, the "correct" recognition is quite as mediate an apprehension as the incorrect ones; it is also a cast, a pairing, an approximation. And let us note in passing that even though it is correct, even though it is borne out by all indices, it may operate quite as effectively to conceal as to discover. When I recognize a strange bird as a sparrow, I tend to dispose of the bird under its appropriate formulation: it is only a sparrow. [p. 215]

Structural linguistics suggests that linguistic *signs* involve both what is signified (a sound or visual image) and the signified meaning. There is no necessary relationship between the two parts; theoretically, any signifier can represent any signified concept. For example, an object is identified by totally different words in different languages, and some languages have no names for some objects or events.

Symbols, on the other hand, involve a rationally meaningful relationship between the two parts. A blindfolded woman holding scales symbolizes justice; other symbols do not. Symbols are forms that embody significance. They also imply an "ideal form" of what they symbolize. The ideal justice suggested by the symbol has qualities of equity, retribution, fairness, and responsibility. Each of these characteristics also implies an ideal. Symbols not only denote; they also exemplify. Symbols do not represent but rather *directly present* the substantive qualities to which they refer. These qualities and the ideals they imply are projected upon objects and events as these are perceived (Parsons, 1988). Even before we intentionally cognitively examine the nature of objects or events, we have assigned meaning to them.

Both signs and symbols are organized into grammars by each culture. These grammars constitute codes of interpretation or rules governing systems whose parts have no meaning outside of the systems. Cultural symbols are what we experience as meaningful qualities. An experience does not depend upon the higher-order mental processes necessary for comprehension in order to become meaningful. Parsons writes, "The meaning content of symbols concerns less conceptions of reality than the very perception of reality itself" (p. 13). Symbols are not projected into an objective reality but rather mediate the constitution of experience and the objective sense of reality itself. Symbols thus are the form and substance as well as the medium and outcome of experiences. As Parsons says, "Linguisitic signs *represent* reality; symbols *present* a world" (p. 13).

Daniel Goleman (1985b) reminds us that every act of perception is an act of selection: the incompatibility of attention and anxiety teaches us to exchange diminished attention for lessened anxiety, and this trade-off profoundly shapes our experience. Goleman bases his thesis on the following three premises (p. 24):

- The mind can protect itself against anxiety by dimming awareness.
- This mechanism creates a "blind spot," a zone of blocked attention and self-deception.
- Such blind spots occur at each major level of behavior, from the psychological to the social.

Goleman's thesis and premises provide the psychological imperative for a transformative theory of learning. Goleman makes it clear that often adult learning is predicated upon distortions the assumptions of which need to be reflected upon and assessed for its justification.

Although the muting of awareness to avoid anxiety has been helpful and perhaps even necessary for human development, our adult reality is often not only shaped but distorted by the resulting self-deception and shared illusions. One of R. D. Laing's "knots," quoted by Goleman (1985), succinctly describes the central learning problem of adulthood:

> The range of what we think and do
> is limited by what we fail to notice.
> And because we fail to notice
> that we fail to notice
> there is little we can do
> to change
> until we notice
> how failing to notice
> shapes our thoughts and deeds. [p. 24]

Comprehension: Learning Through Language

Cognitively construed meaning involves the interaction of speech with the following elements: (1) the habituated symbol system embodying the ideal types, (2) the image in the mind, and (3) the external stimuli. The idealized symbol system is projected onto the external stimuli to form the image in the mind. Thus the qualities and features that the symbol system imposes on the perceived object are actually what is perceived, and it is this "loaded" perception that is objectified through speech. Language is a system of ideal objects expressed in the form of linguistic signs. There is no direct relationship between language and the actual things of the external world.

The Soviet psycholinguist A. A. Leont'ev (quoted in Wertsch, 1979) contends that signs consist of three elements. The first is the "objective content," the system of connections and relations of objects and phenomena in external reality. A second element is the ideal loading, or "ideal content." The third element is the subject's social experience, which is projected onto the sign in his or her consciousness — the "subjective content." According to Leont'ev, meaning presented in consciousness is the result of these three elements. Meanings do not exist for individuals outside of these subjective reflections, which may be in the form of visual or other perceptual images.

We cannot know to what extent the concept of a system of signs is based upon the objective content or on the ideal symbolic content. Perception would be impossible without language, through which a culture communicates its symbols and idealized types in the context of socialization. However, as we have seen, once communicated, symbols may project meanings through perception quite independently of cognitions, which depend upon categories of language. Verbal signification is included in the activity of perception.

Our ideal image of the objective world is present in meanings. Language reflects the qualities, connections, and relationships rightly or wrongly incorporated in our symbolic models. To what extent a system of signs is based upon "objective" content or upon symbolic ideals is always highly problematic. Phenomenology and transformation theory hold that our very perceptions endow events or objects with meaning to give them coherence. To become what is, an entity must be interpreted as an instance of a type; that is, in principle, it must meet certain conditions imposed through meaning schemes and perspectives that constitute a cultural code of interpretation.

A practical implication of the theories just described is that knowledge for the learner does not exist in books or in the experience of the educator. It exists only in the learner's ability to construe and reconstrue the meaning of an experience in his or her own terms.

Functions of Symbolic Models. There is little consensus on the way the mind works, but the emerging thesis of transformation theory is that what we internalize are symbolic models, images, and habits of expectation. Symbolic models serve several constructive functions. One, as we have seen, is to provide us with classificatory schemas pertaining to such properties as direction, dimension, and sequence that enable us to differentiate time and space, direction, entities, and event punctuation. A second function is to enable us to make value judgments. A third function is to make possible what George Lakoff (1988) refers to as "basic-level categories." These are the most common concepts with which we are familiar: objects such as "dog," "cat," "table," "chair"; events such as "party," "fight," "race"; and states such as "dreaming," "joking," "acting." These categories are somewhere between superordinate categories such as "animal," "furniture," or "event," and specific categories such as particular breeds of dogs and cats or specific variations among events ("birthday party") or states ("nightmare"). Basic-level categories involve a single mental image, fast identification, and the shortest, most commonly used words — words that are among the first that children learn.

Such mental processes as scanning, focusing, figure-ground reversal, superimposition, and vantage point shifting are used to process symbolic models. Lakoff explains the dynamic: "Very general innate imaginative capacities (for schematization, categorization, metaphor, metonymy, etc.) characterize abstract concepts by linking them to image-schematic (*symbolic models*) and basic-level physical concepts. Cognitive models are built up by these imaginative processes" (p. 50). Filmore (quoted in Lakoff, 1988) argues that words are defined only in relation to such schemas. Thus *February* is meaningful only in terms of a "months" schema.

It becomes clear that experience is an act rather than a thought. We experience symbolic qualities and, by acting upon them, constitute the world. Reality is constituted by perception through experience. The structure of perception is cultural, and this is mirrored in the structure of language. Of course, perceptually construed experience is prereflective and habitual. It is driven by cues informed by uncritically assimilated cultural symbols (models), which directly present the qualities to which they refer as we differentiate objects and events.

To conceptualize an experience, we use signs to interpret it. Through language we articulate the intentionality implicit in perception. Habitual frames of reference or meaning perspectives (see Chapter Two) constitute practices through which we perceptually enact our world. Although symbolic consciousness has its locus in perception, we can use reflection to assert our control over many of these "conventions of the senses," delineate these cultural symbols, and disengage them from our experience. For Parsons and for transformation theory, *consciousness* is not an inner state; it is a form of action that actualizes the qualities of symbolic models as objects of experience. The intentionality of perception becomes lost when perceptual learning becomes objectified as "categories of the mind." The task of education is to reactivate the intentionality implicit in perception.

Meaning is not experienced symbolically in comprehension, as it is in perception, although, Parsons points out, signs become related as symbols. Philip Johnson-Laird states that "perception yields rich mental models of the world . . . inference depends on the manipulation of mental models . . . and comprehension is a process of constructing models" (1988, p. 110). The initial mental representation of an utterance is used to construct a model of the state of affairs that is described, questioned, or requested. Thus a model including many dogs of many breeds can be evoked by the utterance, "I love dogs." Johnson-Laird writes, "A picture may be worth a thousand words, but a proposition [model] is worth an infinity of pictures" (p. 110). Mental models are provisional and can always be revised by further information.

There is an important distinction to be made between the sense of an expression and that to which it makes reference. The sense of an expression is a function that permits us to place an object of reference in the widest variety of different models. The way words and sentences relate to the world involves truth conditions: When you understand a warning, then you comprehend its truth conditions; you know how the world should be if the assertion is true. To understand any assertion, we must be able to imagine how the world would be were it true. Truth conditions involve the sense of a sentence.

Symbols play a crucial role in construing meaning when

higher-order mental processes are in play, just as they do in perception. Geertz (1973) observes that a poem, which can serve as a symbolic model of the emotional impact of, say, premature death, can similarly transform physical sensations into sentiments and attitudes that enable us to react to such a tragedy not "blindly" but "intelligently." Virtually anything that has been experienced may function as a symbol if it represents, points to, or is a reminder of something else. Geertz suggests that our symbolic models may be drawn from popular culture, from high art, or from formal religious ritual. "Culture patterns—religious, philosophical, aesthetic, scientific, ideological—are 'programs': they provide a template or blueprint for the organization of social and psychological processes, much as a genetic system provides such a template for the organization of organic processes" (p. 216). These symbols and symbol systems are extrinsic sources of information, "extrapersonal mechanisms for perception, understanding, judgment, and manipulation of the world" (p. 216).

Extrinsic Theory. Galanter and Gerstenhaaber (1956) have articulated an "extrinsic theory," which holds that thought consists of the construction and manipulation of symbol systems that are employed as models of other systems (physical, organic, social, psychological, and so on) in ways that allow the structure of the other systems and the ways they may be expected to behave to be understood. Thinking, comprehension, learning, understanding, and making intepretations about the nature of experience consist of matching the states and processes of symbolic models against the states and processes of the wider world. From this perspective, imaginal thinking involves constructing an image of the environment, operating this model faster than the environment, and predicting that the environment will conform to the behavior of the model. In problem solving, these writers assert, we construct a model or image of the "relevant features" of the situation and manipulate this under various hypothetical conditions and anticipated restraints. We observe the outcome of these manipulations and project them onto the environment as predictions. We use comparable external models when we use a map to symbolize roads and our finger running over a route on the map as a model for the relevant aspects of an automobile. Extrinsic theory adds an insightful dimension to transformation theory, explaining how we learn by projecting symbolic models onto our experiences. Transformation theory introduces meaning perspectives, critical reflection, and discourse into this process.

Construing Meaning. The major processes by which we perceive and comprehend are scanning and construal. Scanning involves exploring, differentiating, recognizing, feeling, intuiting, and imagining. There are two interdependent forms of construal. *Presentational construal* is associated with perception and refers to construing immediate appearances in terms of spatio-temporal wholes, distinct processes, and presences: an entity is construed from its unique form or movement, its form is construed from serial occurrences, or its shape or size is construed by its appearance. Presentational construal also includes construing dimension, direction, sequence, and event punctuation by interpreting cues evoked by sense perception. Presentational construal is prelinguistic. *Propositional construal* is associated with comprehension or cognition and involves experiencing things in terms of the concepts and categories that come with our mastery of language, although we may not consciously name or describe to ourselves what we construe (Heron, 1988). As noted earlier, presentational construal can be a significant influence on and serve as a monitor for propositional construal. Feelings, intuition, dreams, and changes in physiological states bring the influences of presentational construal into awareness. Propositional construal similarly monitors presentational construal by introducing rational and reflective interpretations of the meaning of our propositional awareness. Both forms of construal become modified through experience and, obviously, are highly interactive.

Presentational construal is central to perception and propositional construal is central to cognition, although both forms of construal interact in both activities. Each of these forms of construal results in meaning. Tacit meanings arise from presentational construal, and either tacit or explicitly understood meanings result from propositional construal. Thus some tacit meaning derived from presentational construal may be symbolic but does not involve language. We attempt to understand presentational construal through psychoanalysis, dream interpretation, meditation, increased sensitivity to changes in physiological states, and spiritual or mystical exploration.

Rationality and Analysis. For Habermas (1971), rationality is predicated upon the facts that knowledge has a propositional structure and that beliefs can be represented in the form of statements. Rationality has less to do with the possession of knowledge than with learning and action — "how speaking and acting subjects acquire and use knowledge" (p. 8). Knowledge is expressed explicitly in linguistic utterance and, as such, it may be criticized as unreliable or assessed as valid. The rationality of an expression depends on the reliability of the knowledge it embodies.

In addition to perception and recognition, interpretation for comprehension calls for analysis — that is, for determining the perceived similarities and differences between a learner's symbolic models and the learner's experience. Such similarities and differences determine the relevance and fit of the experience within the learner's symbolic frame of reference. This comparative analysis, which is often prereflective, may involve one or more of the physical, instrumental, methodological, linguistic (lexical, syntactic, semantic), psychological, or social dimensions of similarity and difference. The analysis cannot be derived from the facts themselves; it must come from the input of the learner. What becomes fact for us depends upon how we have defined for ourselves the nature of our experience. We produce facts rather than discover them; the "facts" that an adult learns thus are grounded in the orientation and frame of reference of the learner.

The analysis involved in the learning process begins with an analogy, likening an unfamiliar phenomenon in its entirety to a familiar one. It proceeds through an assay of the specific elements of an unfamiliar object or event through further analogies. This process often is expanded as we encounter the same phenomenon in different contexts. We learn not only from our experience but by shaping things to our existing categories of understanding, interpreting the unfamiliar to fit the psychological, cultural, and linguistic constraints of our current frame of reference.

Both the statements derived from the imaginative projection of symbolic models that we use to make interpretations and the inferences that we make in analyzing our interpretations involve assumptions that require validity testing through rational discourse with others in order to arrive at an informed consensus. Giddens points out that "rationality presumes communication because something is rational only if it meets the conditions necessary to forge an understanding with at least one other person" (Bernstein, 1985, p. 99). Habermas believes that rationality lies in the process of achieving mutual understanding by active participation in advancing and objectively weighing evidence and assessing the cogency of supporting arguments. To say that someone is acting rationally or that a statement is rational means that the action or the statement can be criticized or defended by those involved so that it may be justified.

Transformative Logic. James Loder (1981) identifies a general "transformative logic" inherent in every "knowing event" (that is, an event involving comprehension). He claims that this logic is implicit in all major domains of learning — scientific, aesthetic, therapeutic, social, cultural, and spiritual. Transformative logic as defined by Loder has five steps. First is *conflict,* an apparent rupture in the knowing context. This conflict is most potent when it involves a dilemma pertaining to our view of ourselves rather than a mere puzzle imposed from outside. The second step in transformative logic is *scanning:* searching for possible solutions, dissecting errors, keeping some data and discarding others. This stage involves following hunches, sensing direction, and moving intuitively forward.

Step three involves the constructive act of *imagination* and results in insight derived from intuition. Loder borrows Koestler's description of "bisociation" for this imaginative act, which he describes as "two habitually incompatible frames of reference conversing, usually with surprising suddenness, to compose a meaningful unity" (p. 32). A fourth step involves *release and openness:* a release of the energy invested in the conflict and an opening of the knower to him- or herself as conscious of being conscious and to the contextual situation. This step brings forward new possibilities for problem solving.

The final step in transformative logic is "*interpretation* of the imaginative solution into the behavioral and/or symbolic constructed world of the original context" (p. 34). This interpretation involves two elements. One is "congruence," or making explicit the connections between the imaginative construct and the original conditions of the conflict. The other is "correspondence," which makes the apparent congruence public and seeks others' validation of it. Achievement of such validation is easier when the imaginative discovery is something already known by others than when the discovery is new and must be proven to fit an established assumptive world, as when a new scientific discovery challenges supposedly established facts.

Transformation theory incorporates Loder's ideas (which are described further in Chapter Six), but it holds that comprehension involves a conflict, scanning, and construal, during the latter of which a constructive act of imagination occurs, resulting in an interpretation. Problem solving, often using reflection, follows if the interpretation or meaning scheme is found to present a problem.

Remembering

Representational theory, a mainstream position in psychology, holds that perception represents an accurate view of the environment and that perception and recognition are independent functions of the brain. The theory claims that visual, tactile, and auditory stimuli are transformed by the brain into representations of the physical world and that these previously learned images are stored in the brain.

A new and increasingly popular perspective in neurobiology, however, challenges representational theory. This emerging position proposes that the brain categorizes stimuli in ways dictated by present needs and past experience. Perception and recognition are based upon this categorization. What we see depends in part upon what we have seen in the past. Past ways of categorizing stimuli that have led to meaningful or useful behavior become reinforced. What the brain stores and what we remember are not fixed images but procedures that will help us understand the meaning of our experience, and we rely upon recreations to adapt what we know from the past to the present.

Gerald Edelman's theory of "neural Darwinism" (Rosenfield, 1988) provides the biological basis for this approach to memory. Edelman's theory holds that neural networks within the brain are patterned after the brain's system as a whole, in which electrical signals travel among millions of sensors, called neurons, along particular pathways. Neurons generate these signals in response to stimuli. Given groups of neurons respond differently to different stimuli, however, and neighboring groups of neurons respond differently to the same stimuli. Neurons become activated by similar stimuli each time those stimuli appear.

In addition to responding to stimuli, sheets of neural tissue can communicate with each other. This communication makes it possible to create categories of things and events. A "map" is a collection or sheet of neural groups in the brain that preserves the interaction between a sheet of sensory receptors, such as those involved in the skin of one's hand, and the sheet of neural tissue in the brain to which the sheet of sensory receptors can communicate. Edelman's theory states that maps that react to certain groups of stimuli are "selected" and reinforced by use, just as certain species are "selected" in Darwin's theory. Thus, Edelman believes, Darwinian principles of selection can explain the perceptual categorizations that form the basis of memory and recognition. Recognition and memory develop as certain maps or pathways become easier to travel because of frequent use. Interaction among the maps of the brain, which permits a kind of cross-correlation of sensory stimuli, is called *reentry*.

Memory, then, is not an exact repetition of an image in the brain. Rather, it is a recategorization that occurs when the connections between the neurons in different maps are strengthened temporarily. As information is collected in different contexts, maps different from those affected by our initial encounter with the information become activated; this leads to recategorization. Memory is an imaginative reconstruction of our past reactions or experiences plus a limited amount of detail that appears to us in the form of words or images. Rosenfield writes, "Each person, according to [Edelman's] theory, is unique; his or her perceptions are to some degree creations, and his or her memories are part of an ongoing process of imagination. A mental life cannot be reduced to molecules. Human intelligence is not just knowing more, but reworking, recategorizing, and thus generalizing information in new and surprising ways" (1988, p. 193).

Similarly, transformation theory describes memory as the process in which an object or event that we have previously interpreted through projection of our symbolic models, in accordance with acquired habits of expectation or meaning perspectives, is re-cognized when it appears in our experience again. We imaginatively reconstruct an earlier meaning by the same process of projection, interpreting what we know in the new and unfamiliar situational context.

Remembering involves an object or event that usually has been associated with an emotion influential in our initial learning. How well we remember depends upon the strength of this emotion, the degree to which the originally learned event was differentiated from and integrated with past experience in the first place, the context of other events in which the object or event was embedded, and the impact of events that followed the initial learning. We recognize elements in an event that previously gave coherence or strengthened our then current meaning schemes or perspectives. We forget when the event is no longer recognizable because of changes in context or transformations in the meaning schemes and perspectives that provide our conceptual categories. There is a well-established tendency for people to think about their learning increasingly abstractly as time passes.

Skinner (1987) reminds us that the word *remember* comes from the Latin *memor,* which means to be "mindful again. . . . To remember what something looks like is to do what we did when we saw it. No copy [of reality] was needed then and no copy is needed now. We recognize things in the sense of re-cognizing them—responding to them now as we did in the past" (p. 30).

Of course, we know that we do not have conscious access to all that we know and that we have learned things that we have never been conscious of learning, such as understandings that have been culturally assimilated or "introjected" rather than deliberately taught or learned. Such tacit learning includes, for example, our characteristic ways of dealing with rejection or with authority, our ethnocentricity, our stereotypic belief systems, our tolerance for ambiguity, our learning styles, and the way we selectively perceive an event.

Even the most primitive psychomotor learning, such as shock avoidance in psychological experiments, is a function of nonreflective knowledge. The whole process of recognition, sorting, and selection of that of which we become aware takes only milliseconds and occurs outside our field of awareness. A "semantic memory" filters what moves into awareness, and this may well be a function of our habitual frames of reference. Messages that either have no relevance for us or threaten our current habits of expectation are kept out of awareness.

Attention and awareness are different. I can be aware of the existence of the typewriter keyboard as I type without necessarily transferring my attention to the keyboard from the notes I am copying. Memory is limited to what we experience within our span of awareness that will trigger an interpretation to guide our actions. Some of the knowledge we can bring into our span of attention is more accessible than other knowledge. The less used and less currently relevant an interpretation is, the less easily accessible it becomes. Other knowledge can be blocked out by anxiety.

Neurological evidence supports differentiating among episodic, semantic, and implicit memory functions (Tulvig, 1989). Episodic memory refers to remembering and recollecting personal episodes. Semantic memory refers to knowing and recalling impersonal facts learned in the past. Implicit memory refers to repeating skills one exercises automatically, such as riding a bike or speaking grammatically. Neither semantic nor implicit memory appears to decline with age; whether episodic memory declines appears to depend upon individual differences in the way it is used and other circumstances.

It also may be useful to differentiate tacit memory (memory of culturally assimilated habits of expectation that allow us to scan and censor the experience of our senses) from explicit memory (memory that we can produce upon command). Tacit memory plays an indispensable and integral role in making an interpretation. Focal or explicit memory, by contrast, is indispensable in perception and plays an integral role in making an explanation and in reflective action. As used here, interpretation means to construe meaning; explanation refers to a statement of elucidation. We may forget a telephone number we have learned but have tacitly interpreted as insufficiently important to warrant our being able to remember it explicitly. But can we forget what is involved in our tacit memory? Tacit memory does not appear to decrease as one ages. Qualitative changes in learning that appear in older adults, to be discussed in Chapter Six, might well be accounted for by an enrichment of, or greater access to, tacit memory. Moreover, we know that we can transform tacit knowledge by bringing it into our span of attention, explicating it, and reassessing its validity, consequences, and usefulness, as is done in psychotherapy.

The Dynamics of Making Meaning

Remembering involves a reconstrual of the way we imaginatively project symbols to make meaning when we encountered similar sense experiences earlier.

Rationality is a process of assessing the reasons and justification for a meaning scheme. This may involve a review of empirical evidence or a best judgment made through an informed consensus.

Learning involves construing and appropriating a new or revised interpretation for guiding action.

Interpretations are articulations of meaning schemes and involve assumptions that adults in modern society find necessary to validate. Justification of assumptions often involves consensual validation through critical discourse.

There is much evidence to support the assertion that we tend to accept and integrate experiences that comfortably fit our frame of reference and to discount those that do not. It appears that this process is not so much a matter of matching new information with stored information or reconstruing past events as a matter of referring to an existing frame of reference or an already established symbolic model with cognitive, affective, and conative dimensions. Thus, our current frame of reference serves as the boundary condition for interpreting the meaning of an experience.

Figure 1. Interpretation.

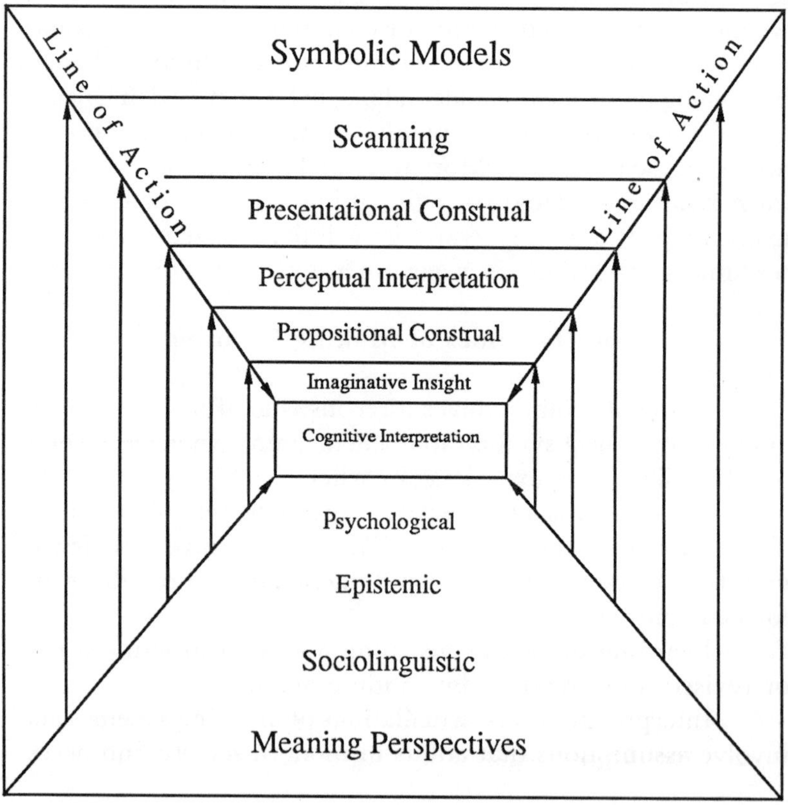

Figure 1 depicts the dynamics involved in making an interpretation — that is, in making meaning. The actions described move in sequence from the outer to the inner part of the diagram. We project symbolic models (outermost area) as we perceive objects or events by scanning and then construing. We resort first to presentational construal and then, if necessary, to propositional construal. Meaning is made both perceptually and cognitively. To move from a perceptual interpretation to a cognitive interpretation requires propositional construal (monitored by presentational awareness) and an imaginative insight. Propositional (cognitive) construal may give coherence to either a new experience or an old one as it becomes validated through reflective assessment.

Influences on the process of making meaning are shown on the bottom part of Figure 1. The process is influenced by meaning perspectives and by the learner's line of action, which provides intention, direction, and drive. Meaning perspectives are sets of habits of expectation that filter perception and cognition. These habits of expectation may be predominantly sociolinguistic, epistemic, or psychological; their nature will be examined in Chapter Two.

Cognitive interpretation can result in appreciation, inspiration, amusement, or some other emotional reaction; in the confirmation or negation of a belief, attitude, or emotional reaction — that is, a meaning scheme; or in a belief or meaning scheme being rendered problematic (defined as a problem). This latter effect is *problem posing*, which often leads to an effort at problem solving. Interpretation involves making a decision among these options. Interpretation can lead to either nonreflective (automatic, habitual) action or to reflective action.

Summary

This chapter has described a basic outline of transformation theory, a constructivist theory of adult learning addressed to those involved in helping adults learn. The chapter has covered the following major points:

1. We learn many of our ways of understanding the world unconsciously in childhood through socialization. These culturally

determined perspectives usually remain unconscious in adulthood, but they are very important in determining the way we interpret experience.

2. Living in the modern world inherently involves the weakening of traditional authority structures and a marked acceleration of change in the lives of adults. These circumstances require that adults be able to solve effectively a wider range of problems with a greater degree of reliance on their own resources than ever before. Culturally prescribed values and belief systems acquired through socialization may no longer be adequate for these tasks.

3. Meaning is an interpretation; to make meaning is to construe experience, to give it coherence. We make interpretations through both perception and cognition; we make meaning both unintentionally and intentionally.

4. We internalize symbolic models through the process of socialization and construe imaginative projections of these models in order to perceive objects, events, and states. Rather than a state of awareness, consciousness may be understood as the form of action of our construing these perceptions. The resulting "loaded" perception is objectified through language. Language is a system of ideal objects in the form of signs that has no direct relationship to the objects and events of the external world.

5. Construal involves projecting our symbolic models, as filtered by habits of expectation, onto objects and events in terms of (a) time and space, direction, dimension, entity, feeling, and punctuation of events, and/or (b) the concepts, categories, and metaphors that come with language mastery. The prelinguistic reality of (a) affects efforts to apply the linguistic concepts of (b) through intuition, and (b) monitors (a) through the use of reason.

6. Meaning perspectives, or generalized sets of habitual expectation, act as perceptual and conceptual codes to form, limit, and distort how we think, believe, and feel and how, what, when, and why we learn. They have cognitive, affective, and conative dimensions. These habits of expectation filter both perception and comprehension.

7. Interpretation involves making a decision that may result in confirmation, rejection, extension, or formulation of a belief or meaning scheme or in finding that that belief or scheme presents a problem that requires further examination. Meaning schemes are the specific beliefs, attitudes, and emotional reactions articulated by an interpretation. They are derived from earlier, often unreflective interpretations. Meaning schemes serve as specific habits of expectation. Meaning perspectives are groups of related meaning schemes.

8. Learning is a process of construing and appropriating a new or revised interpretation of the meaning of an experience as a guide to awareness, feeling, and action. There is much evidence to support the assertion that we tend to accept and integrate experiences that comfortably fit our frame of reference and to discount those that do not.

9. Learning involves five interacting contexts: a meaning perspective, the communication process, a line of action, a self-concept, and the external situation. Other critically important factors in understanding learning include previously learned meaning schemes and the "frames" or paradigms (shared meaning perspectives or definitions of a situation) that organize and govern social action.

10. Our interpretations are fallible and often are predicated upon unreliable assumptions. Examining critically the justification for our interpretations and the meaning schemes and perspectives that they express is the major imperative of modern adulthood.

11. Most significant statements involve sets of assumptions that need to be validated through reflection and discourse. We validate what others mean by assessing empirical evidence or through consensus. In turn, our interpretations of experience through imaginative projection of symbolic models as well as our analysis of these interpretations involve assumptions that may require validation by ourselves or others. Rationality is the process of assessing the reasons and justifications for a meaning scheme.

12. Remembering how we have interpreted objects and events in the past involves repeating the making of an imaginative

projection to interpret sensory stimuli. Frequency of making the same interpretation and the emotional strength of the initial experience condition neural pathways to help us identify similar cues in what we experience and to evoke imaginative projections similar to the ones we made before. The stronger the affective (emotional) dimension of an interpretation and the more frequently it is made, the easier it is to remember.

13. Perception, interpretation, learning, problem solving, remembering, and reflection all are significantly influenced by our line of action, which involves intention, purpose, and conation.

2

❦ Meaning Perspectives: How We Understand Experience

Chapter One introduced the central role played in the learning process by sets of habits of expectation, or meaning perspectives, which serve as selective codes governing perception and comprehension. Dewey described well both the importance of these meaning perspectives and our normal unconsciousness of them:

> A person in pursuing a consecutive train of thoughts takes some system of ideas for granted (which accordingly he leaves unexpressed, "unconscious") as surely as he does in conversing with others. Some context, some situation, some controlling purpose dominates his explicit ideas so thoroughly that it does not need to be consciously formulated and expounded. Explicit thinking goes on within the limits of what is implied or understood. Yet the fact that reflection originates in a problem makes it necessary at some points consciously to inspect and examine this familiar background. We have to turn upon some unconscious assumption and make it explicit. [1933, p. 281]

37

Our meaning perspectives filter the way we project our symbolic models imaginatively to construe what is presented through our senses. Language objectifies and significantly adds to these models, and through propositional construal we use the categories made possible by language to individualize our experience. Meaning perspectives also influence what we remember. If an experience provides interpretations that are compatible with, extend, or help to integrate our meaning perspectives, we are more likely to perceive and remember it. If the emotional stress of a conflict of beliefs causes us to transform a meaning perspective dramatically, that transformation will be remembered. The most significant transformations in learning are transformations of meaning perspectives.

Chapters Four and Five will deal with the transformation of meaning perspectives. The present chapter describes the learning theory of Karl Popper, which anticipates transformation theory. The chapter also examines the nature of meaning perspectives (and their subsets, meaning schemes) by comparing them with the related concept of peceptual filters, concepts of paradigms, psychological frames, ideologies, schemas, personal constructs, and language games. The chapter concludes with a discussion of the role of language in making meaning.

Karl Popper: A Forerunner of Transformation Theory

Karl Popper, the philosopher of science, was also interested in learning theory. His views have direct relevance to our considerations. Popper wrote:

At every instant of our pre-scientific or scientific development we are living in the centre of what I usually call a "horizon of expectations." By this I mean the sum total of our expectations, whether these are sub-conscious or conscious, or perhaps even explicitly stated in some language. Animals and babies have also their various and different horizons of expectations though no doubt on a lower level of consciousness than, say, a scientist whose horizon of expectations consists to a considerable extent of linguistically formulated theories or hypotheses.

The various horizons of expectations differ, of course, not only in their being more or less conscious, but also in their content. Yet in all these cases the horizon of expectations plays the part of a frame of reference: only their setting in the frame confers meaning or significance on our experiences, actions and observations. [Berkson and Wettersten, 1984, p. 7]

According to Popper, we learn in order to change the structure of our expectations rather than to fill in gaps in knowledge. New knowledge resulting from problem solving is a correction rather than an extension of old knowledge. It is relevant for our future discussion to note that Popper's ideas appear to take exception to the hypothetical-deductive model of problem solving, which holds some "variables" constant while exploring the effects of altering others, an approach that systematizes the filling in of gaps in knowledge.

Berkson and Wettersten compare Popper's ideas with theories of the Gestalt school and those of Jean Piaget, which they resemble but from which they also differ. Because Popper's central ideas are compatible with transformation theory, these differences are relevant here.

Popper and Gestalt Theory. Gestalt psychology theorists, like Popper, viewed learning as a problem-solving activity. They defined a problem as a difficulty in achieving a goal. The basic idea of their learning theory was that a gestalt is changed under the pressure of a problem so that the substance previously making up the old gestalt forms a new one. The problem was seen as an incomplete gestalt, and the solution was the "closure" of the gestalt. The process of altering a gestalt was called insight. Insight involved a "recentering" of a gestalt such that a problem situation was redefined to include the problem's potential solution.

While this concept resembles Popper's orientation and that of transformation theory in picturing learning as a change of view, it differs in what Popper and transformation theory emphasize, that new knowledge involves a negation and transformation of past beliefs. Berkson and Wettersten note that Gestalt psychologists did not solve the problem of how gestalts change. It is precisely this consideration to which transformation theory addresses itself.

Popper and Piaget. Whereas Piaget (1967) believed that we develop cognitive skills in order to manipulate the world to our advantage, Popper believed that we are compelled to learn by our search for a coherent and complete horizon of expectations. Piaget was centrally concerned with the growth of intelligence, but Popper, like transformation theorists, focused upon the generation of knowledge. Piaget believed that intellectual development may involve the rejection of some false views, but he did not hold the negation of beliefs to be the central dynamic of progress as Popper did and transformation theorists do. He saw rejection of false views as a by-product of efforts to develop cognitive skills, which improve as the result of both maturation and our need to master the environment. According to Piaget, the gaining of higher-level skills does not involve rejection of the lower; rather, lower-level skills are incorporated into higher-level ones. Skills can fall into disuse but cannot be rejected. Piagetian "formal operations," the adolescent and final stage of cognitive development, were modeled upon the hypothetical-deductive logic of problem solving.

Testing Assumptions. Popper held that all points of view are preconceived. No conscious experience, he wrote, is free from interpretation. Transformation theory agrees with this but holds that experience outside of consciousness also is subject to interpretation. Popper wrote disdainfully of "psychologism," the doctrine that statements can be justified by perceptual experience. He believed that knowledge is not derived from sensation. Rather, he said, new general concepts develop from the conflict between general ideas and particular new experiences.

A problem involves different levels of generality, which stimulate and guide the search for new ideas and thus influence the construction of new expectations or new general theories. Transformation theory suggests that the "general ideas" are understood as symbolic models and meaning perspectives.

Popper and transformation theorists agree that our efforts to understand the world generate the continuous testing of our most fundamental assumptions, not merely the testing of our attempts to extend our knowledge. Popper clearly implied a logic of knowing very different from the deductive hypothesis testing of natural science. Berkson and Wettersten write:

> For Popper, the acts of perception and thinking are like attempts to understand a difficult text: we read one part, guess as to its meaning, look to another part, see if that is consistent, or guess where our interpretations need change and so on. This activity is something we indulge in not occasionally, but rather constantly. We have been born with the task of developing a realistic set of expectations about the world based on the coded messages we receive from it. We can't even be sure of the code but must keep checking on it. [1984, p. 16]

These views of Popper's are incorporated in transformation theory, which focuses on the way that habitual expectations influence our learning and the way that they become transformed through reflection. Transformation theory also suggests that the logic implicit in solving problems in instrumental learning (learning aimed at manipulation) needs to be distinguished from the logic that guides the problem solving involved in understanding what others mean or in transforming meaning perspectives.

Meaning Perspectives

Psychologists have offered general recognition but surprisingly limited analysis of the crucial importance of frames of reference (what transformation theory calls meaning perspectives) in both inquiry and the production of knowledge. Nisbet and Ross (1980) cite workers in a wide variety of psychological fields who have emphasized the vital role of preexisting structures in the mind of the perceiver, but they note how little evidence exists to clarify the property of these structures, define the work they perform, or describe the conditions of their availability, initiation, and use.

The concept of what I refer to as meaning perspectives is equally widespread in philosophy and linguistics. Gidden (1976, p. 142) observes that Wittgenstein's "language games," Castaneda's "alternative realities," Whorf's "language structures," Bachelard's and Althusser's "problematics," and Kuhn's "paradigms" all are used to show that the meanings of terms, expressions or descriptions have to be understood in relation to "frames of meaning." Cell uses the term "maps" to refer to our general beliefs and knowledge, and Foucault's "episteme" refers to the composite "codes of a culture governing its schemes of perception, language, values and the order of its practices" (Gidden, 1976, p. 142).

Similarly, Sztompka (1974, p. 25) reports that a casual review of current sociological literature revealed no less than thirty-three terms signifying the same "metascientific" concept, "a conceptual apparatus with the help of which one defines, describes and explains certain problematic matters."

I want to avoid the suggestion of separation of the cognitive from the conative and affective dimensions of apperception and the psychological from the cultural in the learning process. Since all these dimensions are integrated in the concept of meaning, I have chosen the term *meaning perspective* to refer to the structure of assumptions within which one's past *experience assimilates and transforms new experience*. A meaning perspective is a habitual set of expectations that constitutes an orienting frame of reference that we use in projecting our symbolic models and that serves as a (usually tacit) belief system for interpreting and evaluating the meaning of experience.

There are three types of meaning perspectives. The first,

epistemic meaning perspectives, pertains to the way we know and the uses that we make of knowledge. Sociolinguistic meaning perspectives comprise the second type, and psychological perspectives are the third type. Exhibit 1 presents some of the major influences that shape, limit, and distort meaning perspectives. These are discussed in more detail in Chapter Five.

Exhibit 1. Factors Shaping Meaning Perspectives.

Epistemic Perspectives
Developmental stage perspectives
Cognitive/learning/intelligence styles
Sensory learning preferences
Frequency of events to identify patterns
Scope of awareness
External/internal evaluation criteria
Global/detail focus
Concrete/abstract thinking
Reification
Reflectivity

Sociolinguistic Perspectives
Social norms/roles
Cultural/language codes
Language/truth games
Common sense as cultural system
Secondary socialization
Ethnocentrism
Prototypes/scripts
Philosophies/theories

Psychological Perspectives
Self-concept
Locus of control
Tolerance of ambiguity
Lost functions—childhood prohibitions enforced by
    anxiety in adulthood
Inhibitions
Psychological defense mechanisms
Neurotic needs
Approach/avoidance
Characterological preferences

Meaning Schemes. Meaning perspectives determine the essential conditions for construing meaning for an experience. By defining our expectations, a meaning perspective selectively orders what we learn and the way we learn it. Each meaning perspective contains a number of meaning schemes. *A meaning scheme is the particular knowledge, beliefs, value judgments, and feelings that become articulated in an interpretation.* Meaning schemes are the concrete manifestations of our habitual orientation and expectations (meaning perspectives) and translate these general expectations into specific ones that guide our actions. For example, if ethnocentrism, the basic suspicion of others different from oneself or one's group, is central to the formation of a sociolinguistic meaning perspective, specific negative racial and sexual stereotypes can be recognized as meaning schemes within that perspective that prepare us for particular actions such as shunning someone of a certain race or sex. A meaning scheme may pertain to how to do something (instrumental learning), how to understand what others mean (communicative learning), or how to understand oneself. Meaning schemes are much more likely to be examined critically and transformed by reflection (as defined in Chapter Four) than meaning perspectives.

Meaning perspectives provide us with criteria for judging or evaluating right and wrong, bad and good, beautiful and ugly, true and false, appropriate and inappropriate. They also determine our concept of personhood, our idealized self-image, and the way we feel about ourselves. The perceived content of our experience is determined by the specific meaning schemes included in our meaning perspectives. When our meaning schemes are inadequate to explain facets of our experience, according to Fingarette (1963), we are faced with areas or dimensions of apparent meaninglessness. Our most common reaction to meaninglessness is to become anxious. When inadequate meaning schemes involve self-concept, we fill this void by compensation, projection, rationalization, or other forms of self-deception. Similarly, Fingarette suggests that for meaning schemes involving social roles and relationships such as buyer-seller, parent-child, plaintiff-defendant, and lover-beloved, there are conventional rules or norms, the violation of which leads to social disorder or individual anxiety.

Perceptual Filters. Psychologist Irvin Roth (1990) has identified the following five major categories in the constructed world of the individual. The variables listed after each category suggest specific ways in which meaning perspectives within that category may be organized. Roth's classification provides a useful typology of some significant sources, distortions, and limitations of meaning perspectives. I have shown in brackets the category of meaning perspective in which I place each of Roth's categories.

1. Objects, enduring physical structures: subject to an individual's power (or not); changeability. [Psychological]
2. Persons: similar to self; different from self, and serve as sources of reward and punishment; similar to nonhuman physical objects (a sociopathic perception); subject to individual's power; understandable through patterned behavior, through attributed attitude. [Sociolinguistic]
3. Ways of learning: relative priority of reward and punishment in the learning process; sensory avenues (seeing, hearing, doing); temporal sequences (how often does something have to happen to consider it a pattern; attending to similarities and differences). [Epistemic]
4. Microstructure of attentional processes: clarity of detail, attention to outlines and boundaries, sharpness of differentiation between figure and ground; narrowness or expansiveness of field of awareness; relative emphasis on larger forms and global percepts versus details and specifics. [Epistemic]
5. Temporal structuring: tempo, speed of passage, perception of flow, narrowness of temporal focus, time as figure or ground. [Epistemic]
6. Organization of behavioral sequences: approach versus avoidance; source of outcome specifications and values — external versus internal. [Psychological] [pp. 119–120]

Roth's variables describe the poles between which the characteristic or dominant positions of an individual may be identified. Thus we can see others as similar to ourselves or different, under our control or not, understandable or not, depending upon our perspective. We can get ready satisfaction from learning something or view that learning as a threatening test of self-worth. We can see the behavior of a child in a developmental perspective or exclusively in terms of the immediate situation. We can look at a problem situation as a whole or focus immediately on specific aspects of it. In particular contexts, or as a supplement to the dominant position, we may assume a stance in regard to these variables other than our dominant one. For Roth, "The ideal is for the individual to be capable of functioning at any of the poles, guided by well-developed intuitions about the pole appropriate to the various contexts" (p. 120). Perhaps allowing an individual to function this way is another significant function of presentational construal in transformation theory.

Paradigms, Frames, and Ideologies. What I have called a meaning perspective is similar to what other authors have referred to as a paradigm or personal frame. Thomas Kuhn's seminal book, *The Structure of Scientific Revolutions* (1962), described paradigmatic transformations in scientific knowledge, a counterpart of the process I call perspective transformation. (For a useful interpretive review of the literature on paradigms and adult education, see Sinnott, 1986). Kuhn used *paradigm* to refer to a collection of ways of seeing, methods of inquiry, beliefs, ideas, values, and attitudes that influence the conduct of scientific inquiry. The term has come to be used as a synonym for *model, conceptual framework, approach,* and *worldview. Paradigm* has been characterized by Kisiel as "that which we look through rather than look at in viewing the world" (1982, p. 95). I think of a paradigm as an articulated, theory-based, collectively held meaning perspective. Some comprehensive theories, such as those of Freud, Marx, and Skinner, generate whole new vocabularies and can come to serve as cognitive filters, thus assuming the functions of a paradigm or meaning perspective.

Sociologist Erving Goffman (1974) used the term *frame* to refer to a shared definition of a situation that organizes and governs social interaction. A frame tells us the context of a social situation and how to understand and behave in it. We act differently, for example, depending on whether we are at a play, in a religious service, at an athletic event, on a date, or in a negotiating session. Frames are collectively held meaning perspectives that, unlike paradigms, are tacit. Goleman (1985b, p. 264) refers to frames as "simultaneously activated shared schemes."

Gregory Bateson (1972) delineated the functions of "psychological frames," which I also see as a form of meaning perspective. Bateson tells us that a psychological frame is

1. Exclusive, *i.e.*, by including certain messages (or meaningful actions), . . . certain other messages are excluded.
2. Inclusive, *i.e.*, by excluding certain messages, certain others are included.
3. Related to what we have called "premises." The picture frame tells the viewer that he is not to use the same sort of thinking in interpreting the picture that he might use in interpreting the wallpaper outside the frame . . . . The frame itself thus becomes part of the premise system.
4. Metacommunicative. Any message, which either explicitly or implicitly defines a frame, *ipso facto* gives the receiver instructions or aids in his attempt to understand the message included within the frame.
5. The converse of 4. is also true. Every metacommunicative or metalinguistic message defines either explicitly or implicitly the set of messages about which it communicates, *i.e.*, every metacommunicative message is or defines a psychological frame.
6. Mental processes resemble logic in needing an outer frame to delimit the ground against which the figures are to be perceived . . . a frame whose function is to delimit a logical type. [pp. 187–189]

Some authors have used the term *ideology* to refer to any unconsciously incorporated meaning perspective, but I would like to use this word specifically to mean a distorted, collectively held sociolinguistic meaning perspective. Criteria for designating a meaning perspective as "limited" or "distorted" and the relationship of such perspectives to adult development will be discussed in Chapters Five and Six.

Schemas. The prevailing view in the literature of cognitive psychology identifies *schemas* (or *schemata*) as organized representations of an event that serve as prototypes or norms for what is expected. In current usage, the term *schema* is often differentiated from *concept* in that the former is used to refer to a "mental structure" having a dynamic or relational aspect. When schemas are used to understand the social world, they are often differentiated from propositional statements and belief systems. Event sequence schemas are sometimes referred to as "scripts" (when we open our front door and step out of the house, we expect to step down onto the walk leading to the street; we do not expect to step into the mouth of a whale). Person-prototype schemas, sometimes called "personae," are essentially stereotypes but without the negative connotation of that term (Nisbet and Ross, 1980). Taxonomic, implicational, cause-oriented, and goal-oriented schemas also have been identified in studies of text comprehension (Graesser and Clark, 1985). The availability of a schema is a crucial factor in whether it is used in a particular instance. Schemas, like meaning perspectives, are supposed to guide the way in which we experience, feel, understand, judge, and act upon particular situations.

Unfortunately, the term *schema* often has been stretched to include a variety of different dimensions or processes that possess different levels of abstraction, and the relationships among them and the role of metaschemas have not been clearly described. Transformation theory challenges the common assumptions that suggest that schemas are either images of external reality, knowledge "structures," or memory storage bins.

Differentiating between symbolic models and habits of expectation transforms and refines the schema concept. Building upon Gregory Bateson's (1972) insight that ways of seeing and understanding may be understood as "apperceptive habits" and Karl Popper's emphasis on the role of expectation in learning,

transformation theory differentiates the functions of classificatory schemas that pertain to time, space, direction, dimension,
sequence, and entity from schemas that depend upon the mastery
of language. These functions may be further differentiated from
those exercised by habits of expectation or meaning perspectives, which reflect developmental stage perspectives, cognitive
and learning styles, and perceptual filters as well as social ideologies, professional or academic disciplines, cultural and language
codes, self-concepts, introjected value systems, and predisposi-
tions shaped by personality and neurosis. Rather than simply
serving as frameworks for classifying current experience, meaning perspectives are informed by an horizon of possibility that
is anticipated and represents value assumptions regarding ends,
norms, and criteria of judgment.

Although Goleman sees schemas as "the structures memories are stored in" (1985b, p. 79), he also sees them as guiding
analysis of sensory input, simplifying, organizing, and delet-
ing what is not salient. When they function in this way, schemas
are "lions at the gates of awareness" and "the building blocks
of cognition," embodying the categories and rules that order new
experience. They set priorities, determine relevance, and determine the focus of attention and what will enter our awareness. All this occurs outside of consciousness as the regulatory
function of tacit learning by which we actively select what we
will attend to according to criteria of perceived need, interest,
and perceptual prominence. Only those schemas most activated
in the preconscious reach consciousness. In the terms of Goleman's cognitive psychology, our brains use schemas to scan and
filter stimuli and either relegate them to long-term memory, which
may lead to an unconscious response (an experienced typist
finding the correct keys on a typewriter), or move them into
awareness and possible conscious response. According to Goleman, we also use our repertoire of schemas to classify objects
and events. Goleman (1985a) describes still other functions that
he attributes to schemas:

> Schemas and attention interact in an intricate dance.
> Attention to one facet of experience — it is lunchtime,

say, and you are hungry — activates other relevant schemas — thoughts of nearby restaurants, say, or what is at hand in the refrigerator. The schemas, in turn, guide attention. If you walk down the street with these schemas active, your focus will be on the restaurants, not the other kinds of shops on the street; if you go to the refrigerator, your attention will fix on the cold cuts, not the roast for the evening meal. Schemas choose this and not that; they determine the scope of attention. The interplay between attention and schemas puts them at the heart of the matter of self-deception. Schemas not only determine what we will notice; they also can determine what we do not notice.

From the standpoint of transformation theory, habits of expectation and meaning schemes rather than schemas or "modules of memory" selectively determine the scope of our attention and hence perception and arbitrarily determine the way we categorize objects and events, make associations, and attribute causality within a value system. They provide the basis for reducing complex inferential tasks to simple judgments. They "set us up" with specific expectations pertaining to cause-effect relationships, scenarios of sequences of events, goal orientations, and what others will be like (Archie Bunker, used car salesman, mother-in-law, wimp). These interpretations are always generalized and make provision for exceptions under particular circumstances. Nevertheless, they tend to become self-fulfilling prophecies. Ashley Montague somewhere wrote of "psychosclerosis" or "hardening of the categories."

However closed a schema or meaning perspective may be, we are not locked into Popper's "myth of the framework," which holds that we become so trapped by our radically different perspectives that communication is impossible. We can enter into rational discourse, albeit with difficulty, because there is always some overlap between meaning perspectives in terms of observations, concepts, problems, or standards.

Because of the need to avoid threatening information, we

narrow our perception, and blind spots — what Goleman refers to as "lacunas" and Fingarette calls "patches of meaninglessness" — arise. They operate on attention to filter the flow of information and come to define the shape of both perception and responses. This results in character formation. "The attentional patterns learned in childhood become self-perpetuating; once a certain expectation of threat is learned, the person becomes disposed to look for it and find it — or look away to avoid it" (Goleman, 1985b, p. 148). Goleman quotes Ernest Becker:

> This organization [of our personality] is a process whereby some things have to be valued more than others, some acts have to be permitted, others forbidden, some lines of conduct have to be closed, some kind of thoughts can be entertained, others are taboo — and so on. Each person literally closes off his world, fences himself around, in the very process of his own growth and organization. [1985b, p. 132]

In fencing out the world by focusing on a limited span of things, it seems inevitable that the learner must give a disproportionate weight to some things that do not deserve it and artificially inflate the importance of the limited area that falls within his or her horizon of perception and action. "And you do this," Goleman says, "because it represents an area that you can firmly hold on to, that you can skillfully manipulate, that you can use easily to justify yourself — your actions, your sense of self, your option in the world" (p. 133).

Goleman sees the cardinal human need as being for comprehension that is undistorted by the defensive avoidance of anxiety and for mentors who will not collude with learners' denial of anxiety-provoking information, their self-deceptions, or their shared social illusions. This is the function of investigative reporters, "whistle-blowers," ombudsmen, grand juries, and therapists, all of whom attempt to keep us honest and free of self-deception. It is the thesis of this book that this list must be extended to include all those concerned with the education of adults.

Personal Constructs. George Kelly (1955) wrote of the development of "personal constructs," which fulfill some of the same functions as meaning perspectives in that they are defined as templates that human beings create and attempt to fit over their realities. The fit may not always be a good one, but it is all we have. Because we cannot affirm something without denying something else, constructs are bipolar and channel experience along dichotomous dimensions: good and bad, friendly and unfriendly, threatening and not threatening, accessible and inaccessible, intelligent and stupid, wise and foolish, and so on. Some constructs are superordinate; for example, "good" subsumes kind, generous, empathic, brave, intelligent, and the like. Every individual sets up a hierarchical system of personal constructs.

Constructs do not "represent" or symbolize events but rather represent distinctions between events. They are reference axes that enable us to place and sequence events into arrays and scales, to distinguish among elements of those events and group them by distinguishing polar opposites. Normally, personal construct systems become modified as our expectations of events are either confirmed or found wanting. If they are not modified, they become less realistic. Variation in a construct system is limited by its permeability or openness to new elements and new subordinate constructs. Shared constructs are the basis for social interaction.

Clearly anticipating transformation theory, Kelly states his "Fundamental Postulate" as, "A person's processes are psychologically channelized by the ways in which he anticipates events." He advances the following corollaries:

1. A person anticipates events by construing their replications. [That is, we repeat an earlier construal when we encounter an event similar to one encountered before. We posture ourselves to make the same sense of the event we made before.]
2. Persons differ from each other in their constructions of events.
3. Each person characteristically evolves, for his convenience

     in anticipating events, a construction system embracing ordinal relationships between constructs.

4. A person's construction system is composed of a finite number of dichotomous constructs.

5. A person chooses for himself that alternative in a dichotomized construct through which he anticipates the greater possibility for extension and definition of his system [chooses in favor of elaborating a system that is functional for anticipating events].

6. A construct is convenient for the anticipation of a finite range of events only.

7. A person's construction system varies as he successively construes the replication of events.

8. The variation in a person's construction system is limited by the permeability of the constructs within whose ranges of convenience the variants lie. [New experiences and events can be added to those that the system already embraces.]

9. A person may successively employ a variety of construction systems which are inferentially incompatible with each other.

10. To the extent that one person employs a construction of experience which is similar to that employed by another, his psychological processes are similar to those of the other person.

11. To the extent that one person construes the construction processes of another, he may play a role in a social process involving the other person. [pp. 103–104]

    It is provocative not only to speculate that meaning perspectives may be structured as Kelly suggested but also to note that his superordinate value constructs, which provide major mapping coordinates (that is, points of reference for getting one's bearings), bear a striking resemblance to the "eternal verities" of the Platonic Idealist philosophers—Truth, Beauty, Goodness, Justice, and so on. Perhaps these may be understood not as metaphysical concepts but as acquired meaning coordinates that epistemologically structure the way we think and learn.

Kelly's delineation of the way that personal constructs function suggests the psychological dynamics of meaning perspectives as well.

Language Games. Wittgenstein's (1958) "language games" are activities played according to various rules that provide the context within which we learn. In the terminology of transformation theory, the rules are assumptions constituting meaning perspectives; they pertain to such activities as describing appearances, giving and obeying orders, and justifying behavior. Understanding consists of being able to follow a rule correctly and respond correctly to a situation. We know that someone has learned something because the learner acts in a way that is judged correct, given the rules for that particular language game, or responds correctly to the situation by following the rules of the game.

Language games refer to the tacit agreement that we share about the way language is to be used in specific contexts. We agree on the definition of words, the situations to which they pertain, and the results of using them. In order to understand the sentence "John is six feet tall," we must agree on what we mean by the word *six*—that is, on the conditions under which we use this word. Similarly, we must agree on the conditions under which we use the word *feet,* and on the nature of the implied process of measurement in feet. These agreements, among others, constitute the rules of the language game played by communicating that "John is six feet tall." Only after a consensus is reached on these rules by members of the language community can we attempt to judge the truth of the assertion about John's height. The agreement we reach through rational discourse provides "objective" criteria for judging validity or correctness.

There are nonverbal games as well. If a masked man points a gun at me on a dark street and demands money, there is a common set of expectations that we both understand about how each of us will behave during the ensuing "conversation of gestures." I will stand still and raise my hands and avoid quick movements. He will take my wallet and possibly my watch. If

I cry out or fight, I increase the probability that he will shoot me. If I give him my wallet, the possibility is greater that he will not harm me. If I avoid eye contact, he may be less likely to interpret my gaze as a challenge. If I speak to him sarcastically or insultingly, on the other hand, I invite a violent response. Sets of mutually understood, though tacit, expectations like these are accepted by those interacting as the cultural and linguistic conditions for communication. The social norms that establish these conditions for interaction have validity only insofar as they are mutually understood and accepted by both parties. Inasmuch as this episode of commuication is largely unspoken, one can understand it only by understanding the meaning perspective that is shared in the context of the situation and the interacting participants' "lines of action."

To explain how or why people learn, we must be attentive to the meaning perspectives they share — the language games they play. It is crucial to identify the rules they are following. What they know is known within the context of the meaning perspective or the language game being played. Learners learn to respond to conditions in appropriate and sometimes in inappropriate ways. Maladaptive or bizarre behavior results when the learner has learned to respond to rules that are inappropriate for particular circumstances.

For Wittgenstein, the beliefs that we experience are not the actual causes of our actions, even though we often offer these beliefs as the reasons why we did what we did. Rather, the conditions in which we find ourselves and the ways we have learned to deal with such conditions cause us to act as we do.

For the educator or the therapist, the relevant questions are "How does the learner respond to the situation?" and "What assumptive rules does he or she follow?" In attempting to describe the rules that the learner follows in a specific situation, the educator must take into account both the way the learner indicates the rules he or she follows and the perceptions of others familiar with the learner.

We learn the rules of various "games" as we learn to react to situations in particular ways. The educator teaches the learner to play new language games by treating the learner as though he or she were already playing each new game and following its rules. The educator who wishes to facilitate transformative learning provides different meaning perspectives that offer new ways of responding to a situation according to new rules that the learner is taught to follow. The educator then encourages the learner to apply the new perspectives (rules) in specific problem situations. Perspective transformation is never complete until action based upon the transformative insights has been taken.

Transformation theory adds dimension to Wittgenstein's ideas. Language games, which transformation theorists would call sociolinguistic meaning perspectives, are understood as habits of expectation assimilated primarily from one's culture. Language games are changed by reflection upon their premises. Even for instrumental learning, in which the truth of assertions may be established empirically, the process always develops in the context of a consensus about the paradigms used. Transformative learning is learning through action, and the beginning of the action learning process is deciding to appropriate a different meaning perspective.

Meaning, Language, and Culture

Sociolinguistic meaning perspectives include both cultural and language codes. The making of meaning in comprehension is primarily a linguistic activity, although a meaning perspective can position us for visual, auditory, or kinesthetic as well as verbal action (Cell, 1984). The way language shapes, limits, and distorts our beliefs needs to be fully recognized. We create and share meanings through signs and symbols. By attaching our wants and impulses to agreed-on meanings, we transform them into desires and purposes. Wants and impulses become desires and purposes only when they are communicated. What wants and impulses mean is defined by the terms used to describe them.

Our common language bonds us into a dialogic community. It is through the dialogic process of consensually determining the conditions under which a sentence or an expressed idea is true or valid that its meaning is substantiated. Consequently, participation in dialogic communities is profoundly important for anyone who wants to understand and facilitate adult learning, autonomy, responsibility, and freedom.

The Cultural Content of Language. Knowledge is a function of association and communication. As such, it depends on tradition — that is, upon symbolic constructs and methods of understanding that are culturally transmitted, developed, and sanctioned. Cultural codes regulate patterns of thought and behavior. Bowers observes, "The range of intentional awareness, the ability to make complex interpretations, and the possibility of imaging alternative future possibilities are all restricted by limited language codes that communicate a life world of recipe knowledge" (p. 47). Norms, rules, institutions, values, and interpretations, including such foundational categories as those that organize our thoughts in such polarities as either-or, cause-effect, or right-wrong, become embedded in language. Language does not adequately communicate intermediate shading, context, intentionality, or subjective meaning. Hanna Pitkin (quoted in Shapiro, 1981, p. 231) refers to the fact that our "language membership" constitutes a set of internalized and obligatory norms that an individual cannot manipulate effectively because their significance derives from collective rather than individual experience.

Cultural codes are the tacit regulatory principles that establish power relationships and the nature of appropriate discourse both within a given body of knowledge or area of specialization and among such bodies and areas. They also are the principles behind the assumptions implicit in our social norms. For Foucault (1972), an "episteme" was the model of interest and power relationships that informs a specific body of knowledge to give it meaning. These relationships create knowledge systems. Foucault held that transformations in knowledge systems are not cognitive but instead emerge as the result of changing social interests that locate persons in various roles and distribute authority and responsibility differently.

Meanings, ideas, feelings, and concepts are not contained in words, sentences, and paragraphs or books, plays, and poems.

They are in the mind of the originator of communication (Reddy, 1979). These systems of signs, which contain partial meaning, can stimulate a reconstruction of meanings, ideas, or feelings in the other person involved, based on his or her own experience — a different experience from that of the originator of the communication. We give meaning to experience in large part by participating in dialogue with others. This includes understanding what is valid in the assertions made by others and achieving consensual validation for our own assertions.

It has frequently been observed that because our reality is prestructured by our linguistic symbol systems, we do not live through language so much as language lives through us. Through language we find concepts with which to punctuate the flow of experience, to locate it in time and space, and to identify objects, events, feelings, circumstances, and contexts. Indeed, language does not merely describe things and events that we experience but constructs them. We cannot conceive the world of our experience without some presuppositions about the boundaries that separate one object or event from another. Statements are not merely about objects or events but are complex utterances governed by rules that rely on implicit norms or standards — tacit knowledge — to typify experiences. In *The Social Construction of Reality* (1966, p. 22), Berger and Luckmann write:

> The language used in everyday life continuously provides me with the necessary objectifications and posits the order within which these make sense and within which everyday life has meaning for me. I live in a place that is geographically designated; I employ tools, from can openers to sports cars, which are designated in the technical vocabulary of my society. I live within a web of human relationships, from my chess club to the United States of America, which are ordered by means of vocabulary. In this way language marks the coordinates of my life in society and fills that life with meaningful objects.

Michael Shapiro (1981) suggests that in any society or culture, language contains rules that provide boundaries around phenomena and thereby produce the objects and events that are the referents of our speech. For example, we do not usually purposefully decide that we will regard certain persons as children. We tacitly designate certain persons as children because our language (and thus consciousness) contains the rule-governed category "child." This category fits into a pattern of life reflected in our use of the language. The "political" content of language becomes apparent here in the presupposition of a set of culturally specific authority and responsibility relationships with implications of legitimation, influence, and control. With Foucault, Shapiro holds that an adequate examination of the problem of meaning must be oriented toward uncovering the political presuppositions inherent in language and in alternative speech practices, that is, in sociolinguistic meaning perspectives. Speech is a form of activity, and meaning inheres in the uses to which utterances are put. The meaning of a statement is to be understood in the contexts in which it is expressed—meaning perspective, self-concept, line of action, and situation.

Linguistic Horizons of Expectation. Symbolic models are imaginatively projected, within the unreliable context of our habits of expectation, to construe objects and events. The central thesis of J. N. Hattiangadi's book *How Is Language Possible?* (1987), is that the meaning of a word or an expression is also a set of expectations or beliefs ("theories"), each of which is "a hypothesis that might conceivably be false, even though we may provisionally accept it unconditionally" (p. 35). Validity testing becomes central to understanding meaning. Words or combinations of words are "crystallizations" of these expectations to which sounds are attached. Each meaningful group of sounds can combine with others to form sentences.

As an example, we come to understand the meaning of *big* by identifying all kinds of big things. Each of us associates "big" with somewhat different dimensions and things. The total meaning of *big* thus includes many different meanings for different people. In a descriptive sentence beginning "Big things are . . . ," someone can be in error or resort to superstition, stereotypes, or other distortions. Nonetheless, there are some common elements of the meaning that let us communicate.

Broad participation in dialogue is necessary to reconcile different meanings of the same thing. Our understanding of language is approximate. Fortunately, although we may never understand the same languages, we do understand largely similar ones. For Hattiangadi, the meaning of a word is not defined by the uses to which it can be put or by the rules governing it but by all those things people believe it could be. It is this variability in meaning combined with common elements that permits us to adapt language to new experience.

When a concept contradicts a deeply entrenched perspective, it may contradict meanings embedded in our words or even presupposed by the perspective that provides us with grammatical categories. Our everyday speech, which reflects our entrenched meaning perspectives, can become challenged through reflection, however. We then attempt to express ourselves more tentatively, as a "manner of speaking," perhaps using new words or combinations of words.

Transformation of linguistic meaning perspectives is inherent in language learning. New expectations (meaning schemes) can bring forth changes in concepts because they contradict beliefs embedded in the meaning of old words. We learn by understanding a problem for which we prepare a "theory" or meaning scheme. This provides us with new words that we can use to state a new problem. The new problem is solved by a new scheme, the new meaning scheme provides some more specialized language, and so on. Hattiangadi writes:

> In my view, transcending the presuppositions of the language is far from extraordinary; it is commonplace. Every child learning a language is constantly transcending the presupposed views of its own language. The key to this process is in the particular ability of a language to allow us to entertain views which are contrary to its own presuppositions. The

means by which this is accomplished is the institutionalization of forms of speech, divorcing them somewhat from their original significance. It is this which allows us to transcend our languages, to understand each other. [p. 15]

Summary

This chapter has elaborated on the nature of meaning perspectives and meaning schemes by comparing them to similar terms used by other authors. These terms include horizons of expectation (Popper), perceptual filters (Roth), paradigms (Kuhn), frames (Goffman, Bateson), ideologies, schemas (Goleman and others), personal constructs (Kelly), and language games (Wittgenstein).

The chapter also explained ways that culture and language contrive to create the meaning perspectives and schemes that constitute what Popper calls our horizons of expectation. These ways of understanding, believing, and feeling are seldom intentionally learned in adulthood. They involve the selection and construal of symbols and signs through which instances in experience may be identified.

Words and sentences also may be understood as habits of expectation. Because we each experience somewhat different instances of these habitual categories for construing meanings, dialogue is essential to permit us to validate consensually our particular interpretations. From this perspective, the critiquing of assertions based upon culturally assimilated habits of expectation that distort reality and produce dependence, leading to transformation of these expectations, is seen as the most significant developmental task of adults in a modern society.

Propositions from various sources discussed in this chapter include the following:

1. Meaning perspectives are rule systems of habitual expectation (orientations, personal paradigms), and meaning schemes (knowledge, beliefs, value judgments, and feelings that constitute a specific interpretation) are specific habits of expectation. Both influence the way we define, understand, and act

upon our experience. Meaning perspectives generate meaning schemes.

2. Meaning perspectives are structures of epistemic, cultural, and psychic assumptions within which our past experience assimilates and transforms new experience. In addition to providing a framework for classifying experience, they are informed by a horizon of possibility that is being anticipated and that represents value assumptions regarding ends, norms, and criteria of judgment.

3. Because meaning perspectives are structures of largely prerational, unarticulated presuppositions, they often result in distorted views of reality. Negation or transformation of inadequate, false, distorted, or limited meaning perspectives or schemes is central to adult learning; this involves the testing of fundamental assumptions rather than mere extension of knowledge. Meaning perspectives and schemes can be transformed through a reflective assessment and critique of the presuppositions upon which they are based.

4. We learn in order to add to, extend, or change the structure of our expectations, that is, our meaning perspectives and schemes; learning to change these structures of meaning is fundamentally transformative.

5. Some of what other authors have called *schemas* may be better understood as *symbolic models,* which are organized by and projected through mediating meaning perspectives, as dictated by a line of action; their projection results in an interpretation or *meaning scheme.* Other schemas are sets of habits of expectation or *meaning perspectives.* Transformation theory also differentiates between schemas that are dependent upon language categories and those that are not.

6. Meaning perspectives may serve as bipolar axes or coordinates in construing the nature and values of our experiences. The axes enable us to place and sequence events and to distinguish between elements and groups of elements in experience by distinguishing polar opposites. Meaning perspectives can position us for action that involves visual, auditory, and kinesthetic as well as linguistic modes.

7. Our language binds us into a dialogic community that

has common meaning perspectives concerning the contexts and meanings of words. Dialogic communities strive to achieve consensus regarding the conditions under which an expressed idea is considered to be true or valid. Dialogue is necessary to validate commonly held meanings.

8. We trade off awareness for avoidance of anxiety when new experiences are inconsistent with our habits of expectation, which can result in areas of meaninglessness. To provide meaning, we may resort to the psychological mechanisms of self-deception.

3

∝ Intentional Learning: A Process of Problem Solving

This chapter focuses on a fundamental distinction between two interacting domains of intentional learning, the instrumental and the communicative. This distinction was derived from Habermas, whose work also provides the sociolinguistic theoretical context for transformation theory. The chapter suggests that communicative learning is predicated on a logic different from the logic that guides instrumental learning. Metaphors rather than hypotheses play a central role in the logic involved in communicative learning. In this form of learning, problematic beliefs and meaning schemes are validated through critical discourse and action. The chapter also describes reflective learning, a process that affects both instrumental and communicative learning. This kind of learning involves reflection on assumptions and premises, which can transform meaning schemes and perspectives. Finally, the chapter describes four forms of adult learning, two of which are transformative.

The Sociolinguistic Context of Transformative Learning

Jurgen Habermas is considered to be the most influential contemporary German social theorist. As a philosopher and

sociologist, he has produced an extraordinary range of specialized writings in the social sciences, linguistics, and philosophy
that combine to present a comprehensive and provocative theory of knowledge, human interest, and rationality in communication that is of particular import for educators of adults. His
roots are in the tradition of German thought that extends from
Kant to Marx. He is the present leading representative of the
form of critical social theory associated with the Frankfurt School,
which (through the work of Horkheimer, Adorno, Marcuse,
Fromm, and others) pioneered in the study of the relationship
between the ideas of Marx and those of Freud. Habermas's *Theory of Communicative Action* (1984, 1987) has been widely hailed
as a major contribution to contemporary social theory. It also
suggests a new foundation for understanding adult learning and
the function and goals of adult education. This work is sum-
marized in the following subsections.

Validity Testing. Dialogue or communicative action (spoken
or written communication) occurs whenever an individual with
particular aims communicates with another person in order to
arrive at an understanding about the meaning of a common experience so that they may coordinate their actions in pursuing
their respective aims. In short, reaching an understanding is
the inherent purpose of human linguistic communication. Being able to participate in communicative action requires a universal core of basic attitudes, a tacit consensus about norms and
values and fundamental rules — that is, meaning perspectives —
that we must master in order to speak a language. This core
of basic attitudes includes agreed-upon ways of establishing the
validity (justification) of a given communication. Drawing upon
the prior learning represented by these attitudes, we are able
to incorporate the way that the person with whom we are communicating defines the situation about which we speak so that
it becomes possible to arrive at a common definition by which
we may coordinate our points of view.

Dialogue or communicative action allows us to relate to
the world around us, to other people, and to our own intentions,
feelings, and desires. Dialogue in any of these areas involves

either implicit or explicit claims regarding the justification or validity of what is said, implied, or presupposed. The meaning of an utterance is inherently connected with the validity claims it makes. Giddens (in Bernstein, 1985, p. 99) explains: "When I say something to somebody else, I implicitly make the following claims: that what I say is intelligible; that its propositional content is true; that I am justified in saying it; and that I speak sincerely, without intent to deceive. All of these claims are contingent or fallible, and all except the first can be criticized and grounded in by offering of reasons."

Habermas refers to the application of validity criteria as "grounding": "'Grounding' descriptive statements means establishing the existence of states of affairs; 'grounding' normative statements, establishing the acceptability of actions or norms of action; 'grounding' evaluative statements, establishing the preferability of values; 'grounding' expressive statements, establishing the transparency of self-presentations; and 'grounding' explicative statements, establishing that symbolic expressions have been produced correctly" (Habermas, 1984, p. 39).

Our claims to valid knowledge about objective facts, social norms, and the authenticity of our subjective experience are refined through speech. As Habermas says, "The meaning of sentences, and the understanding of sentence meanings, cannot be separated from language's inherent relation to the validity of statements. *Speakers and hearers understand the meaning of a sentence when they know under what conditions it is true.* Correspondingly, they understand the meaning of a word when they know what contribution it makes to the capacity for truth of a sentence formed with its help" (1984, p. 276, my italics).

Figure 2 depicts the processes involved in validity testing. Movement in the validation process, dictated by the learner's purpose or line of action, goes from the identification of a problem through reflection, empirical or consensual validation, and imaginative insight to making a new interpretation. Every phase of the validation process is affected by our meaning perspectives, which may be transformed as a result of premise reflection (see Chapter Four). This aspect of the validation process

is indicated by the arrow pointing from the new interpretation
to the meaning perspectives.

Figure 2. Validation of Learning.

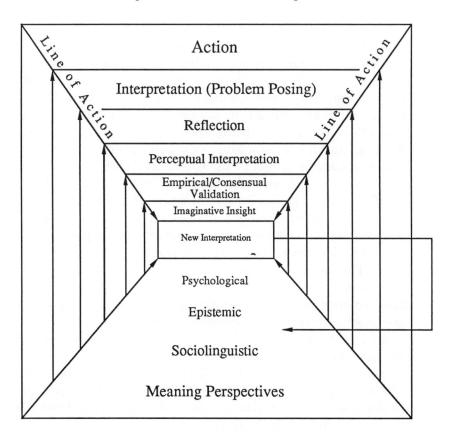

Rationality. Rationality for Habermas is inseparable from
the processes of making meaning, understanding, and testing
the validity of what we communicate. Rationality means validity testing by reasoning—using reasons and weighing evidence
and supporting arguments—rather than by appealing to authority, tradition, or brute force. Habermas rejects the traditional

cognitive-instrumental concept of rationality as the process through which an individual acquires and uses knowledge to control and manipulate the environment. He sees rationality as applicable to all validity testing; our concern with making meaning by assessing the validity of statements, he says, cannot be limited to questions of propositional truths or means for attaining ends.

Habermas uses the term *argumentation* to refer to that process of dialogue in which implicit validity claims are made explicit and contested, with an effort to criticize and vindicate them through arguments. An argument contains reasons or grounds that are relevant to supporting a validity claim. Rationality is indicated by being open to argument. One agrees or disagrees "in light of reasons or grounds; such positions are the expression of insight or understanding" (1984, p. 38). Argumentation, in short, is the process of applying rationality to validity testing. In the context of communicative action, the responsible and autonomous adult is one who is a member of a communication community that is able to participate fully in discourse devoted to assessing criticizable validity claims.

The rational arguments we use in reviewing the grounds for claiming validity are adapted to cultural traditions. They also are institutionalized in many kinds of institutions, which are concerned with determining the truth of propositional statements; the legal system, which is concerned with determining the rightness of action; and the art establishment, which is concerned with determining the authenticity of creative expression. These are specialized dialogic communities with consciously articulated standards for making informed, objective, and rational consensual judgments concerning validity claims.

Because validity claims can be criticized rationally, it is possible to correct mistakes and learn from them. We can not only revise errors in prior learning but challenge and revise inadequate meaning schemes and perspectives by critical reflection on the formerly unexamined assumptions that led us astray in earlier interpretations.

Communicative competence is the ability to participate in rational assessment of the evidence and arguments that support an implied or explicit claim of the validity of a linguistic communication act—that is, to apply rationality to dialogue. For Bowers, communicative competence may be understood simply as "the individual's ability to negotiate meanings and purposes instead of passively accepting the social realities defined by others" (1984, p. 2). Although children must rely upon adult authority to provide guidance in the validation process, self-directedness is inherent in the way our culture defines adulthood, and communicative competence is the essence of self-direction. It follows that freedom from coercion is an indispensable requirement for communicative competence.

The Dynamics of Communicative Action

Three interrelated dynamics are involved in communicative action. They are the dynamics of the lifeworld, learning, and social interaction. This section will examine these different dynamics in detail.

The Lifeworld. The symbolically prestructured world of everyday life, or "lifeworld," is a "culturally transmitted and linguistically organized stock of interpretive patterns" or perspectives. This daily universe of social activity that we take for granted, this prereflective lifeworld that provides the "context-forming horizon" of learning, is made up of a vast inventory of unquestioned assumptions and shared cultural convictions, including codes, norms, roles, social practices, psychological patterns of dealing with others, and individual skills. Communicated through language, it provides learners with a basis from which to begin negotiating common definitions of situations.

The processes by which the lifeworld is reproduced—cultural reproduction, social integration, and socialization—are based upon the understanding, coordination, and sociation functions of communicative action. These functions become manifest in what Habermas calls propositional, illocutionary, and expressive speech acts. The illocutionary refers to what a person is purposefully doing when he or she makes an utterance. If I say to you, "Look out, it may explode," what I am doing is giving you a warning. The illocutionary speech act specifies "which validity claim a speaker is raising with his utterance, how he is raising it, and for what" (p. 278). Illocutionary acts have an internal connection with reasons, and this infuses them with the inherent possibility of mutual recognition based on insight rather than on external force.

Learning. The second dynamic of communicative action, according to Habermas, involves the transformative nature of the learning process. Through our capacity to become critically reflective we can diminish the "prejudgmental power" of the lifeworld over communicative practice in everyday life. Once our experiences are translated into speech acts, they become transformed into judgments and are connected with a validity claim. We can become empowered to "own" our mutual understandings because they have been arrived at through our own adult interpretations and positions on criticizable validity claims.

If meaning is understood when we know under what conditions an expressed idea is true, as Habermas suggests, we must attend closely to the process of validity testing in order to learn. In dialogue what we say most commonly involves either descriptive, normative, or expressive contents. The validity of these contents can be challenged through argumentative discourse that raises questions of truth, justice, and self-deception respectively. Consequently, there are three major types of discourse. The first pertains to knowledge we hold about the world. Their claim to truth may be challenged. When it is, the ensuing dialogue is called by Habermas *theoretical discourse.* Claims to truth may be validated by empirical tests.

The second type of discourse pertains to utterances that involve social norms, ideals, values, and moral decisions. When these are challenged, it is not their truth but their rightness (or the rightness of the norms used as standards) that is at issue. The challenge gives rise to *practical discourse.* Validation of claims in practical discourse is achieved by a consensus arrived at through rational dialogue. The third type of speech acts involve feelings or intent and pertain to a person's subjectivity. They may be challenged in terms of their authenticity. *Therapeutic dis-*

course attempts to determine whether they indeed represent true
feelings or intentions or instead involve falsehood or self-deception.

There are two additional types of discourse. One is "aesthetic criticism," which challenges the value standards implicit
in any effort to interpret feelings and desires. The other is "explicative discourse," which raises questions about the comprehensibility or rightness of linguistic expressions. It is through
these forms of critical discourse that the validity of a speech act
is called into question that the learner has the opportunity to
make a new interpretation of his or her experience, which in
turn can transform meaning schemes and perspectives.

For Habermas, the very idea of developing an individual sense of identity centers around the ability to realize one's
potential for critical self-reflection. He adapts the Piagetian concept of "decentration" as the process of moving away from an
egocentric understanding of the world toward a progressive willingness and ability to participate in rational argument about
the validity of what is communicated. When a person becomes
decentered, "Communicatively achieved understanding" replaces
the willingness to take for granted the "normatively ascribed
agreement" prescribed by the background convictions of the
lifeworld. Rationality applied to communication relates a decentered understanding of the world to the possibility of participating in discourse to assess criticizable validity claims.

Social Interaction. The third dynamic of communicative action is the self-regulating system of society and social interaction, the patterns of material reproduction, that serve as a
"boundary-maintenance system" of the lifeworld. Traditional cultures usually involve closed worldviews. Through social evo-
lution and the decentering of worldviews, modern cultures
generally are more open to modification in the light of their
members' learning experiences. The more advanced the decentering process, the less assured is a consensus predicated only
upon established beliefs and codes of behavior.

"Mechanisms of modernity," such as the organization of
exchange relations in a market economy and the institutionalization of political power in public bureaucracies, tend to become

quasi-autonomous subsystems that organize and steer social interaction in ways that can corrupt the process of seeking mutual understanding through rationally settling validity claims. Professionalization has emerged as a further barrier to fostering critically reflective dialogue among ordinary people in everyday life. Rather than active agents seeking mutual understanding of their world, adults become "clients," citizens are reduced to objects of mass manipulation, and workers become commodified. These "system" forces tend to subjugate or "colonize" the lifeworld and to distort rational decision making and adult learning processes. Social integration and the supports that the economy and public policy require become jeopardized.

The encroachment of economic and administrative subsystems on communicative interaction can be suffocating. Nonetheless, there is a potential for emancipation and resistance through social movements concerned with the quality of life: the civil rights, ecology, peace, women's, popular democracy, and other movements concerned with maintaining the essential conditions for active participation in critically reflective dialogue by all. Habermas deems it essential that we develop the institutions and the communicative competence necessary to secure an effectively functioning public sphere in which practical questions can be resolved through public discussion and decided on the basis of discursively achieved agreement.

Instrumental Learning

In his *Knowledge and Human Interests* (1971), Habermas describes three broad areas in which human interest generates knowledge: the technical, the practical, and the emancipatory. They are grounded in our relationships to the environment, other people, and power, respectively. Each area is "knowledge constitutive" because it has its own distinctive categories for interpreting experience, methods for discovering knowledge, and methods for validating assertions pertaining to it.

Habermas sees the first two human interests as representing distinct learning domains — the domains of instrumental and communicative learning, respectively — while the emancipatory interest involves a learning dimension of critical reflection with implications for both of the other two. The two interests each also requires a different mode of personal learning, with different learning needs and different implications for facilitators of adult learning. Habermas makes a fundamental distinction between the dynamics of learning to control and manipulate the environment (instrumental learning) and the dynamics of learning to understand others (communicative learning). Differences in the nature of these two basic interests mandate a fundamentally different methodology of systematic objective inquiry for each type of learning.

The first of the three areas of cognitive interest, the technical or "work" area, concerns the ways we control and manipulate our environment, including other people. This involves "instrumental"—or, in the case of controlling or manipulating people, "strategic"—action. Instrumental action always involves predictions about observable events, physical or social, which can prove correct or incorrect. Such action is based upon empirical knowledge and is governed by technical rules. Choices in the process of instrumental action involve strategies based upon this knowledge and deduced from rules of a value system or from rules of investigation. These strategies may be correctly or incorrectly deduced. Choosing the best strategy depends upon correctly assessing alternatives. The criteria of effective control of reality determine which choice is appropriate or inappropriate.

The domain of instrumental learning centrally involves determining cause-effect relationships and learning through task-oriented problem solving. Dewey's (1933) concept of reflection in the context of problem solving has particular relevance here. Dewey explains that we respond to an indeterminate situation by formulating hypothetical courses of action, anticipating the consequences of each, acting upon the most plausible hypothesis, and testing its validity by the results of the action. We deduce generalizations from hypotheses. Piaget described this hypothetical-deductive form of reasoning in terms of "formal operations" and saw it as a final developmental stage of human beings, emerging in adolescence.

Put in terms of transformation theory, meaning is acquired

deductively in task-oriented problem solving by testing a hypothetical meaning scheme that we believe will more effectively
influence a cause-effect relationship so as to permit greater control over a problem situation. We begin by developing a prediction (hypothesis) that describes how it is possible to make something work better by doing something differently. To hit a golf
ball so that it will land closer to the hole, for example (cause-
effect), we might analyze the relevant variables — both those that
have to do with style and technique and those that have to do
with conditions of distance, wind, and terrain — and decide that
we have reasons to believe that we may achieve greater control
by changing the way we hold the club (hypothesis). We then
test this hypothesis by holding the other variables constant and
altering our grip on the club. If the resulting swing places the
ball closer to the hole than before, we can take the hypothesis
as truth. In other words, the truth of the meaning scheme
hypothetically attributed to an external reality is proven or dis-
proven through the control and manipulation of variables following the protocols of empirical-analytic inquiry, a prescriptive form of inquiry.

It should be noted parenthetically that behind this learning scenario is a set of *consensually,* rather than empirically, established meanings; the meaning of cause and effect, of a game,
of the game of golf and the function of a golf ball and golf clubs,
of the meaning of successful performance in golf and in general,
and of the meaning of the very words and sentences with which
we conceptualize this reality. Instrumental learning and empirical verification are based on and dependent upon a foundation
of communicative learning.

Instrumental learning always involves a prediction about
observable things or events. A proposition can be established
as "valid" — that is, justified or supportable — by demonstrating
its empirical "truth," that is, its being in accord with what is,
and the correctness of the analyses involved. Experience is organized to ensure the success of these operations. Learning is
directed toward determining cause-effect relationships.

The "empirical-analytic" natural sciences have been developed expressly to assist us in understanding material related
to our technical interest. Habermas contends that the very form

of this way of knowing necessitates the analysis of objects and events into dependent and independent variables and the identification of regularities among them. Our efforts to control and manipulate the environment have dictated a uniquely appropriate approach that uses hypothetical-deductive theories and permits the deduction of empirical generalizations from lawlike hypotheses through controlled observation and experimentation.

Communicative Learning

The second area of cognitive interest is what Habermas identifies as "practical." The domain of learning associated with this area is called communicative. Its purpose is communication: learning to understand what others mean and to make ourselves understood as we attempt to share ideas through speech, the written word, plays, moving pictures, television, and art. Most significant learning in adulthood falls into this category because it involves understanding, describing, and explaining intentions; values; ideals; moral issues; social, political, philosophical, psychological, or educational concepts; feelings and reasons. All of these things are shaped decisively by cultural and linguistic codes and social norms and expectations.

Communicative action is a way of knowing distinctly different from instrumental action. Communicative action, Habermas writes, "is governed by binding consensual norms, which define reciprocal expectations about behavior and which must be understood and recognized by at least two acting subjects. Social norms are enforced through sanctions. Their meaning is objectified in ordinary language communication. While the validity of technical rules and strategies [pertaining to instrumental learning] depend on that of empirically true or analytically correct propositions, the validity of social norms is grounded only in the intersubjectivity of the mutual understanding of intentions and secured by the general recognition of obligations" (1971, p. 92).

Consensual Validation. Communication — that is, symbolic interaction — involves assertions about the meaning of a vast range of experience in several dimensions, extending from the concrete to the poetic. We are continually confronted with having to determine the validity of reports, predictions, explanations, arguments, and denials as well as the implicit claims of validity involved in justifying commands, requests, excuses, and recommendations. We must decide what is right or wrong, bad or good, correct or incorrect, appropriate or inappropriate, beautiful or ugly. In the domain of communicative learning, as Habermas noted, validity cannot be determined through the empirical-analytic kind of inquiry used in instrumental learning. Rather, validity testing takes the form of consensus reached through rational discourse.

In the absence of empirical tests, we learn what is valid in the assertions of others and gain credence for the validity of our own ideas by either relying on tradition, authority, or force or relying on as broad a consensus possible of those who are most informed, rational, and objective. The consensus involved in validating expressed ideas ideally implies a universal agreement, just as a judgment by a jury in a court trial ideally would remain the same regardless of whether one or two jurors became ill and alternative jurors took their place. The verdict should be the same because an informed and objective review of the evidence and arguments should result in the same decision regardless of the change in jurors. In fact, however, universal agreement is difficult, if not impossible, to obtain, and the validity of consensual judgments arrived at through rational discourse must be provisional because new information and new paradigms may always emerge. Gouldner (1976) appropriately suggests that we think of this group consensus as a mediation and a continuing dialogue.

Because a consensus may be reached through coercion, it becomes essential that the standards pertaining to arriving at a consensus be examined before a specific consensus can be accepted as reasonable. The threat of infinite regression implied by observing that these standards must also be the product of group agreement is ameliorated by recognizing that every group involved in rational discourse must win acceptance of its procedures and conclusions from some larger group. Gouldner (1976) points out that even in the context of scientific inquiry, "the scientists' actions must be deemed reasonable by the larger community of non-specialist scholars, because it conforms to some grammar of rationality or culture of critical discourse it accepts which cuts across the diverse paradigms of each science" (p. 20). Gouldner goes on to observe, "Such validity as truth-claims possess, then, are to be understood as proposals and counterproposals in a dialogue in a community of the interested who share a culture of critical discourse. They are moments in an ongoing process of talk; responses to what has been said before, as well as remarks about a world outside the speakers" (p. 21).

In rational discourse, in contrast to everyday dialogue, principles and operations are made linguistically explicit. Thus, Gouldner says, such discourse is likely to be more independent of context and less closely linked to local social structures, relationships, or situations than ordinary dialogue. Rational discourse has been institutionalized in, for example, courtroom proceedings, university seminars, scientific inquiry, psychotherapy, and responsible journalism (at least in their ideal forms). We resort to discourse when we have reason to question the comprehensibility, truth, appropriateness (in relation to norms), or authenticity (in relation to feelings) of what is being asserted or to question the credibility of the person making the statement. When this happens, further dialogue becomes impossible until these questions can be resolved.

The Conditions of Rational Discourse. Because validity testing of contested meaning is so central to understanding the conditions under which the meaning of a communicated idea is true and because so much of what we need to understand must be consensually validated, the very nature of communication implies the existence of a set of optimal conditions for participation in rational discourse. Under these optimal conditions, participants will:

- have accurate and complete information
- be free from coercion and distorting self-deception
- be able to weigh evidence and assess arguments objectively
- be open to alternative perspectives

- be able to become critically reflective upon presuppositions and their consequences
- have equal opportunity to participate (including the chance to challenge, question, refute, and reflect and to hear others do the same), and
- be able to accept an informed, objective, and rational consensus as a legitimate test of validity.

These conditions provide the grounds for determining criteria for judging the level of development of meaning perspectives, the educational process, and social goals and practices as well. They become the bridge between the *is,* the present nature of the adult learning process, and the *ought,* an educational and social philosophy, as we will see in Chapter Seven.

Participation in rational discourse under these ideal conditions will help adults become critically reflective of the meaning perspectives and arrive at more developmentally advanced meaning perspectives. A developmentally advanced meaning perspective is one that is:

- more inclusive, discriminating, and integrative of experience
- based upon full information
- free from both internal and external coercion
- open to other perspectives and points of view
- accepting of others as equal participants in discourse
- objective and rational in assessing contending arguments and evidence
- critically reflective of presuppositions and their source and consequences, and
- able to accept an informed and rational consensus as the authority for judging conflicting validity claims.

The Limits of Rationality. There are limits to the process of rational discourse. Issues such as those involved in the "constrained" versus "unconstrained" visions of society described by Sowell (see Chapter Five) or the debate over abortion do not lend themselves to this process because the presuppositions of the opposing groups are often irreconcilable. When rational discourse fails, we turn to other forms of authority to resolve our differences. In the United States, we resort—all too readily—to a political solution or one imposed through the courts, or we turn to religious dogma. It is in all of our interests to minimize the number of these imposed solutions and not to allow the dictates of political, legal, or religious systems to become substitutes for rational discourse. In a sense, politicians, lawyers, and dogmatic religious leaders represent an entrenched establishment who have acquired a hegemony over problem solving that encroaches upon the lifeworld of both adult learners and adult educators. When the educators fail, the politicians, lawyers, and religious leaders move in and impose solutions. Of course, any of these professions may—and sometimes do—play the role of adult educator and foster rather than usurp the role of critical discourse and consensus.

Differences from Instrumental Learning. Understanding and inquiry in the communicative domain do not have as their aim technical control and manipulation, as they do in the instrumental domain. Rather, their aim is the clarification of conditions for communication and "intersubjectivity," the process of relating to another as a psychological subject (an agent like oneself) rather than as an object to be controlled and manipulated. As a result, the process of problem solving in this learning domain is fundamentally different from that of the task-oriented problem solving involved in instrumental learning.

In communicative learning, the learner actively and purposefully negotiates his or her way through a series of specific encounters by using language and gesture and by anticipating the actions of others. This process is governed by social norms, which provide the frame of reference and the preconditions for understanding in the form of a set of reciprocal expectations.

The form of inquiry involved in communicative learning is designative, as opposed to the prescriptive form found in instrumental learning. We learn to understand what is designated rather than to dictate what we should do. We have all read a poem or viewed a painting without fully comprehending it or have left the theater unclear about the meaning of a play or film. Only later something we read or the insightful remark of a friend or critic suggests a meaning scheme that makes our experience click into focus and provides understanding. As with the domain of instrumental learning, however, consensual judgments can be reached through reasoning and argumentation.

The focus of communicative learning is not establishing cause-effect relationships but increasing insight and attaining common ground through symbolic interaction. Action in this learning domain is communicative rather than instrumental. Rather than testing the truth of a hypothesis, the problem-solving process in communicative learning involves the identification and validation of explanatory constructs.

The distinction between instrumental and communicative learning is extremely important to point out because instrumental learning has been too commonly taken as the model of all learning. Nonetheless, this differentiation should not be understood as an attempt to establish a dichotomy. As I emphasized in the earlier example of learning to improve one's golf game, instrumental learning occurs within a context of communicative learning; most learning involves both instrumental and communicative aspects.

Learning Through Metaphors. Just as hypotheses are the reasoning tools of instrumental learning, metaphors are the tools of communicative learning. We confront the unknown by making associations with what we know. We begin with partial insights to direct the way we collect additional data. We compare incidents, key concepts, or words and relate them to our meaning schemes. Often understanding comes from finding the right metaphor to fit the experience analogically into our meaning schemes, theories, belief systems, or self-concept.

Learning through metaphors transcends simply identifying isolated similarities; it may refer to whole ranges of similarities and associated implications. Metaphors often are based upon correlations between the experience perceived and something known. For example, in perceiving the correlation between the amount of time a task takes and the amount of labor it takes, we become able to view time and labor metaphorically as resources and to see similarities between them. In this way similarities are *created*. Another type of correlation is illustrated by the metaphor "Life is a gambling game," in which actions in life are experienced as gambles with chances of winning or losing (Lakoff and Johnson, 1980).

Of course, metaphors connoting the attributes associated with a known event or object focus selectively upon some attributes and ignore and obscure others. When we say, "George is flaky," we create similarities by likening an intangible, elusive psychological orientation to a solid object, a snowflake. We focus on certain attributes of a snowflake, such as fragility, lightness of weight, and directionlessness of movement, and ignore others, such as beauty and structural complexity.

Meaning schemes and perspectives dictate both the selection and the composition of metaphors. Lakoff and Johnson note, "A sentence is virtually never understood on its own terms without the evocation of some larger gestalt that specifies the normal range of natural dimension (e.g., purposes, stages, etc.). Whichever gestalt is evoked, we understand much more than is given directly in the sentence. Each such gestalt provides a background for understanding the sentence in terms of an experiential category of our culture" (p. 168). Many concepts, such as understanding, argument, idea, love, happiness, health, and morality, can be described only in terms of metaphors.

Donald Schön (1979) identifies two traditions in understanding metaphors. One tradition treats them as a language anomaly to be overcome in order to make possible the formulation of a general theory of reference or of meaning. However, Schön writes, there is also another tradition, "one which treats metaphor as central to the task of accounting for our perspectives on the world: how we think about things, make sense of reality, and set the problems we later try to solve. In this second sense, 'metaphor' refers both to a certain kind of product — a perspective or frame, a way of looking at things — and a certain kind of process — a process by which new perspectives on the world come into existence" (p. 254). Metaphors resulting from this process, which Schön calls "generative metaphors," are significant only as symptoms of a particular way of seeing something as something else, "of carrying over frames or perspectives from one domain of experience to another" (p. 254).

One of Schön's examples of a generative metaphor involves a group of product development researchers who were attempting to improve a new paintbrush with synthetic bristles. They were unable to do this until one observed that "a paintbrush is a kind of pump!" This metaphor focused attention on the way paint is forced through the spaces between the bristles of a paintbrush when the brush is pressed against a surface. The original metaphor insight permitted the researchers to draw upon all their associated notions about pumps and pumping and to apply them to the painting situation, thus transforming the initial ideas of both painting and pumping. For example, seeing paint flowing through channels made between the bristles, they could experiment with ways of changing the bristles to compress the channels, thus affecting the pumping of liquid through them. It is important to note that the process did not begin with the researchers noticing specific similarities between paintbrushes and pumps. They started with only a notion or feeling of similarity. Formulation of an analogy between paintbrushes and pumps occurred only after the perception of both had been restructured so that their elements and relationships could be analyzed. Still later the researchers were able to construct a generalized model with other applications.

Because so much of what we communicate and of what we understand in what others communicate is construed metaphorically, it is essential that we become aware of and able to criticize tacit generative metaphors. Such critical awareness will increase our effectiveness in analyzing problems by allowing us to examine the analogies, including possibly false or limited analogies, that are being used to attribute meaning to an experience.

Confronting the Unknown. Because communicative learning involves dealing with the ideas of others, it frequently requires us to confront the unknown. When we confront the unknown — that is, when the properties of an experience do not fit our expectations or further differentiation is called for — our reflection may result in the creation of new meaning schemes or habits of expectation to integrate these properties. Over time, a limited initial understanding may become transformed through metaphorical thought as we come to discover the significance of this understanding in other experiential, theoretical, literary, or aesthetic contexts. Each datum is a building block of understanding and is clarified and extended by the discovery of other building blocks in a dialectical symbiotic relationship. We continually move back and forth between the parts and the whole of what we seek to understand. Initial expectation and its revision, the dialectical movement between preconception and confirmation and between meaning scheme and experience, is captured in Hans-Georg Gadamer's concept of the "hermeneutic circle," which also can refer to mediation between whole and parts and between past and present (Wolff, 1975).

The process of learning in the communicative domain involves the identification and validation of explanatory constructs. Concepts become constructs as we actively explore them in new contexts by searching out other experiences in which they seem operative, much in the same way that theoretical sampling guides grounded theory research (Glaser and Strauss, 1967). In theoretical sampling, one selects cases for study that can best contribute to understanding inductively derived patterns of commonality and difference.

Imagination is indispensable to understanding the unknown. We imagine alternative ways of seeing and interpreting. The more reflective and open to the perspectives of others we are, the richer our imagination of alternative contexts for understanding will be. Intuition also can play a central role in identifying a strange experience. Intuition refers to immediate recognition of the experience's meaning or significance without going through the process of intentional analysis. In Chapter One we identified intuition as the major link between presentational and propositional construal. Intuition can guide us when we encounter the unknown, suggesting metaphoric analogies and directions for abductive thought. It is also a resource that can provide insight during the process of problem solving or reflection. We appear to be especially receptive to intuition when we are just falling asleep or awakening.

Barer-Stein (1987) provides us with a phenomenological

analysis of learning as a process of experiencing the unfamiliar. She delineates a five-phase model for this process. The first phase, *being aware,* is a reflective pause during which a decision is made to proceed toward understanding an object or event. This phase involves an awareness of current or retrospective interest but does not involve explanations. It involves the desire to know more and the motivating belief that we can achieve understanding. The dominant question in this phase is, "What is this?"

A second phase is *observing.* This involves taking a closer look at the phenomenon and becoming aware of our own interest. The dominant question here is "How does this compare what what I know?" *Acting*—looking at alternative meaning perspectives and judging them—is the third phase. The dominant question is "Shall I try it?" The fourth phase involves *confronting,* coming face-to-face with the unfamiliar and recognizing that it is unknown and will not yield meaning. Faced with this developmental dilemma, we can ignore the confrontation, do battle with it, withdraw by retreat into ourselves or into the comfortable and familiar, or go on to the final phase of *involving.* The dominant questions of confronting are "Do I know this? Do I want to?"

Involving refers to reflecting, validating, judging. It is the phase in which the unknown is appropriated into our meaning framework. This mode of thought in Barer-Stein's system is known as *Sh'ma* (derived from *shema,* to hear) in the Judaic tradition. It involves a fourfold theme of hearing/listening and reflection/heeding (appropriation). Dominant questions in the involving phase are "How did this come to be?" "What are the possibilities?" "Which makes sense?" and "What is the relevant meaning for me?"

Barer-Stein notes the existence of an important anomaly, "the paradox of involving": the more profound the involvement, the more is appropriated and taken for granted; "The better you know something, the less you are aware of knowing it" (p. 101). Ellen Langer (1989) has similarly observed that assumed expertise implies mindlessness.

Problem Solving by Metaphorical-Abductive Logic. The logic of communicative learning is *metaphorical-abductive,* as distinct from the hypothetical-deductive logic of instrumental learning. It moves from the concrete to the abstract rather than from the abstract to the concrete. In communication, we try to understand what someone else means "abductively," that is, by drawing upon our experience to explain theirs. Abduction explains what *may be,* deduction what *must be,* and induction what actually *is* operative (Hanson, 1981).

In solving a problem in the communicative domain, we start by making a metaphoric association between what is known, that is, what has been interpreted within a current meaning scheme, and a new experience. What we know then suggests the next step in problem solving; in abduction, each step suggests the next one. We understand parts in terms of an initial impression of the whole, shaped by habits of expectation (meaning schemes); this interpretation of the whole becomes modified or revised in light of closer analysis of the parts. Movement is toward an interpretation of the whole in which our detailed knowledge of the parts can be integrated without conflict (the hermeneutic circle). We test perceptions against this process of data development; the more we know, the less feasible it is to apply arbitrary preconceptions in very different contexts.

This "problem-solving" process of attempting to understand requires an openness to different perspectives so that a learner becomes reflective or critically reflective in the course of interpretive activity. The learner must view an experience in terms of a conceptual framework or meaning scheme different from that in which it was originally understood as meaningful. Making meaning in this situation occurs through the creation of new meaning schemes or the modification of old ones. McCarthy (1973) compares the process to translation: "[Just] as the translator must find an idiom which preserves, so to speak, the rights of the mother tongue and at the same time respects the foreignness of his text, so too must the interpreter conceptualize his material in such a way that, while its foreignness is preserved, it is nevertheless brought into intelligible relation with the concepts and beliefs of his own culture" (p. 365).

Research in the Communicative Domain. The methods of the empirical-analytic sciences are not appropriate for studying learning in the communicative domain. Such study requires systematic inquiry that seeks the understanding of meaning rather than the delineation of causality. Habermas says that the "historical-hermeneutic" sciences are most relevant to this task of understanding communication. Hermeneutics is the science of interpretation and explanation. It is derived from the branch of theology that, through textual analysis, defines the laws by which the meaning of the Scriptures must be ascertained. The historical-hermeneutic disciplines include descriptive social science, history, aesthetics, legal, ethnographic, literary, and other studies that interpret the meaning of communicative experience.

Habermas compares the approach of the historical-hermeneutic sciences to that of the empirical-analytical sciences (the so-called hard sciences, such as physics and biology):

> Here [in the historical-hermeneutic sciences] the meaning of validity of propositions is not constituted in the frame of reference of technical control. . . . Theories are not constructed deductively and experience is not organized with regard to the success of operations. Access to the facts is provided by the understanding of meaning, not observation. The verification of lawlike hypotheses in empirical-analytic sciences has its counterparts here in the interpretation of texts. Thus the rules of hermeneutics determine the possible meaning of the validity of statements in the cultural sciences. [1971, p. 309]

The historical-hermeneutic disciplines differ from the empirical-analytic sciences in the "content" studied, methods of inquiry, and criteria for assessing alternative interpretations. An example of a study in such a discipline is the writer's grounded theory study of perspective transformation of women in college reentry programs (Mezirow, 1975), in which we used a hermeneutic approach to attempt to understand common patterns in the process of perspective change, which we identified as a prevailing learning process from transcripts of our interviews.

Emancipatory Learning: The Reflective Dimension

In addition to the technical and the practical, Habermas identifies the emancipatory as the third general area of human interest in which we generate knowledge. The emancipatory interest is what impels us, through reflection, to identify and challenge distorted meaning perspectives. It is interest in the knowledge resulting from self-reflection, including interest in the way our history and biography have expressed themselves in the way we see ourselves, our assumptions about learning and the nature and use of knowledge, and our roles and social expectations and the repressed feelings that influence them. Emancipatory knowledge is knowledge gained through critical self-reflection, as distinct from the knowledge gained from our "technical" interest in the objective world or our "practical" interest in social relationships. The form of inquiry in critical self-reflection is appraisive rather than prescriptive or designative.

The emancipation in emancipatory learning is emancipation from libidinal, linguistic, epistemic, institutional, or environmental forces that limit our options and our rational control over our lives but have been taken for granted or seen as beyond human control. These forces include the misconceptions, ideologies, and psychological distortions in prior learning that produce or perpetuate unexamined relations of dependence. Although for Habermas emancipatory interest focuses upon critical self-reflection, critical reflection clearly constitutes an integral element in the process involved in validating learning about the environment and other people as well as ourselves; that is, in both instrumental and communicative learning.

When self-reflection is critical, it involves a searching view of the unquestioningly accepted presuppositions that sustain our fears, inhibitions, and patterns of interaction, such as our reaction to rejection, and their consequences in our relationships. Knowledge gained through self-reflective learning may be distorted, and all learning about oneself is not necessarily reflective (see Chapter Four). Most of what we have learned about ourselves has not been examined for unconsciously incorporated assumptions about the stability of our roles, internal prohibitions, or patterns of thought, perception, and response.

Empirical tests cannot be used to validate the authenticity of our assertions regarding how we feel, but such assertions are consensually validated (or not) through dialogue among those who know us best. We, in turn, validate or question the assertions of others about their feelings; we may decide, for example, that one person's protestations of love are insincere, that another tends to exaggerate or be a chronic complainer, that a third's expressions of feeling arise from self-interest, and so on. Thus, self-knowledge is clearly a function of communicative learning — of how others interpret us — but it is also gained in important ways through instrumental learning by getting feedback on our competence to perform.

All critical reflection is appraisive rather than prescriptive or designative. Emancipatory learning often is transformative. In emancipatory learning, the learner is presented with an alternative way of interpreting feelings and patterns of action; the old meaning scheme or perspective is negated and is either replaced or reorganized to incorporate new insights. In emancipatory learning we come to see our reality more inclusively, to understand it more clearly, and to integrate our experience better. Dramatic personal and social changes become possible when we become aware of the way that both our psychological and our cultural assumptions have created or contributed to our dependence on outside forces that we have regarded as unchangeable. Habermas follows Hegel and Marx in rejecting the notion that a transformed consciousness can be expected to lead automatically to a predictable form of action in a specific situation. One cannot become emancipated through indoctrination. However, learning to understand our individual historical and biographical situation more fully contributes to the development of autonomy and responsibility in deciding how to define our problems and the course of action that is most appropriate under particular circumstances.

When Habermas points to critical social theory as the process of systematic inquiry most appropriate to study material related to our emancipatory interest, my impression is that he is referring to critical reflection upon cultural or, more specifically, ideological assumptions in the domain of communicative learning. As a critical science, psychoanalytic therapy has its most obvious relevance to self-reflective learning in studying the way we come to challenge those psychological assumptions, repressed in childhood, that influence our adult patterns of interaction. In Chapter Seven we will explore other approaches to the systematic study of reflective learning.

It is important to emphasize that both the instrumental and the communicative dimensions are involved in most acts of learning about the world, other persons, and ourselves. Adult learning cannot be understood, facilitated, or researched by defining it exclusively in terms of behavior change. Most adult learning is multidimensional and involves learning to control the environment, to understand meaning as we communicate with others, and to understand ourselves. It often involves critical reflection as well. This suggests that any analysis of adult learning or adult learning gains must address both instrumental and communicative learning, including learning about oneself, as well as the nature, extent, and impact of critical reflection in both domains.

The Nature of Adult Learning

Now that we more clearly understand the dynamics of different types of learning and the function of reflection in transforming established meaning schemes and perspectives, we can identify the forms and levels that learning can have. These forms and levels have been described in different ways by Gregory Bateson, Edward Cell, and transformation theory.

Gregory Bateson's Learning Theory. Gregory Bateson's (1972) ideas about learning are particularly relevant to understanding how meaning perspectives are transformed. Bateson's learning theory rests centrally on the changing of contexts rather than on the mere acquisition of data. His epistemology is predicated upon the belief that we each create our own world in that we look at our reality through our own presuppositions, premises, and expectations. These form the contexts within which we learn. We open ourselves to some interpretations but block out others that make us uncomfortable and often fail to recognize that our own perceptions are only partial. Bateson insisted on the crucial importance of our inescapable biases, our own parochialisms. "For me," writes Bateson, "the moral question is which of my premises I shall be dogmatic about. True, many premises are culturally relative; some are, I believe, both wrong and pathogenic. Alas, the culture can foster premises of this last kind!" (May, 1976).

Because of the parochialism and dogmatism with which we separate ourselves from the perspectives of others and from reality, we need to take part in some form of consensual validation. In his study of communication, which anticipated Habermas, Bateson focused particularly upon communication in which validity depends on belief, such as statements of principles of ethics or aesthetics. Communication and the relationships through which it takes place—relationships of family, work, and community—constitute the context for understanding human beings. Form, pattern, and order inhere in these relationships. Bateson believed that sense organs can receive only news of differences, so phenomena are perceived only when they differ from something else.

According to Bateson, there are four categories of learning. "Zero Learning" involves extending a preexisting habitual response (meaning scheme) to cover additional facts. Neither error nor creativity is possible in Zero Learning. Learning I includes learning about our own habitual responses. In this stage our meaning schemes or perspectives do not change; we are still learning within established meaning schemes. Learning I would include thoughtful action without reflection. (See Chapter Four for a description of the differences between the two.)

Learning II involves learning about contexts (meaning schemes). It is "a change in the process of Learning I, *e.g.,* a corrective change in the set of alternatives from which choice is made, or it is a change in how the sequence of experience is punctuated" (p. 293). Learning through cultural assimilation or introjection is part of Learning II, which also includes our learned traits of character. The premises based upon which we learn may become changed during this stage, although we are unaware of such changes, and consequently we learn how to learn in a different way. When the perceived contexts of meaning become changed, the "facts" we have learned assume new meanings as well. Learning II might be interpreted to involve content or process reflection, the processes by which we make changes in our meaning schemes (see Chapter Four).

Learning III involves transformations of the sort that occur in religious conversion, Zen experience, and psychotherapy. These are perspective transformations, through which we can become aware that our whole way of perceiving the world has been based on questionable premises. "Learning III is a change in the process of Learning II" (p. 293), Bateson writes. Such learning about the "context of contexts" implies learning that involves a change in the whole assumptive frame of reference within which our habits of expectation have been formed.

Bateson describes six changes that might be characterized as Learning III:

1. The individual might learn to form more readily these habits of forming which we call Learning II.
2. He might learn to close for himself the "loopholes" which would allow him to change the habits acquired by Learning II.
3. He might learn to change the habits acquired by Learning II.
4. He might learn that he is a creature which can and does unconsciously achieve Learning II.
5. He might learn to limit or direct his Learning II.
6. If Learning II is a learning of the contexts of Learning I, then Learning III should be learning the contexts of those contexts. [pp. 303–304]

Edward Cell's Learning Theory. Edward Cell (1984) also interprets learning as involving four different levels of change that may take place either separately or in combination. He calls these levels response learning, situation learning, transsituation learning, and transcendent learning.

In response learning, we change the way we are prepared to respond, either by adding a new response to our repertoire or by substituting a new response for an old one. Much of this kind of learning proceeds by trial and error. It includes conditioned responses and rote learning.

Situation learning involves a change in the way we interpret a situation. Interpretations, for Cell, involve placing a value on something in the situation and judging how things work in the situation. It is through situation learning that we create alternatives from which to make choices. Situation learning may involve either an active reinterpretation of the situation or a reflective reinterpretation by which we remove ourselves from the action to examine the situation critically. Cell maintains that we adopt an interpretation only when we embody it in our behavior. We interpret a situation by dividing it into a sequence of events or subsituations and learn responses to each subsituation that is rewarding or leads to consequences we desire. By doing this, we organize experience in ways that have meaning for us. We can learn by operant conditioning within this context of interpretation.

Transsituational learning is learning how to change our interpretations of a situation. This involves interpreting our acts of interpretation and reflecting on our powers of reflection.

The development of the ability to modify concepts or to create new ones for interpreting individual situations is what Cell calls transcendent learning. Examples of the results of transcendent learning include the theories of Newton, Freud, Marx, Skinner, and Maslow, creative contributions that provide new tools for interpretation of specific situations.

Cell's analysis usefully extends the discussion of learning and reflection in Chapter One. However, the reader should note that transformation theory assumes that interpretation is involved in *all* learning, including response learning. Learning that a flame burns one's fingers is considered a prereflective form of interpretation. As Popper points out in his critique of stimulus-response psychology, "A stimulus will always be a stimulus as interpreted by the individual, and a repetition will be a repetition from the viewpoint of the individual" (Berkson and Wettersten, 1984, p. 17).

Transformation Theory. Bateson's pioneering analysis of transformations in learning and Cell's differentiation of reflective learning into transsituational and transcendent categories are valuable contributions to the development of a transformation theory of adult learning. This latter theory identifies four distinct forms in which adult learning may occur.

The first is *learning through meaning schemes* — that is, learning to further differentiate and elaborate the previously acquired meaning schemes that we take for granted, or learning within the structure of our acquired frames of reference. For example, in the instrumental domain, we learn that we must keep our head down as we swing a golf club if we want to improve our drive. In the communicative domain, we learn that honesty can refer to self-disclosure as well as to abiding by the law. In the case of self-reflection, we learn the limits of our tolerance for ambiguity.

This form of learning includes habitual and stereotypic responses to information received through preexisting, known categories of meaning — what has been aptly described as "recipe learning" — as well as rote learning, in which one behavior becomes the stimulus for another behavior. The only thing that changes within a meaning scheme is a specific response.

The second form that learning can take is *learning new meaning schemes* — that is, creating new meanings that are sufficiently consistent and compatible with existing meaning perspectives to complement them by extending their scope. Instrumentally, we learn how to take tests, for example; communicatively, we learn how to play a new role; in self-reflection, we learn to think of ourselves in terms of a new category of description, such as introverted/extroverted.

In this form of learning, our meaning perspective does not change fundamentally, even though it is extended. The prevailing perspective is strengthened rather than negated because the understanding of new areas of experience that the new meaning scheme makes possible resolves inconsistencies or anomalies within the older belief system. New meaning schemes may be assimilated consciously or unconsciously in the course of socialization. Identification with others often plays a large role in this form of learning.

A third form of learning is *learning through transformation of meaning schemes.* This is learning that involves reflection on assumptions. We find that our specific points of view or beliefs have become dysfunctional, and we experience a growing sense of the inadequacy of our old ways of seeing and understanding meaning. For instance, a woman attending an early evening class at a local college who feels obligated to rush home to prepare dinner for her husband may come to question the meaning scheme that produces that compulsion as she encounters other women who do not feel a need to fulfill this stereotypical sex role. Often other meaning schemes derived from the same stereotypical role become similarly transformed at about the same time. This accretion of transformed meaning schemes can lead to a transformation in meaning perspective.

Learning through perspective transformation is the fourth form that learning may take — becoming aware, through reflection and critique, of specific presuppositions upon which a distorted or incomplete meaning perspective is based and then transforming that perspective through a reorganization of meaning. This is the most significant kind of emancipatory learning. It begins when we encounter experiences, often in an emotionally charged situation, that fail to fit our expectations and consequently lack meaning for us, or we encounter an anomaly that cannot be given coherence either by learning within existing schemes or by learning new schemes. Illumination comes only through a redefinition of the problem. Redefinition in turn is achieved by critically reassessing the assumptions that support the current meaning scheme(s) in question. Such epochal transformations often are associated with a life crisis that impels us to redefine old ways of understanding. Chapter Four deals with the way premises and other assumptions undergirding prior learning are assessed.

Learning as Problem Solving. Problem solving is central to all four forms of learning described in transformation theory.

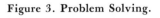
Figure 3. Problem Solving.

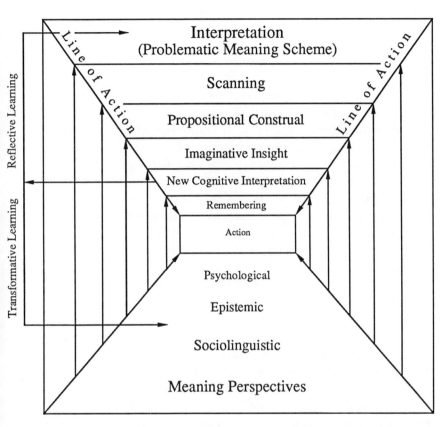

Figure 3 details the problem-solving process, following the sequence of the learner's line of action. The process begins with a doubtful or problematic meaning scheme (outer area) and moves to scanning—exploring, analyzing, remembering, intuiting, imaging. Scanning in turn leads to propositional construal, imaginative insight, and making a new interpretation. As we remember this interpretation and use it as a guide to subsequent decisions or action, we learn. The interpretation may lead to a reflective change in our original meaning scheme, elaborating, supplementing, or transforming it. When the new interpretation successfully challenges an entire meaning perspective, it can result in a perspective transformation. Every phase of problem solving is influenced by our meaning perspectives.

Summary

This chapter has suggested a theory of adult learning embedded in the broader cultural context of Habermas's theory of communicative competence. It emphasized Habermas's distinction between two major domains of intentional learning, instrumental and communicative. It also discussed a process or dimension, that of emancipatory or reflective learning, which affects them both. The two domains of learning differ from each other in a number of significant ways. It should be emphasized that much adult learning involves both domains.

Other key points covered in this chapter include the following:

1. Communicative action occurs whenever an individual with particular aims communicates with another person in order to arrive at an understanding about the meaning of a common experience so that they may coordinate their actions in pursuing their respective aims. Reaching an understanding is the inherent purpose of communicative action.

2. During communicative action it becomes necessary to test the validity claims made by utterances. Rationality is validity testing by reasoning—using reasons and weighing evidence and supporting arguments—rather than by appealing to authority, tradition, or brute force.

3. Communicative competence, a condition necessary for significant learning and development in adulthood, involves an individual's ability to negotiate meanings and purposes instead of passively accepting the social realities defined by others—in other words, to participate in rational communicative action.

4. The three dynamics involved in communicative action are those of the lifeworld (the unquestioned world of everyday social activity), learning, and social interaction.

5. Human learning can be divided into two interactive domains or areas based on interest: the instrumental (concerned with manipulating parts of the environment) and the communicative (concerned with understanding and being understood by other people). Reflectivity involves examining the assumptions and premises of either domain. Each domain has its own purpose, method of problem solving, logic, and way of validating statements.

6. Problem solving or learning in the instrumental domain is done through hypothetical-deductive logic; that is, we respond to an indeterminate situation by formulating hypothetical courses of action, anticipating the consequences of each, acting upon the most plausible hypothesis, and testing its validity by the results of our action.

7. Problem solving or learning in the communicative domain involves validity testing of assertions by consensus. Consensus making is a continuous process; each consensus is a provisional judgment that is open to new evidence and arguments and to new paradigms of understanding.

8. The meaning of a statement is understood when we know the conditions under which the statement is true. Thus validity testing becomes crucial to establishing meaning. The broader the opportunities for discourse, to examine the varied conditions under which an assertion has been found to be true or valid in the lives of participants, the more reliable the assertion's meaning will be.

9. The ideal conditions for rational discourse, through which we validate problematic assertions in the communicative learning domain, suggest fundamental criteria for effective adult learning and education.

10. In communicative learning and problem solving, we reason by metaphors rather than hypotheses. The logic involved is called metaphorical-abductive logic. This type of logic helps us make sense of the unknown by comparing it to aspects of our previous experience.

11. The emancipation in emancipatory learning is freedom from libidinal, linguistic, epistemic, institutional, and en-

vironmental forces that limit our options and our control over our lives. We achieve this emancipation by examining our own assumptions. Emancipatory reflective learning can be involved in both instrumental and communicative learning but has broader implications for the latter.

12. Adult learning may assume any of the following four forms: learning through existing meaning schemes, learning new meaning schemes, learning through the transformation of meaning schemes, and learning through the transformation of meaning perspectives.

4

ᏚᏚᏚ Making Meaning Through Reflection

Art critic Arthur Danto (1990) suggests that the defining factor of modern times is our becoming conscious of living in history, rather than looking backward at what had been history — in short, as he puts it, being aware that we are living in the Age of Warhol. We recognize how our perception of reality has been shaped by our cultural and antecedent circumstances rather than by an understanding of history as an impersonal account of the past. This individual and collective awareness of the influence of our own history and biography on the way we make and validate meaning also celebrates the emergence in our culture of an age of reflection. The appearance of reflection as an increasingly influential mode of making sense of experience is anticipated by Habermas's view of modernity (described in Chapter Three) as the attenuation of established authority structures, which mandates a new self-directedness in learning.

Reflection is the central dynamic in intentional learning, problem solving, and validity testing through rational discourse. Intentional learning centrally involves either the explication of the meaning of an experience, reinterpretation of that meaning, or application of it in thoughtful action. Most theoretical work and research on learning have focused on problem solving and the roles of perception, recognition, recall, and memory in this process. There has been an egregious disregard for the function of reflection, which makes enlightened action and reinterpretation possible, and especially for the crucial role that reflection plays in validating what has been learned.

One reason for the underemphasis on reflection may be the lack of clarity of this concept in psychological theory and in common usage. The term *reflection* generally is used by learning theorists as a synonym for thoughtful action. However, as Chapter One explained and this chapter will review, transformation theory holds that thoughtful action does not necessarily imply reflection.

In his *Essay Concerning Human Understanding,* Locke held that mind was a product of sensation and reflection, but for him reflection was simple awareness of our own process of thinking and writing. A man was reflective when he was "conscious to himself that he thinks." Locke described reflection as having both cognitive and conative dimensions: "[It] is the perception of the operation of our own mind within us, as it is employed about the ideas it has got; which operations . . . are perception, thinking, doubting, believing, reasoning, knowing, willing, and all the different actings of our own minds; which we being conscious of, and observing in ourselves, do from these receive into our understandings as distinct ideas, as we do from our bodies affecting our senses" (Klein, 1984, p. 215).

John Dewey made the seminal analysis of reflection. This chapter builds upon his concept to formulate a definition, analysis, and interpretation of the nature and function of reflection in transformative learning and the problem-solving process. The chapter also reviews the way the concept of reflection has been treated by other learning theorists and social scientists.

Dewey on Reflection

John Dewey's definition of reflection is most widely quoted when this topic is discussed in the context of learning or education. Dewey defined reflective thought as "active, persistent and careful consideration of any belief or supposed form of knowledge in the light of the grounds that support it and the further conclusion to which it tends" (1933, p. 9). "Grounds" refer to evidence by which the reliability and worth of a belief can be established so as to justify its acceptance. Dewey's "reflection" is what transformation theory calls validity testing. Boud, Keough, and Walker (1985) extend Dewey's definition to include attending to the grounds of one's feelings as well as one's beliefs. There has been sporadic, if not explicit, recognition of the conative and affective as well as the cognitive content of reflection, and transformation theory affirms this by recognizing the roles of line of action and intuition in the learning process. Clearly, not every act of introspection (becoming aware of thoughts or feelings) is reflective. For purposes of understanding how to facilitate adult learning, educators will gain insight by confining the concept of reflection to Dewey's definition: *Reflection means validity testing.*

Dewey dealt with reflection in the context of rational problem solving, "putting the consequences of different ways and lines of action before the mind to enable us to know what we are about when we act" (p. 17). Reflection involves a review of the way we have consciously, coherently, and purposefully applied ideas in strategizing and implementing each phase of solving a problem. This process follows the hypothetical-deductive model, which, as we have seen, is integral to instrumental learning: identification and formulation of the problem, reasoning from evidence, developing of hypotheses, testing of hypotheses, and their reformulation based on feedback from research. Dewey referred to this reflective process as "critical inquiry." Although reflection as defined by Dewey ends by formulating an outcome as a conclusion, it also involves a review of the evidence supporting the conclusion (a "grounded" or "warranted" assertion). This review process results in formulation of the premises upon which the assertion rests.

Although Dewey understood reflective thought as the process of examining assumptions and validating assertions, he did not explicitly differentiate the function of reflection on the content of a problem or on the process of problem solving — that is, critically reviewing the grounds for assumptions pertaining to the strategies and procedures of problem solving — from the function, designated here as premise reflection, that

involves the critique of presuppositions (which postulate a preexisting condition upon which subsequent reasoning rests). He
also did not examine systematically how habits of expectation
(meaning perspectives) affect reflective thought — as in problem
posing — or how reflective thought might affect them — as in consciousness raising or psychotherapy.

In *How We Think,* however, Dewey did note that the ability of two persons to converse intelligently is made possible because common experience provides a background of mutual understanding upon which they are able to project their respective
remarks. "If, however, the two persons find themselves at cross-
purposes, it is necessary to dig up and compare the pre-suppo-
sitions, the implied context, on the basis of which each is speaking.
The im-plicit is made ex-plicit; what was unconsciously assumed
is exposed to the light of conscious day" (1933, p. 280). Dewey
also wrote about the unexamined presuppositions that gave rise
to public school curricula. In *The Public and Its Problems,* furthermore, he described a "social pathology" that weakens effective inquiry into social institutions and conditions, idealizes the
past, glorifies things as they are, intimidates dissenters, and stifles
thought "with subtle and unconscious pervasiveness" (Greene,
1986, p. 434).

Dewey held consistently that the process of critical inquiry
and reflective thinking requires an awareness that a true problem exists for which the solution is uncertain. He referred to
awareness of a problem situation as the "pre-reflective" stage
of critical inquiry. Transformation theory holds that the application of reflection to this prereflective stage of awareness, the
process that we call premise reflection — a fault-finding review
of presuppositions from prior learning and their consequences —
is central to meaning and value realization and to significant
transformations in meaning perspectives in adulthood. Through
reflection we *see through* the habitual way that we have interpreted
the experience of everyday life in order to reassess rationally
the implicit claim of validity made by a previously unquestioned
meaning scheme or perspective. This dimension of reflection
is missing in other contemporary learning theories.

Reflection in Theories of Adult Learning

The most familiar view of reflective thinking, following Dewey, limits it to the interpretation of data, application of facts and principles, and logical reasoning (Knowles, 1975). Gagne's (1972) delineation of types of learning confines higher-order functions to identification of classes of similar objects and events, application of principles, and problem solving. Knox (1977), who reviews over 1,000 studies of adult development and learning, only once mentions critical thinking, which he characterizes as including "the ability to interpret data, weigh evidence, and engage in deductive thinking" (p. 446). Neither Knox's nor Long's more recent (1983) review of adult learning makes more than passing reference to the process of reflection. Halpern's (1984) book on critical thinking makes no mention of reflection and defines critical thinking merely as "thinking that is purposeful and goal directed" (p. 3).

Kolb's experiential learning theory (1984) counterposes "reflective observation" and "active experimentation" as dialectical opposites but does not present the grounds for making this polar distinction, although he makes reflective observation central to his learning theory. His discussion of the meaning of reflection is limited to the following passage:

> An orientation toward reflective observation focuses on understanding the meaning of ideas and situations by carefully observing and impartially describing them. It emphasizes understanding as opposed to practical application. A concern with what is true or how things happen as opposed to what will work; an emphasis on reflection as opposed to action. [p. 68]

The writings of philosophers Edward Cell (1984) and Peter Jarvis (1987) provide notable exceptions to this disregard of reflection among learning theorists. Jarvis's ideas are less germane to transformation theory, but Cell elaborates very compatible concepts. Cell differentiates active and reflective reinterpretation. Active reinterpretation, Cell explains, is made rather spontaneously in response to a change in our situation. Cell's "active reinterpretation" refers to thoughtful learning with reflection. In this stage we may either arrive at an interpretation that we are aware has gradually taken shape subconsciously, or we may be aware only that we are beginning to look at things differently. What Cell calls reflective reinterpretation, by contrast, involves removing ourselves from the action to enable ourselves to see more critically what has been happening. Transformation theory calls this retroactive reflection:

> The principal difference between the two forms of reinterpretation, Cell writes, concerns our ability to correct distortions in our reasoning and narrowness in our attitude. When we are transacting with others, our thinking is often creative but tends to embody our prejudices, our provincialisms, our rationalizations. When we are reflecting on our transactions, we are better positioned to use what discipline and skill we have achieved in overcoming such distortions. [p. 84]

Three Forms of Reflection

Reflection is the process of critically assessing the content, process, or premise(s) of our efforts to interpret and give meaning to an experience. Because so much of our learning is cast in the form of problem solving, it was natural for Dewey to deal with reflection in the context of hypothetical-deductive problem solving, the logic followed with such success by the natural sciences. He was correct that we reflect on the content or description of a problem. However, we also reflect on the strategies and the procedures of problem solving, sometimes in the course of taking action and sometimes afterward, to check the decisions we have made. This is what we do when we "stop and think" about what we do or have done. As we attempt to solve a problem, furthermore, we reflect to find similarities and differences between what we are currently experiencing and prior learning — to identify principles, make generalizations, identify patterns of data, select appropriate ways of expressing our concepts, create metaphors for extending meaning beyond the data as given, and decide on next steps in problem solving.

If the problem is to determine whether Joe is telling the truth about his age, for example, reflection on content might focus our attention on physical clues, such as the color of Joe's hair, the lines in his face, or the year he completed school. Reflection on process might lead us to assess the adequacy of our efforts to find relevant and dependable clues in order to improve our performance in solving similar problems in the future. Reflection on the premise of the problem might lead us to question the merit and functional relevance of the question: Why do, or should, we care how old Joe is? We might conclude that if Joe is physically healthy, active, and productive, his age does not really matter to us. If the problem were in the communicative rather than the instrumental learning domain, reflection on premise might involve an assessment of the validity of norms, roles, codes, "common sense," ideologies, language games, paradigms, philosophies, or theories that we have taken for granted. Depending on the nature of the problem, we might also reflect on epistemic or psychological presuppositions.

Reflection involves the critique of assumptions about the content or process of problem solving. Premises are special cases of assumptions. The critique of premises or presuppositions pertains to problem *posing* as distinct from problem *solving*. Problem posing involves making a taken-for-granted situation problematic, raising questions regarding its validity. While all reflection is inherently critical, as is pointed out in the writings of Brookfield (1986, 1987b), Marsick (1987), and many others, including my own, the term "critical reflection" often has been used as a synonym for reflection on premises as distinct from reflection on assumptions pertaining to the content or process of problem solving.

Reflection on the content, process, and premises of problem solving is not limited to expediting learning related to hypothetical-deductive problem solving; it is also the way we learn in metaphorical-abductive problem solving. If we are to facilitate learning, we must differentiate among these three types of reflection and between the two forms of logic used in problem solving so we may design appropriate educational interventions for each.

Nonreflective and Reflective Action

We can use higher-order cognitive functions without consciously focusing on and deliberately examining the validity of prior learning; the resulting action in this case is thoughtful but nonreflective, as when we identify a pattern of relationship, recognize a theory, name objects or events, make a judgment, generalize, or explain. In reflection, we check back on our problem-solving process: were our generalizations based upon a representative sample, our inferences warranted, our logic sound, our control of the variables appropriate, our anticipated consequences of alternative actions inclusive, our analysis fully discriminating, our evidence convincing, and our actions consistent with our values? Reflection is more than simple awareness of our experiencing or of being aware of our awareness; process reflection involves both reflection and critique of how we are perceiving, thinking, judging, feeling, and acting, and premise reflection involves awareness and critique of the reasons why we have done so. Much of the current confusion in academic circles about the nature of critical thinking is the result of failing to differentiate among the three functions of reflection and to distinguish between reflective and nonreflective action.

Nonreflective Action. In Chapter One two kinds of action were identified as nonreflective. Much prior learning that originally involved deliberate effort, practice, and concern for the validity of our insights, such as learning to type, ride a bicycle, or drive a car, becomes *habitual action,* freeing us to act while focusing our attention elsewhere. Habitual action takes place outside of focal awareness in what Polanyi (1967) refers to as tacit awareness. A second type of action that may be nonreflective falls within focal awareness. This is *thoughtful action,* which involves higher-order cognitive processes to guide us as we analyze, perform, discuss, and judge.

In thoughtful action, we direct our attention to ongoing action but draw upon our prior learning to remember and make inferences, generalizations, analogies, and discriminations, judgments, analyses, and evaluations. Although we make tacit judgments regarding what knowledge is relevant, thoughtful action involves a selective review of prior learning rather than a deliberate appraisal or reappraisal of it; we are not attending to the grounds or justification for our beliefs but are simply using our beliefs to make an interpretation, like deciding on the next action move when involved in an intensive physical sport. Cognition is not the same as reflection. Learning under these circumstances remains within preexisting meaning schemes and perspectives and focuses on planning the next moves in a sequence of action.

Introspection refers to thinking about ourselves, our thoughts or feelings. We feel good about ourselves or are aware of how much we are enjoying an experience, for example. Introspection does not involve validity testing of prior learning and hence is also nonreflective.

We resort to *reflection* only when we require guidance in negotiating a step in a series of actions or run into difficulty in understanding a new experience. Reflection can be integrated into the active process of instrumental problem solving and can become an integral part of the process of thoughtful action — we assess what we have defined as our options in order to make the most appropriate next move (reflection on the content of the problem) — or it can occur only when the action stops because of a block, in which case it becomes part of a retrospective assessment of process or premise. Sometimes only then do we check prior learning to determine why our strategies or procedures of problem solving have not worked as they should to solve the problem.

An example may clarify the differences among these processes. Becoming aware of, say, negative feelings toward an acquaintance named John is *introspection,* simply being aware of ourselves feeling, perceiving, thinking, or acting. Deciding that "John is bad" is a *thoughtful action,* making a judgment based upon evidence or prior learning. This involves *content reflection* — reflection on *what* we perceive, think, feel, or act upon. *Process reflection* is an examination of *how* we perform these functions of perceiving, thinking, feeling, or acting and an assessment of our efficacy in performing them. We might, for example, ask ourselves whether we could have misinterpreted some incident that we used as evidence in concluding that "John is bad." The act of *premise reflection* leads us to question whether *good* or *bad* is an adequate concept for understanding or judging John. Premise reflection involves our becoming aware of *why* we perceive, think, feel, or act as we do and of the reasons for and consequences of our possible habits of hasty judgment, conceptual inadequacy, or error in the process of judging John. Premise reflection involves the process of "theoretical reflectivity" (Broughton, 1977). Theoretical reflectivity may cause us to become critical of epistemic, social, or psychological presuppositions such as those we will examine in the next chapter.

Reflective Action. Reflective action is making decisions or taking other action predicated upon the insights resulting from reflection. The path of reflective action is depicted in Figure 4. The process begins with posing a problem and ends with taking action. Major subprocesses include scanning, propositional construal, reflection, imaginative insight, a resulting interpretation that can lead to a change (a transformation) in a meaning scheme or, in the case of premise reflection (dotted line), to the transformation of a meaning perspective. We subsequently remember our interpretation in order to guide our actions. Thoughtful action with reflection is shown as involving content reflection, process reflection, or both. Retroactive reflection may involve premise reflection as well as content and/or process reflection. Transformative learning here may refer to content and process reflection, which can lead to transformation in meaning schemes (but does not always do so; it may result in an elaboration, confirmation, or creation of a scheme), and to premise reflection, which can lead directly to transformations in meaning perspective.

    Our perceiving, thinking, feeling, and acting may be carried out either habitually or thoughtfully, but in either case these modes of action can be influenced significantly by errors in con-

Figure 4. The Process of Reflective Action.

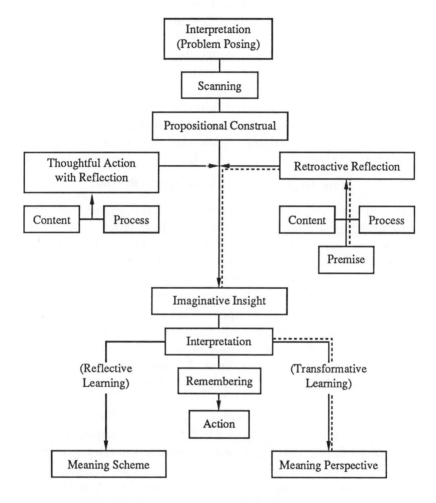

tent or process as well as distorted by unwarranted epistemic, social, or psychological presuppositions resulting from prior learning. Thus our continued learning becomes dependent upon a reflective review of what we have learned, how we have learned it, and whether our presuppositions are warranted.

Learning about ourselves can be the result either of thought-ful action or of action based upon content (with self as object), process, or premise reflection. We can gain an enhanced sense of confidence from performing with increased competence through thoughtful instrumental action. We can learn a new dimension of our personality, such as our limited tolerance for ambiguity (a new meaning scheme), through reflective action. We can reassess and negate previously unexamined assumptions regarding the consequences of behaving in a particular way (sexually, assertively, competitively, and so on) that was prohibited by parents in a traumatic childhood encounter and repressed from consciousness but enforced in adulthood through anxiety and guilt. This is critical self-reflective action based on premise reflection.

The Importance of Premise Reflection

It becomes necessary for us to reexamine and challenge our presuppositions and premises less frequently than to critique content or our process strategies and tactics. But it is this premise reflection that opens the possibility for perspective transformation. Critique and reassessment of the adequacy of prior learning, leading potentially to its negation, are the hallmarks of reflection. This is why Popper was correct in believing that negation is the critical dynamic for learning. Although content or process reflection may become an integral part of thoughtful action, premise reflection cannot. It must involve a hiatus in which a problem becomes redefined so that action may be redirected.

Premise reflection involves its own logic, an inferential logic which I have characterized as "dialectic-presuppositional." The dialectic is a "developmental movement through forms [cognitive structures]" (Basseches, 1984, p. 22; see also Chapter Five of this book). Presuppositional logic is found in some theories of formal semantics. In these theories, sentences alone may not be judged true or false without also identifying the relevant presuppositions behind each and assigning a truth value to these as well. For example, to judge what is falsely communicated in the sentence, "The president of Hawaii is a conservative," we must recognize the error in the presupposition that Hawaii has a president. In his taxonomy of inferences, Collins differentiates between inferences based on knowledge, which involves induction and deduction, and those based on "metaknowledge," which depends on what a person knows about his or her own knowledge (Graesser and Clark, 1985, p. 17). Presuppositional logic is defined differently in communication-based theories of learning. Graesser and Clark (p. 28) give this example:

Speaker S presupposes P and the time T if at T
Speaker S believes or assumes:
(a) P
(b) other members of the conversation also believe or assume P
(c) other members recognize that speaker S believes or assumes (a) and (b)

The significance of differentiating content, process, and premise reflection becomes clear when we realize that content and process reflection are the dynamics by which our beliefs — meaning schemes — are changed, that is, become reinforced, elaborated, created, negated, confirmed, or identified as problems (problematized) and transformed. Premise reflection is the dynamic by which our belief systems — meaning perspectives — become transformed. Premise reflection leads to more fully developed meaning perspectives, that is, meaning perspectives that are more inclusive, discriminating, permeable (open), and integrative of experience.

Reflective learning can be either confirmative or transformative. It becomes transformative when assumptions are found to be distorting, inauthentic, or otherwise unjustified. Transformative learning results in new or transformed meaning schemes or, when reflection focuses on premises, new or transformed meaning perspectives — that is, in perspective transformation. While not all adult education involves reflective or transformative learning, reflective, and hence transformative, learning surely should be considered to be a cardinal objective of adult education.

Other Interpretations of Reflection

Several psychologists have made reflection, or something closely allied to it, a significant part of their theories. Terms used in these theories that are more or less synonymous with what transformation theory calls reflection include *metacognition, reflection-in-action,* and *mindfulness.* An examination of the concepts represented by these terms can add dimensions to our understanding of reflection.

Reflection as Metacognition. Psychologists who write of "metacognition" are referring to reflection, but they almost never explicitly refer to premise reflection. As noted earlier, their theories have shown little interest in the conative or affective dimensions of reflection. According to these writers, metacognition refers to knowing about our "cognitive states" and their operations. Its function is to inform and regulate cognitive routines and strategies. For example, Borkowski writes, "The mature problem solver is assumed to integrate metacognitive knowledge with strategic behaviors (control processes) in solving problems. This dynamic interchange not only enables the learner to select, modify and invent strategies but also to enlarge the contents of metacognition through successful problem solving" (Yussen, 1985, p. 114).

Borkowski associates "planfulness," self-monitoring, and inventiveness with metacognition and understands metacognition to be central to the generalizing of cognitive strategies. He perceives failures in cognition as deficiencies in understanding the how, where, when, and why of using cognitive strategies. Bruner (1986, p. 67) concludes that "metacognitive activity (self-monitoring and self-correction) is very unevenly distributed, varies according to cultural background, and, perhaps most important, can be taught successfully as a skill."

"Reflection-in-Action." Donald Schön has coined the term "reflection-in-action" to describe the way various professionals he studied deal with situations of uncertainty, instability, uniqueness, and value conflict. They respond to surprise by turning thought back on the process of knowing implicit in their action:

They may ask themselves, for example, "What features do I notice when I recognize this thing? [pro-

cess reflection] What are the criteria by which I
make this judgment? [premise reflection] What procedures am I enacting when I perform this skill?
[process reflection] How am I framing the problem that I am trying to solve?" [premise reflection]
Usually reflection on knowing-in-action goes together with reflection on the stuff at hand [content
reflection]. [Schön, 1983, p. 50; my brackets]

Schön makes a persuasive argument against the traditional
model of "technical rationality," which sees intelligent practice
as an *application* of knowledge to instrumental decisions, and in
favor of practice as reflective action. The results of reflection-
in-action in one case may be generalized to other cases, thus
contributing to the practitioner's repertoire of exemplary themes
from which he or she may compose new variations. Thoughtful action with reflection often can mean an almost intuitive kind
of content reflection, with which we get a "feeling for" and critically assess our actions as we take them, like jazz musicians who
improvise. As Schön says:

They [the musicians] can do this, first of all, because their collective effort at musical invention
makes use of a schema—a metric, melodic, and har-
monic schema familiar to all participants—which
gives a predictable order to the piece. In addition,
each of the musicians has at the ready a repertoire
of musical figures which he can deliver at appropriate moments. As the musicians feel the direction
of the music that is developing out of their inter-
woven contributions, they make new sense of it and
adjust their performance to the new sense they have
made. [p. 55]

Schön asserts that tacit "theories-in-action" or "frames"—
what we have called meaning perspectives—provide a set of operating assumptions that govern actions. These theories-in-action
are derived from repertoires of relevant examples, models, or

generative metaphors. A theory-in-action supplies language from which to construct descriptions and themes from which interpretations are possible, rather than providing a rule for predicting or controlling an event.

A professional frames his or her role in a way that allows professional knowledge to take on the character of a system. "The problems he sets, the strategies he employs, the facts he treats as relevant, and his interpersonal theories of action are bound up in his way of framing his role," Schön writes (p. 210). In the language of transformation theory, a professional role frame constitutes a sociolinguistic meaning perspective. Our characteristic ways of framing a problem, our theories-in-action, can constitute epistemic or psychic meaning perspectives as well.

Schön suggests that problem solving turns into a "frame experiment": the practitioner uses a frame to probe the situation metaphorically in search of an interpretation, then makes adjustments based on feedback from the situation. Reflecting on the consequences of efforts to fit the initially chosen frame to the situation, the professional frames new questions and new ends.

Framing a problem thus becomes an experiment in shaping a new situation to a theory-in-action or meaning perspective. Means and ends are framed interdependently and involve a transaction with the situation encountered in which knowing and doing are inseparable. Perception of similarity and difference in a situation precedes articulation of that perception.

Reflection as Mindfulness. Habitual action is called "mindlessness" by psychologist Ellen Langer (Yussen, 1985, p. 267–285), who defines this term as a routine reliance on categories and distinctions already formed. She contrasts this approach with "mindfulness," or being fully engaged in making distinctions and creating categories. Mindfulness is described as being aware of content and multiple perspectives. It is what transformation theory calls reflective action. Behavior based on mindlessness is rigid and rule governed, while that based on mindfulness is rule guided. Mindfulness is not effortful or difficult, although there is much psychological research to support the contention that people frequently try to reduce their cognitive activity and to use minimal cues to guide their action.

Langer has marshalled extensive empirical research evidence to support and elaborate her concepts of mindlessness and mindfulness (Langer, 1989). Mindfulness may come into play either after many repetitions of a particular experience or after only a single exposure as when the situation triggers an over-learned sequence of behavior (like copying familiar text on a typewriter we have used for years). People are more likely to be mindful and to have accurate perceptions when they are attending to the unfamiliar and the deviant than when they are dealing with the familiar. Mindfulness is described as welcoming new information, involving more than one view, and focusing on process before outcome, control over context (meaning perspective), and creation of new categories.

An individual's lack of awareness of the difference between mindlessness and mindfulness can result in difficulties and inaccuracies in reading, writing, and speaking because it can cause mindlessness and mindfulness to be used inappropriately. Mindfulness is sometimes maladaptive; when riding a bicycle in heavy traffic, for example, it is better not to have to pay attention to the mechanics of riding the bike. We also tend not to be mindful of information that appears irrelevant, is given by a non-threatening authority figure, or concerns a subject about which we have no prior knowledge.

In learning and education, mindlessness is associated with a goal rather than a process orientation, what Langer calls "education for outcomes" — instrumental learning — rather than a learning orientation that focuses on the processes of creative problem solving. Mindlessness often involves "premature cognitive commitments," clinging to a previously formed mind-set when we encounter a similar but new situation. Mindlessness leads to the uncritical acceptance of labels, self-induced dependence on external authority, simplistic attributions, diminished self-image, and reduced growth potential.

Langer differentiates mindfulness and mindlessness from Piaget's concepts of assimilation, the process of cognitive growth by which the external world is fitted to our cognitive representations of it, and accommodation, the process by which we adjust our representations to fit the external world. She interprets mindlessness and mindfulness (or nonreflective and reflective action) as states of passive or active involvement with experience. They are the ways in which the individual carries out the processes of assimilation and accommodation. Assimilation may be either mindless or mindful. Accommodation is usually mindful because when we have no established way of dealing with an object or event, we must create new distinctions and categories.

For the typical individual, mindfulness occurs only when significantly more effort is demanded by the situation than was originally demanded by similar situations; when external factors prevent the completion of a behavior; or when there are negative or positive consequences of prior enactments of the same behavior (Yussen, 1985). Such consequences either pose a problem or a tentative hypothesis or interpretive metaphor to try out in making our next interpretations.

Langer has found that mindfulness on the job can increase productivity, satisfaction, flexibility, innovation, and leadership ability (1989, p. 133). Among the aged, it is significantly related to greater activity, independence, confidence, alertness, vigor, sociability, and length of life (p. 86).

Summary

This chapter has presented an analysis of the nature and function of reflection. Its major propositions include the following:

1. Validation of prior learning, or attending to the grounds or justification for our beliefs, is the central function of reflection. When we find reason to doubt the truth, validity, or authenticity of assertions made or implied about our physical environment, our social interactions, and our personal world of feelings and intentions, we must resolve these issues before we can continue to learn.

2. Reflection is the central dynamic involved in problem solving, problem posing, and transformation of meaning schemes and meaning perspectives.

3. We may reflect on the *content* or description of a problem (or a problematic meaning scheme), the *process* or method of our problem solving, or the *premise(s)* upon which the problem is predicated.

4. Content and process reflection can play a role in thoughtful action by allowing us to assess consciously what we know about taking the next step in a series of actions and consider whether we will be "on course" in doing so. Thoughtful action may or may not involve reflection; we do not always question our methods of or reasons for doing something, even when we thoughtfully analyze and act upon a situation.

5. Premise reflection involves "dialectic-presuppositional" logic, a movement through cognitive structures guided by the identifying and judging of presuppositions.

6. Through content and process reflection we can change (elaborate, create, negate, confirm, problematize, transform) our meaning schemes; through premise reflection we can transform our meaning perspectives. "Transformative learning" pertains to both the transformation of meaning schemes through content and process reflection and the transformation of meaning perspectives through premise reflection.

7. Reflective learning involves the confirmation, addition, or transformation of ways of interpreting experience. Transformative learning results in new or transformed meaning schemes or, when reflection focuses on premises, transformed meaning perspectives. Not all adult education involves reflective learning; however, fostering reflective and transformative learning should be the cardinal goal of adult education.

8. We reflect on the results of our efforts to project our symbolic models, as selected and organized by our meaning perspectives, metaphorically to interpret a situation. This is the central dynamic in communicative problem solving, a fitting and refitting of our theories-in-action to the situations we encounter and being responsive to feedback as we do so.

9. Reflective action or "mindfulness" is associated with greater accuracy of perception of the unfamiliar and deviant, avoidance of premature cognitive commitments, better self-concept, greater job productivity and satisfaction, flexibility, innovation, and leadership ability.

5

ᐇ Distorted Assumptions: Uncovering Errors in Learning

We have seen in earlier chapters that we construe meanings by projecting symbolic models via meaning perspectives onto our sense impressions and making metaphorical inferences to form the meaning schemes—the specific knowledge, beliefs, judgments, and feelings—that constitute interpretations of our experience. Because symbolic models, meaning perspectives, metaphors, and meaning schemes are all or almost all products of unreflective personal or cultural assimilation, the possibility of distortion of assumptions and premises makes reflection and critical discourse essential for validation of expressed ideas. A distorted assumption or premise is one that leads the learner to view reality in a way that arbitrarily limits what is included, impedes differentiation, lacks permeability or openness to other ways of seeing, or does not facilitate an integration of experience.

This chapter examines the nature of assumptions and premises for reasoning and action and the ways they are acquired. It first reviews common misconceptions about the process of reasoning and distorted assumptions that cause logical and methodological errors in the problem solving involved in instrumental learning. It then turns to communicative learning to describe how typical premise distortions occur in epistemic, sociolinguistic, and psychological meaning perspectives. The term *distortion* here is extended to include perspectives of adults that have not been fully developed, such as those occurring at stages of epistemic development prior to critical judgment in Kitchener and King's (1990) model, which is described in this chapter.

Crucially important though correcting distortions is, the value of identifying them goes deeper. As Roth notes, distortion is inescapable, but we can hope to identify and artfully use our distortions and other modelling processes by refining and contextualizing them better (1990, p. 118). Becoming aware of our limitations can help us learn how to compensate for them. Awareness involves recognition of how we have been influenced by our culture and biography to acquire these limitations in the first place.

Distorted Assumptions About the Reasoning Process

Many errors that lead us astray, especially in the domain of instrumental learning, are logical and methodological. They concern the process of reasoning and involve fallacies in the principles of logic and violations in the rules of interference. Technical and methodological distortions occur in both instrumental and communicative learning, but they are more prominent in the former.

Informal fallacies (Angeles, 1981) refer to reasoning that does not follow the forms and rules of logic or to arguments whose conclusions are inadequately supported or do not necessarily follow from the reasons given. One category of informal fallacy is material fallacies having to do with the facts or content of an argument, including fallacies of evidence, in which an argument does not provide the required factual support for its conclusion, and fallacies of relevance, in which an argument's supporting statements are irrelevant to its conclusion. A second category involves linguistic fallacies, in which arguments have been corrupted by ambiguous use of language such as shifts in meaning, imprecision or vagueness, or incorrect use of words. The third category is strategic fallacies, in which arguments are presented in ways that appeal to prejudices, biases, loyalties, fears, guilt, and the like.

Errors in inferential rules or assumptions encountered in everyday life have been carefully analyzed by Nisbet and Ross (1980). Such distortions are rooted in what these writers refer to as "knowledge structures," which they define as "preexisting systems of schematized and abstracted knowledge — beliefs, theories, propositions and schemas" (p. 7). From a transformative learning viewpoint, knowledge structures are meaning perspectives. Some of our knowledge structures are made up of beliefs, theories, and schemas that inaccurately represent the external world. We may label objects and events inaccurately or process them through inappropriate knowledge structures.

Among the sources of distortion identified by Nisbett and Ross are cognitive strategies, heuristics, or "rules of thumb" for reducing complex tasks of inference to simple matters of judgment. These "judgmental heuristics" include a *representativeness heuristic,* which makes it possible to reduce many inferential tasks to simple judgments about similarities. Such a heuristic enables us to assign an object or event to a conceptual category into which its principal features most nearly fit. When known features or perceived similarities cannot be relied upon for an accurate judgment, statistical considerations often become important. People generally have little understanding of the relevance of such considerations as correlation coefficients and measures of central tendency. Meaning schemes can mislead when they involve poor symbolic representations of external reality or when they block out or substitute for attention to the details of the actual object at hand.

We judge the frequency, probability, and causality of objects or events to the extent that they are readily remembered. This serves us as an "availability heuristic." The problem here is that factors other than frequency, probability, and causal efficacy affect our being able to remember objects and events.

Nisbet and Ross identify another heuristic, which involves weighting the relevance of one's data. People assign weight to data in proportion to its perceived salience and vividness. This weighting determines what data will be attended to, retained, and retrieved. The problem is that vividness is not a dependable quality for assessing evidence. As "intuitive scientists," ordinary adults perform problem-solving operations comparable to those that guide the scientist, but they lack the scientist's degree of careful, reflective assessment, including conscious adherence to established standards pertaining to these operations. Preexisting knowledge structures can distort the way we characterize an event. When a learner generalizes from samples, available samples are necessarily limited to the events that the learner can remember. When the learner attempts to generalize from the characteristics of the sample to those of the population it represents, there is evidence that most learners have little understanding of the significance of either the size of the sample or its freedom (or lack of freedom) from bias. Moreover, research suggests that the average adult learner is very poor in assessing the relationships between events. Nisbett and Ross write, "It appears that *a priori* theories or expectations may be more important to the perception of covariation than are the actually observed data configurations. That is, if the layperson has a plausible theory that predicts covariation between two events, then a substantial degree of covariation will be perceived . . . even if it is totally absent" (p. 10).

Common errors pertaining to causal inference include letting prior theories of causality make the learner oblivious to implications about covariation presented in the evidence, relying on distorting and arbitrary predilections for attributing causality, and applying causal schemas or analytic strategies inaccurately. Adult learners also are ordinarily prone to making poor predictions because they tend to ignore variations among populations or relative frequencies of outcome possibilities.

A type of *premise distortion* that causes particular problems in instrumental learning (though it can affect communicative learning as well) is metaphoric. It involves an inadequate problem definition or system of categorization. For example, Donald Schön (1979) points out, an urban planner might have a metaphoric assumption that causes him or her to see a slum as a "sick" area that can be restored to "health" only be removing dilapidated buildings and designing a new environment. Instrumental learning and reflection might cause the planner to exchange this metaphor for one that likens a slum to a natural community. This alternative metaphor places an emphasis on preserving social integration, home stability, and informal networks of mutual support and strengthening these community assets through a combination of outside assistance and self-help.

Serious logic distortions often are involved in making attributions. For example, Nisbet and Ross (1980) describe what they call the "fundamental attribution error," which sees behavior as caused primarily by enduring and consistent dispositions toward action rather than by the particular characteristics of situations to which the actor responds. This error results in meaning schemes such as the beliefs that successful people are more motivated and ambitious than unsuccessful people and that a person's fate eventually mirrors his or her character. Relatedly, although many people tend to explain others' behaviors as dispositional, they usually explain their own in situational terms.

Different distortions in the attribution process have been identified by other researchers. For example, we underutilize the opinions and experiences of others, that is, consensus information, in making judgments. We are more likely to take credit for good outcomes than blame for bad ones, and we take more credit for joint outcomes than is our due. Fiske and Taylor (1984, p. 99) hold that overall, these biases in the attribution process suggest that, rather than being a naive scientist as suggested by Nisbett and Ross, "the social perceiver can be a self-centered, conservative charlatan who distorts reality in a personally advantageous manner."

Errors in reasoning and in instrumental learning typically involve inappropriate use of a particular heuristic or "rule of thumb," theory, or metaphor. The problem is not only that adults are overly eager to apply simple heuristics and immediately available knowledge structures but that once these inappropriate knowledge structures are used, subsequent considerations fail to exert significant impact in modifying them. As Nisbet and Ross note, "Once formulated or adopted, theories and beliefs tend to persist, despite an array of evidence that should invalidate or even reverse them. When 'testing' theories, the layperson seems to remember primarily confirmatory evidence. . . . When confronted forcibly by disconfirmatory evidence, people appear to behave as if they believed that 'the exception proves the rule'" (p. 10).

Nisbet and Ross nonetheless conclude that, despite the lack of "rigor" in the intuitive strategies of most adults, these strategies enable people to get by in everyday life because of the collective nature of many inferential tasks. In collective problem solving, our most significant errors are likely to be challenged by others. The importance of validity testing in learning and knowing thus becomes self-evident.

Epistemic Premise Distortions

Writers in psychology and learning theory have identified a number of epistemic premise distortions — that is, distorted assumptions about the nature and use of knowledge. Some of these distortions are common at early stages of intellectual development (in childhood), but they linger on in certain adults as well.

The Development of Reflective Judgment. Kitchener (1983, 1990) follows Dewey in placing reflective thinking within a context of a hypothetical-deductive model of problem solving but observes that while some problems have correct solutions, many others do not. The former, such as mathematics problems, she calls puzzles. For others, such as questions of public policy, there are provisionally preferred solutions based upon informed opinion derived from an objective assessment of evidence and reasons — that is, through consensual validation. Kitchener contends that only the latter type of problem (comparable to problems of communicative learning) presents a truly problematic situation in the Deweyan sense. For such problems, reflective thinking cannot be reduced to a set of skills or steps to be mastered because they are predicated upon a particular set of epistemic assumptions on which reflective thinking is based. These meaning perspectives, which have been established empirically by several studies, involve the degree to which objective reality is deemed knowable, the nature of objective knowledge, and the way beliefs are justified.

Kitchener describes seven stages in the development of reflective judgment, ranging from Stage 1, the most prone to what we have called epistemic premise distortions, to Stage 7, the most reflective and rational. As an example of Stage 1, consider Harry, who assumes that objective reality exists as one sees it — that is, that reality and knowledge about it are the same, are absolute, and are known through the individual's sense perceptions and prior learning. If an individual is not in a position to perceive the answer to a question directly, he or she can learn the absolute truth from authorities. Truth is not problematic: right answers exist, and information or points of view that disagree with them are simply wrong. For Harry, beliefs are as real as physical objects; they are not derived, and they do not need to be explained. Differences of opinion are not perceived, so justification is unnecessary. Harry sees all problems merely as puzzles. Given Harry's assumptions that one must accept authority as the basis of all knowledge and that discrepant information is simply wrong, Kitchener holds that reflective thinking is uncalled for because there is no real uncertainty.

Jane's point of view is very different from Harry's. She assumes that there is an objective reality against which ideas and assumptions must be tested and that, although our knowledge of reality is subject to our own perceptions and interpretations, it is possible through critical inquiry and rational argumentation to determine that some judgments about reality are more correct than others. For Jane, knowledge is the outcome of a process of reasonable inquiry that, because it is fallible, may not always lead to correct claims about the nature of reality. Knowledge statements must be evaluated as more or less likely approximations to reality and must be open to the scrutiny and criticisms of other rational people. Jane assumes that beliefs reflect solutions that can be justified as most reasonable using general rules of inquiry or evaluation, although criteria for evaluation may vary from one area, such as literature, to another, such as science or religion. Jane represents Stage 7, the highest stage in Kitchener's model.

There is a world of difference in the way Harry and Jane would approach the same problem. Harry would be convinced that his inability to find the "true solution," even if in fact the problem had none, reflected his lack of success in finding an authority with the knowledge required. He might simply resolve to try harder in his quest. Jane, however, would weigh carefully the quality of the assumptions, evidence, and rational arguments in support of alternative approaches to arrive at a "best bet" for dealing with the problem under the given circumstances.

Kitchener identifies five intermediate stages or levels of development between the extremes represented by Harry and Jane. The structure of each level of development "appears to underlie some superficially unrelated beliefs, including the validity of authorities' claims, the way beliefs can be justified as better or worse, and understanding of bias and interpretations" (Kitchener, 1986, p. 83).

The major presupposition of Stage 1 is that beliefs need no justification because there is an absolute correspondence between what is believed and what is true. People at this stage therefore find no need whatever to engage in reflective thinking or validate their assumptions.

Stage 2 has the view that knowledge is absolutely certain but may not be immediately available. We can know either directly or through authorities. The epistemic assumption at this stage is that beliefs are either unjustified, unexamined, or justified through an authority. There is a right answer to most issues.

Learners at Stage 3 believe that knowledge is absolutely certain or only temporarily uncertain. When it is temporarily uncertain, we can know only through our intuition or biases. These learners assume that in areas in which answers exist, beliefs are justified through authorities; in areas in which answers do not exist, there is no rational way to justify beliefs.

At Stage 4, knowledge is seen as idiosyncratic, since such situational variables as incorrect reporting of data or data lost over time conspire to keep us from knowing with certainty. The assumption here is that beliefs may be justified by giving idiosyncratic reasons or choosing the evidence that fits the beliefs. Decisions appear as a combination of reasoned and arbitrary.

People in Stages 3 and 4 are skeptical about rationally knowing anything. Although they believe that objective truth exists, they feel that knowledge can be temporarily uncertain until the truth can be found. Authorities may not be the absolute source of knowledge. Beliefs are justified because they "feel right." Unless truth is known, all opinions are equally unjustified. Assumptions underlying reflective thought and the process of rational inquiry are rejected as sources of knowledge.

For learners at Stage 5, knowledge is contextual and subjective. We cannot know the world directly; we can know only interpretations of it, made through our perceptual filters. These learners assume that beliefs may be justified within a particular context only via the rules of inquiry that pertain to that context. Because justifications are assumed to be context specific, choosing between competing interpretations is often difficult and therefore is resisted.

At Stage 6, learners see knowledge as personally constructed, based upon evaluations of evidence and arguments across contexts so that we may know our own and others' personal constructions of issues. The assumption at Stage 6 is that beliefs may be justified by weighing the evidence and arguments on different sides of the issue or across contexts and constructing a solution that is evaluated by personal criteria, such as our individual values or the pragmatic need for action.

In Stages 5 and 6, belief in objective reality or truth is abandoned. People in these stages believe that all knowledge is personal, subjective, problematic, and uncertain. Because judgments are based upon subjective interpretations, they cannot lead to knowledge in a more objective sense. Assumptions influence interpretations, and points of view must be understood in the context of a particular time, place, and situation. Different points of view are necessary in problem solving, but judgments, even those based upon rational inquiry, can have no meaning beyond our own subjective interpretation.

Kitchener designates as "reflective judgment" the mode of justification that characterizes Stage 7 of her model, that is,

Jane's perspective. The four presuppositions involved in reflective judgment include: "(1) there is a reality against which ideas and assumptions must ultimately be tested; however, (2) the process of inquiry is itself fallible, (3) knowledge claims rest on the process of rational inquiry, and (4) justification is, therefore, based on a rational evaluation of evidence and interpretation" (1983, p. 80).

Kitchener goes on to write, "The sequence described in the reflective judgment model implies that before an individual reaches the point at which his or her thinking can be called 'reflective' in the Deweyan sense, he or she must have passed through six prior steps or stages in which he or she holds assumptions about reality and knowledge which are not compatible with reflective thinking" (p. 80). In general, movement is through the stages from dogmatism through skepticism toward rationality.

Kitchener and King (1990) offer evidence that reflective judgment increases with both age and education. Samples of students selected for high scholastic aptitude were found to be functioning in the range of Stages 2–3.5 in high school, the 3–4.5 range in college, and the 4.5–6.5 range in graduate school. After two years, modal scores on a test that these authors devised to identify people's place on their seven-stage model had increased by one stage for all groups, but only the former graduate students (90 percent of whom scored at stages 6 or 7) were using reflective judgment. Thus it appears that an individual may attain reflective judgment only in adulthood. Movement toward reflective judgment "continues into the young adult years as long as individuals continue their formal education, but development plateaus after leaving educational institutions" (p. 86). Obviously, this suggests a strong case for the usefulness of adult education and counseling programs that facilitate reflective learning after one leaves school.

Kitchener's interpretation of Dewey's concept of reflection is not easily reconciled with our present understanding that the criteria of reflective thought involved in validating knowledge in the instrumental domain are different from those used in the communicative domain and that Dewey's hypothetical-deductive model of inquiry may be relevant primarily to the instrumental domain. Nor is Kitchener's model concerned with distinctions among functions of reflection. However, her finding of the existence of stages of development of epistemic meaning perspectives is provocative both for its instructional implications for adult educators and for the suggestion that a qualitatively superior perspective can serve as an educational objective. It is particularly interesting that Kitchener and her colleagues have established empirically a meaning perspective of reflective judgment that is remarkably compatible with that projected by Habermas when he wrote of identity development and of the quality of participation involved in an ideal speech situation.

Common Epistemic Distortions. Geuss (1981) has identified three types of distorted epistemic premises. One is assuming that propositions are meaningful only if they can be verified empirically. A second is assuming that a phenomenon (the Law, the Church, the Bomb, the Government) produced by social interaction is immutable and beyond human control (that is, reified). A third is using concepts that are descriptive (life stages, learning styles, personality characteristics) as prescriptive.

In reviewing traditional psychological research on typical modes of perceiving, remembering, thinking, and problem solving in children and youth, Knox (1977, pp. 447–448) describes the concept of "cognitive style" as being composed of the following nine dimensions:

1. Tolerance of perceptions that differ from conventional experience
2. Consideration of various possibilities before making a decision
3. Susceptibility to distraction
4. Intensity of attention and span of awareness
5. Blurring and merging of similar objects and events in memory
6. Construal of the world in a multidimensional and discriminating way
7. Categorization that uses many different concepts (thematic, functional, descriptive, class membership)

8. Perception of items as discrete from their backgrounds and contexts
9. Preference for a category range that is broad and inclusive rather than narrow and exclusive.

Long (1983) suggests that Kagan's "risk taking versus cautiousness" should be added to the list.

Distortions in cognitive style mentioned by Geuss (1981) include focusing on either the analytical or the global when the other is appropriate, focusing or not focusing when appropriate, defining categories too broadly or too narrowly, being either reflective or impulsive when the other is appropriate, and dealing with either the concrete or the abstract when the other is necessary for understanding. These distortions focus on dimensions similar to those described by Roth (1990) as "perceptual filters" (see Chapter Two).

Kitchener's findings suggest that "cognitive style" may be considered as a developmental progression from a more limited and distorted viewpoint to a way of understanding that is more inclusive, discriminating, and integrative of experience. The distortions that failure to attain complete development produces on these "stylistic" dimensions of knowledge production may be interpreted as epistemic in nature. Educators can help learners overcome these, like other epistemic distortions, by fostering reflective and critical reflective dialogue to assess the validity of problematic assumptions.

As another example of an epistemic distortion reflecting incomplete development, Larry Daloz (1988) tells the story of one of his adult students, Gladys, who had run a nursing home and was encouraged to write about it. An instructor had given Gladys a modest grade because of her inability to distance herself from her writing so that she could think about what she was saying in a more critically reflective way. Daloz, Gladys's mentor in a nontraditional degree program, was sympathizing with her. Gladys protested, "I mean, what does he know about nursing homes? How can he give me a C about my life's work?"

Daloz thought, "She is so concrete. She's just not separating form from content; she thinks he is criticizing her when he is talking about her writing style. She still hasn't made that leap from *being* her ideas to *having* them; she is still embedded in her experience. He's absolutely right: she is her experience, she doesn't 'have' it" (p. 6).

Daloz tried to have Gladys write about the "ideal" way to care for the aged as a tactic for helping her gain a perspective from which she could become more critically reflective. This did not work. Gladys simply wrote about all the ways she would improve her existing home if she had unlimited money, changes that had no discernible principles underlying them. "It appeared simply beyond her to imagine that nursing homes might not have to exist at all — that the principle of care for the aged might be honored in other ways. In order to do that, she would have had to uproot her most basic assumptions, question the premise on which she had built her entire life." In addition to offering an intriguing educational challenge, Gladys presents a distorted view of ways of knowing, the failure to be able to think abstractly and in a critically reflective way.

Langer (1989) describes how notions of entropy and linear time also can serve as limiting mind-sets. Entropy is the gradual breaking down of an entity or pattern of organization within a closed system, as embodied in the view of the universe as a great machine running down. This perspective leads to a belief in fixed limits, whereas the view that reality is socially constructed suggests that it is relatively amenable to human control. The concept of linear time means that one must accept that time "runs out," which leads to the notion that cognitive skills and psychological and physical health are predictably related to age.

In this section we have seen a wide range of epistemic distortions that are related to the fact that each learner is embedded in his or her particular life situation and stage of intellectual development. We have seen in earlier chapters how these distortions in meaning perspective are decisive in filtering perception and comprehension.

Sociolinguistic Premise Distortions

Factors creating sociolinguistic premise distortions include all the mechanisms by which society and language arbitrarily shape and limit our perception and understanding, such as implicit ideologies; language games; cultural codes; social norms, roles, and practices; and underdeveloped levels of consciousness, as well as theories and philosophies. All contain values and behavioral expectations, and all are implemented through "recipe" knowledge.

For the most part we take for granted and are unaware of these social norms and cultural codes, which distribute power and privilege. Our meaning perspectives mirror the way our culture and those individuals responsible for our socialization happen to have defined various situations. Our parents' location in the social structure and their own personal biographies and idiosyncrasies influence our conception of reality. As children, we internalize the rules, roles, conventions, expectations, and attitudes of our parents or mentors in the context of an emotionally charged relationship. We then apply them in abstract form to the rest of society. "Primary socialization," write Berger and Luckmann (1966, p. 135), "thus accomplishes what (in hindsight, of course) may be seen as the most important confidence trick that society plays on an individual—to make appear as necessity what is in fact a bundle of contingencies, and thus make meaningful the accident of birth."

When ideology tends to legitimate existing society, institutions, and ways of life as natural, good, and just, it becomes what Gramsci (1971) calls hegemonic. As such, it contains the dominant, most widely shared beliefs and attitudes expressed in social practices and institutions. Ideologies can vary from sophisticated theory to blind prejudices or biases such as racism, sexism, and chauvinistic nationalism. Such prejudices produce a "restricted"—that is, limited and stereotyped—linguistic code. Hegemonic ideologies define the limits of discourse by setting the political agenda, defining the issues and terms of debate, and excluding opposing ideas. They cause discourse to degenerate into fixed, rigid sets of stereotypes that misrepresent the complexity of social life. Ideology becomes "false consciousness" by reducing complex social processes to simple, apparently natural and stable states of affairs. Purportedly universal ideas or interests mask private interests, social contradictions are glossed over, and alternatives are suppressed. Fortunately, because ideologies occur in many phases of life, there is always a good possibility of contradictions among them. This can provide leverage for reflective analysis and, ultimately, transformation.

Language-Based Distortions. Learning a language involves internalizing various interpretive schemes that have been socially defined, such as brave little boys and sweet little girls, patriots and traitors, success and failure, and other polarities that Kelly (1963) called personal constructs (see Chapter Two). We also internalize rationales to explain why we must behave according to these schemes. Such rationales may be expressed as proverbs, parables, or myths, or they may be superstitions or other simplistic distortions of reality.

Experience can be arbitrarily shoehorned into categories of meanings or typifications simply because of the nature of language. We must name a thing in order to bring it into active consciousness, and when we name an experience, we change it. By articulating the positive feelings we have toward another person as "love," we transform a reality by adding a variety of expectations and obligations to it. Similarly, hate, envy, greed, lust, treachery, heroism, good sense, patriotism, courage, and ignorance can come to be reified (regarded as part of objective reality) simply by being named.

A persuasive case can be made for saying that conceptual systems and human thought processes are largely metaphoric since metaphors serve functions other than just being a logical form of communicative learning. The very logic of communicative learning is metaphorical-abductive. However, the immense potential for distortion implicit in metaphors is illustrated by Lakoff and Johnson (1980), who show how trapped we are, for example, by the prevailing metaphor that argument is war:

Argument is War

Your claims are *indefensible*
He *attacked every weak point* in my argument
His criticisms were *right on target*

> I *demolished* his argument
> I've never *won* an argument with him
> You disagree? Okay, *shoot!*
> If you use that strategy, he'll *wipe you out*
> He *shot down* all of my arguments (p. 4)

It is not just that we talk about argument in terms of war, Lakoff and Johnson point out. We literally win or lose arguments, see those with whom we argue as opponents, attack and defend positions, win and lose ground, abandon positions, and take up new lines of attack. These are things we *do*, not just talk about. Conventional ways of having and talking about arguments thus are governed by a metaphor, so commonly accepted as to be unconscious for most of us, that becomes dysfunctional when the purpose of argument is to seek consensual agreement.

The tricks metaphors can play show very clearly in the metaphor of labor as a resource. Material resources can be quantified, assigned a value per unit, employed to serve a purposeful end, and used up progressively. Hidden assumptions behind this metaphor include the beliefs that a clean distinction can be made between labor and nonlabor, that inactivity cannot be productive, that work cannot be play, that all labor serves a clear purpose and is worthwhile, and that labor is independent of the person who performs it, how he or she experiences it, and what it means in his or her life (in other words, that workers are more or less interchangeable) (Lakoff and Johnson, 1980, pp. 65–67).

Because what we interpret as the realities of our social life are actually the products of linguistic use, culture itself can be understood as "an ambiguous text constantly in need of interpretation by those who participate in it" (Bruner, 1986, p. 66). For Goleman, culture is a "basket of frames" (1985b, p. 209). Culture may be understood as a collective store of associative images and chains that suggest the nature of coherence, probability, and "sense" within a given world. As Bruner says, "So if one asks the question, where is the meaning of social concepts — in the world, in the meaner's head or in interpersonal negotiation — one is compelled to answer that it is the last of these. *Meaning is what we can agree upon or at least accept as a working basis for seeking agreement about the concept at hand.* If one is arguing about social 'realities,' like democracy, or equity or even gross national product, the reality is not the thing, not in the head, but in the act of arguing and negotiating about the meaning of such concepts. Social realities are not bricks that we trip over or bruise ourselves on when we kick at them, but the meanings that we achieve by sharing of human cognitions" (1986, p. 122; my italics).

The true nature of such social "realities" often is buried in persuasive or distracting linguistic tactics. Tactics such as intimidation, threat, appeal to authority, insult, belittling, challenge to authority, evasion of the issue, bargaining, and flattery all can be presented as "reasons," as in, "because if you don't I'll . . . ," "because the boss says so," or "because you're so stupid (or so smart)." Such tactics are common in everyday dialogue. However, in several subcultures, such as the academic, scientific, legal, diplomatic, ecclesiastic, and journalistic worlds, people make a sustained and deliberate attempt to bar their use. These tactics can still creep in, but the prevailing norms in these dialogic communities disapprove of them because each of these communities in its own fashion is consciously committed to validating contested meaning claims in a rational way.

The reality of everyday life maintains itself by being embodied in routines. "Recipe knowledge" involves frequently repeated action being cast into a pattern so that the pattern comes to be apprehended as the action. Once meanings become embedded in routines, they are taken for granted. People classify habituated actions by types of actors and roles in order to help themselves anticipate the actions of others—the selfless parent, the psychologically aware teacher, the just judge, the honest policeman. These concepts become institutionalized and are passed on to others as external and sometimes coercive facts, the supposed "inherent nature" of reality. Mary Rogers writes of a "paradox of rationality": "the more habitualized the pattern of action within a population, the less its elements are available for scrutiny" (1982, p. 193).

Distortion Through Selective Perception. We have noted in Chapter One how meaning perspectives or viewpoints that do not fit into the prevailing ideology tend to be dismissed as aberrations or even blocked out entirely. We see only what we prefer to see. Goleman (1985b, p. 201) writes, "Any frame at all defines the narrow focus where the relevant schemas direct attention, and a broad ignored area of irrelevance." An ideology or reified frame is insulated against unwelcome perceptions and points of view that it deems irrelevant. We can deal with the anxiety generated by the homeless who sleep on our urban streets or starving Third World peasants by simply not focusing on them, by entering what George Simmel called an "urban trance." Social roles are frames that direct how, under what circumstances, and how much we give our attention to the role players. Both social norms and cultural codes are involved in role identity.

Tact, "the well-mannered deployment of attention," also conspires to limit perception and cognition. How natural it is to simply block out someone we meet at a dinner party who insists on airing a social philosophy or political point of view diametrically opposed to our own. We all avoid discourse and confrontation when they clearly are fruitless. By contrast, what a relief it is to discover that a stranger shares our meaning perspective! We are spared the threat of a confrontation or the strain of a polite evasion; anxiety is allayed and ceases to govern how we see and think about the other person. By reacting in these "natural" ways, however, we escape the insight that can come only from a different perspective and a questioning of cherished assumptions. This is why Maxine Greene entitled her 1973 book *The Teacher as Stranger.* As Greene points out, those who would educate others must help them understand a viewpoint of one who is not embedded in their particular cultural orientation and is not constrained by their restrictive language codes. We can learn best as strangers and from strangers, if we can feel sufficiently secure to do so.

Sociolinguistic Distortion and Levels of Consciousness. Paulo Freire has defined *conscientization,* the central concept in his theory of learning and education, as the process by which learners "achieve a deepening awareness of both the sociocultural reality which shapes their lives and of their capacity to transform that reality through action upon it" (1970b, p. 27). Freire has identified four culturally conditioned levels of consciousness in the Third World. The lowest is intransitive consciousness, the level at which people are preoccupied with meeting elementary needs and are unaware of problems other than basic biological ones. People at this level lack historical consciousness and are unable to comprehend their sociocultural situation.

A second level of consciousness is "semi-intransitivity" or magical consciousness. This is the level found in societies ruled by dictators and in many emerging Third World countries. In such "cultures of silence," the existing sociocultural reality is taken for granted. Life is perceived in terms of fate or destiny and seen as beyond human control. The oppressed internalize the values of their oppressors, resulting in emotional dependency upon them and self-deprecation.

At the third level, naive or semitransitive consciousness, people engage in questioning their lives and can understand that sociocultural reality is determined by human beings. However, questioning is naive. People at this level of consciousness are easily impressed by populist leaders and are very vulnerable to manipulation.

Through conscientization, learners can reach a fourth level of consciousness. They can then participate in a dialogic educational process that focuses on validity testing of assumptions concerning social norms, cultural codes, and ideologies that foster dependency and oppression. This entails a rigorous critique of the dehumanizing social, political, and economic structures supported by ideologies. Through praxis, the union of reflection and action, learners engage in action to bring about social change. Freire clarified what he means by praxis and action:

> Let me emphasize that my defense of the praxis implies no dichotomy by which this praxis could be divided into a prior stage of reflection and a subsequent stage of action. Action and reflection occur

simultaneously. A critical analysis of reality may, however, reveal that a particular form of action is impossible or inappropriate *at the present time.* Those who through reflection perceive the infeasibility or inappropriateness of one or another form of action (which should accordingly be postponed or substituted) cannot thereby be accused of inaction. Critical reflection is also action. [1970b, p. 123]

Although Freire sees premise reflection as a form of action, when he writes of transformation he means social transformation. He does not differentiate dependency-producing epistemic or psychic presuppositions from those that are sociolinguistic; he views all distorted assumptions as ideologies that become legitimated and enforced by social structures. For him a transformation in meaning without further action to transform the social structures recognized as oppressive is only an "intellectual game" (Evans, Evans, and Kennedy, 1987, p. 222). This view is shared by leading social action educators in the United States as well (for example, Heaney and Horton, 1990).

Constrained and Unconstrained Visions. Thomas Sowell (1986) identifies a pair of pervasive prerational, usually unarticulated sociolinguistic meaning perspectives that he calls "constrained" and "unconstrained" visions of society. The constrained vision sees human beings as hopelessly flawed. In this view, the best humankind can hope for is a perilous prosperity and a fragile peace, which are most likely to be gained by conservatively following tradition and the collective wisdom of society. Reason alone cannot make the world better because humans have insufficient knowledge to achieve this end. The unconstrained vision, by contrast, rejects the notion of inherent limits on humanity and holds that it is within our power to perfect ourselves and to eradicate social evils through will and reason.

It is easy to see how these meaning perspectives become the foundations for, respectively, conservative and liberal social and political meaning schemes. For example, the unconstrained vision values sincerity in pursuit of social good, while the constrained exalts fidelity to duty. In the constrained view, a business executive is obligated to protect the interests of the business's stockholders but not to improve society, and an educator should promote the intellectual processes of learners but should not intentionally encourage learning that might change the social or economic system. The unconstrained vision encourages exactly opposite priorities.

Sowell is alarmed by the way people with these differing visions tend to label and dismiss people with the opposite view, thus preventing the use of rational discourse to arrive at an understanding. As we have seen, similar problems occur with other distorted sociolinguistic meaning perspectives.

Psychological Premise Distortions

Psychological premise distortions produce ways of feeling and acting that cause us pain because they are inconsistent with our self-concept or sense of how we want to be as adults. They are artifacts of our earlier experience—ways we have learned to defend ourselves after childhood traumas—that have become dysfunctional in adulthood. Through premise reflection we can understand how they have come to shape the way we feel and act and their consequences. Such reflection is thought of as occurring mainly in psychotherapy, but it is a natural form of transformative learning that often occurs in adult life, especially during major life transitions, without the intervention of either a therapist or an educator.

In childhood we all learn simple rules, such as "Hold your mother's hand when you cross the street." With additional experience, this rule becomes modified. We learn that we need not always hold Mother's hand, but we must cross the street at the corner when the traffic light is green. Later, the rule becomes further modified as "Look both ways before you cross the street." The original prohibition becomes a general rule-of-thumb about being careful when crossing the street.

Rules of this sort may be quite useful. However, when a parental prohibition becomes learned in an emotionally charged and traumatic episode involving what is perceived as a severe threat of withdrawal of love, frightening physical punishment, or humiliation and shame, the prohibition can become frozen in place long after the episode is forgotten and continue to monitor feelings and control ways of interacting with others throughout adulthood by means of anxiety feelings. Whenever we anticipate violating the prohibition, which we interpret as an order "never" to behave in a certain way or feel certain feelings, our stomach muscles tighten, our palms perspire, and our throats get dry. The hidden prohibition may say "never" confront, never be sexual or sensual, never succeed, never fail, never take a chance, never be playful, never express feelings, or many others. The possibility of violating such a prohibition evokes the child's wildly exaggerated nightmare of catastrophe — uncontrolled violence, total rejection, public humiliation, abandonment — even though we are now adults and know that such a vision is unwarranted by any rational adult assessment of the consequences of our actions.

As psychiatrist Roger Gould (1989) explains it, such a prohibition blocks a necessary adult function. Educators might see it as a learning block. To compensate for the loss of function, people often develop defensive "shells" or action patterns to avoid the threat of anxiety. Such shells include being a "workaholic," "perfect," a "people pleaser," a "clown," a "follower," a "martyr," a "bully," and many others.

The adult burdened with such a psychological block often becomes aware that he or she is not functioning well, that something is getting in the way of being the autonomous and responsible adult he or she aspires to be. This latter vision is the self-concept, identified in Chapter One as a major context of learning, monitoring the learning process through intuition. Taking appropriate action, despite the inhibiting feelings of anxiety and exaggerated fear of calamity, becomes essential to regain the lost function. However, the fears of and resistance to taking such action are very real. Gould calls the common litany of these fears "the analysis of regret" because the individual knows that he or she should take a specific action but hesitates to do so because of fears that he or she will regret it. Gould identifies five implicit assumptions — distorted meaning perspectives — involved in the "analysis of regret":

1. I may regret taking this action because it might not be the right act.
2. I may regret taking this action because it might disturb an important relationship in my life.
3. I may regret taking action because I may fail and feel worse about myself.
4. I may regret taking action because I may succeed and it will change my life in a way that makes me feel uncomfortable.
5. If I take action, it might disturb some inner balance and I might find out something about myself that I don't want to know. [p. 119]

To recover a blocked function, a learner must be assisted to understand the psychodynamics of his or her situation and to bring the presupposition impeding the needed action into critical reflection. An educator or therapist may help the learner identify the specific problem to be resolved, its symptoms and the pain it evokes, the ways of dealing with the problem that are not working, and the learner's willingness to change. The potential solution or needed action is identified among several possibilities, and an action plan is formulated. The strong feelings that impede action also must be dealt with before transformation can occur; simply understanding the situation is insufficient to effect transformative learning. Transformative learning may involve progressively greater risk taking in deciding action steps.

An example of Gould's thesis is the case of Richard, a lawyer in his early fifties, for whom the practice of his profession had lost its appeal. "Midcareer burnout" was the way Richard characterized his malaise. He was the partner in a successful law firm but found that his management duties and the nature of his practice precluded his spending much time in court, where he preferred to be. In his law firm, as in many others, tradition had it that as a partner became older and more experienced, he was given less of a case load and more of the desirable and financially rewarding cases. As a young lawyer, Richard had played by these rules, but he now was confronted by much younger partners who challenged the grounds for this preferential treatment. Richard felt that he was being treated unfairly by having his "perks" challenged. He found that he could not discuss the matter without losing his temper or withdrawing to avoid talking about it. This issue became the straw that broke the camel's back. Richard had been attracted to the law because he loved to represent clients in court, and he had gotten very skilled at it. Now this attraction had faded, and he thought he would quit and change careers or just take early retirement.

When Richard heard that Gould was giving a workshop for people who were having difficulty going through life transitions, he decided to attend. His greatest insight came when he arrived at one session of the workshop red-eyed and upset. His neighbor in the next apartment had kept his television blaring until four in the morning. Richard, who was still clenching his fists at the thought of it, said he "could have slugged the guy" and in fact came close to pounding on his door and doing just that. When asked why he hadn't knocked on his neighbor's door and asked him to turn down his TV, Richard could only shrug and roll his eyes.

It became apparent in the ensuing discussion that although Richard was attracted to the law because he enjoyed confronting on behalf of his clients, he was unable to confront people on behalf of his own interests. As a child he had made the mistake of confronting his father at a bad moment, and his father's frightening overreaction had so traumatized Richard that he felt he could never confront anyone on his own behalf again. This was why he found confronting for others so satisfying and became so good at it as a lawyer. Yet at the same time his wife and friends were attracted to him because of his gentleness and nonthreatening demeanor.

Coming to understand his dilemma, and specifically writing and reading aloud to the workshop an unsent letter to his father telling him how he planned to change and why and how he intended to go about it, helped Richard deal with the anxiety feelings involved in becoming self-reflective and challenging the presupposition that impeded his taking action to confront people when this was necessary. He then found it possible to present his viewpoint to his young partners and to argue his case forcefully without getting angry. Richard had to work things out with his wife and children, too, because they felt threatened when he regained his lost capacity to confront others if he felt that they were taking unfair advantage of him.

Jesse also showed up one evening for a workshop on life transitions. A beautiful black woman of about thirty, she had been going nowhere in her career as a writer for documentary films when suddenly she was selected to head a major urban adult education program. She was delighted with her new job but soon found herself stuck in a strange way. She could not seem to bring herself to make the decisions necessary for selecting instructors, setting budget priorities, developing programs, and recruiting personnel. She would take her pile of papers home and bring them back to the office the next day, only to take them home again. She hired an administrative assistant, but the problem would not go away, so she decided to try the workshop.

It soon became apparent that Jesse's problem was that she always had trouble finishing what she started. As this became clearer, her earlier frustrations with her writing career came into perspective. Jesse came to realize that underlying her problem was the fact that she was a perfectionist. Dr. Gould explained to her that most people realize that they are good at some things, not so good at others, and poor at some. They average out their performances and end up feeling that they are o.k. For a perfectionist, however, every performance is a final test of self-worth. No wonder Jesse could not finish anything!

When asked, Jesse was able to explain exactly how she had become a perfectionist. She grew up in a home with an angry and violent father who, in his rages, beat her mother. Jesse spent much of her childhood hiding in a closet with a pillow over her head so that she would not have to hear what was going on. In one of his violent episodes, Jesse's father spotted her report card, which had one C on it. He grabbed her, held her up close to his angry face, and shouted, "Don't you ever come home again with a rotten grade like that. The world is full of those white bastards pushing everyone out of their way. You have got to be twice as good as any of them. DO YOU HEAR ME?!!!"

But, of course, no one can be twice as good as everyone else all the time. Fearing failure in terms of the impossible standard her father had set, Jesse avoided the possibility of failing by never finishing the tasks she started. Insight into her feelings, an unsent letter to her father read in the workshop, and a plan to make the easier and safer decisions at work first got her back on track.

As priorities change during an adult's life cycle, new attitudes and new behaviors become necessary, and these often generate internal conflict that is manifested as inhibitions, defenses, or rigid character patterns. An adaptive response leading toward perspectives that are more inclusive, discriminating, and integrative of experience requires freedom from these underlying conflicts. Learners can attain this freedom by resolving the conflict that caused them to be rigid or limited in their responses to changing situations. In effect, they recover a necessary function when they become able to be critically reflective of the distorted presuppositions that blocked action appropriate to a situation.

It is important to acknowledge that the preceding description of the process of psychological distortion is based upon familiar Freudian assumptions. There are many other explanations for psychological "hang-ups." In Chapter Six, for example, we will examine the work of Robert Boyd, which explains transformative learning from a Jungian orientation (Boyd and Myers, 1988; Boyd, 1989; Boyd, Kondrat, and Rannells, 1989).

Summary

In this chapter we reviewed the ways in which we can become misled by errors in the process of reasoning or problem solving and by distorted and underdeveloped epistemic, sociolinguistic, or psychological meaning perspectives. We have detailed how these distortions in the premises underlying our belief systems can block adult development toward more inclusive, discriminating, permeable, and integrative meaning perspectives. Major points in the chapter include the following:

1. Meaning perspectives may be more or less fully developed; they are subject to epistemic, sociolinguistic, and psychological distortions. Each meaning perspective involves a set of assumptions that may be dysfunctional in adult life.

2. In instrumental learning, distortions are likely to be logical or methodological; errors are made in applying rules of inference or reasoning.

3. Reflective judgment — acceptance of consensual validation through rational discourse — involves a developmental sequence that becomes complete only in adulthood. Development of reflective judgment also appears to be correlated with formal schooling in which abstract thought is emphasized.

4. Epistemic distortions are derived from perspectives held over from earlier developmental stages; cognitive, learning, and intelligence styles; narrow scope of awareness; inappropriate use of global/detail focus or concrete/abstract thinking; emphasis on entropy and linear time; and others.

5. Dysfunctional meaning schemes may arise from distorted sociolinguistic premises involving specific ideologies, prescribed norms and roles, cultural and language codes, language games, role expectations derived from secondary socialization, prototypes, anticipated scenarios of interaction, and philosophies and theories that serve to frame experience selectively.

6. Psychological distortions arise from anxiety generated by parental prohibitions learned under traumatic circumstances in childhood. These distortions take the form of "lost" adult functions (mature ways of feeling and acting) blocked by inhibitions, psychological defense mechanisms, and neurotic needs. The distorted assumptions suggest that to feel or act in ways forbidden by the prohibition will result in disaster, even though such an expectation usually is unrealistic in adulthood.

6

ᘓᕽ Perspective Transformation: How Learning Leads to Change

This chapter examines the development and dynamics of perspective transformation and reviews studies that deal directly with this concept. The chapter will show how a wide range of scholars in various disciplines have identified and analyzed this phenomenon of adult learning and development from different viewpoints. We will see the remarkable similarities in their findings, which represent the research base for transformation theory. Previous chapters have located the process of perspective transformation in the context of adult learning; this chapter locates it in the context of adult development. Collective transformations are also discussed.

Development of Meaning Perspectives and Critical Reflection

This section will examine the factors in early development that set the stage for an adult to acquire the ability to become critically reflective. It will define and discuss such central concepts as the development of cognitive structures and the developmental processes of decentration, symbolization, self-awareness, perceptual consciousness, role and perspective taking, bracketing, and hypothesizing.

As we mature, we improve our ability to anticipate reality by developing and refining our meaning schemes and perspectives so that we may use them more effectively to differentiate and integrate experience. Experience strengthens our personal category systems by reinforcing our expectations about how things are supposed to be and about the circumstances in which the rules for a particular language game are appropriate. What we actually experience nonetheless remains a category that is evoked by a particular stimulus, not an occurrence in the real world. That is, we construct a model of the world with our system of categories, come to expect certain relationships and behaviors to occur, and then experience our categories, making imaginative projections to construe experience.

Jerome Bruner (1957) sees a universal direction of intellectual development moving from action — knowing by knowing how to do — to symbolic representation, which primarily involves the use of language, specifically rules for forming and transforming propositions and permitting representations not only of what is but also of what is not and what might be. To make the crucial distinction between our own psychological reactions and external events requires the development of our capacity for self-consciousness. This self-awareness is also a precondition for developing the capacity to categorize the same stimuli according to several different criteria or points of view. Through symbolic representation, we can dialogue with ourselves and, in imagination, construct the perspective of another person as well.

The process of conceptual development increases the tendency to group together things that share a common attribute (superordinate grouping), as opposed to the earlier mode of grouping things that fit together in another way, for example, in a story. The narrative form groups related ideas to give coherence to the story being told rather than categorizing characteristics that are somehow similar. "The transition from the earlier to the later mode of grouping is handled by 'egocentrism.' Things are alike by virtue of the relationship that 'I' or 'you' have to them, or the action taken toward them by 'I' or 'you'" (Bruner, 1973, p. 27).

Culture can impede or facilitate the development of self-consciousness and the ability to make symbolic representations. Thus schooling in traditional societies can make a very special difference by fostering the sort of self-consciousness essential for children and sometimes for illiterate adults to distinguish between their own thought or description about something and the thing itself. This involves the cultivation of individual subjectivity.

Bruner and others have found that cultures vary in the degree to which they encourage the expression of the functions of things in terms of one's personal interaction with them. Some, like the Wolof of Senegal and the Eskimo of Anchorage, value self-reliance and suppress expression of individualism. Their children are less likely to set themselves apart from others and the physical world, are less self-conscious, and place less value on themselves.

The etiology of critical reflection is illuminated by Bruner's work on the Piagetian concept of "decentration." In Piagetian theory, decentering refers to the process by which an egocentric cognitive position is replaced by a more "objective" one in order to reconcile disjunctions between conceptual schemes and empirical experience. Piaget's theory of equilibration suggested that cognitive structures generate higher and more stable forms by resolving contradictions that the existing forms cannot resolve (Piaget, 1967). Transformation theory emphasizes that people make an intentional movement in adulthood to resolve these contradictions and to move to developmentally advanced conceptual structures by transforming meaning schemes and perspectives through critical reflection.

Several cultural dimensions in the use of language have been found to correlate with the ability to achieve decentration. Lower-class children were found far less able to achieve decentration than middle-class children (Bruner, 1973, p. 147). Middle-class children more commonly tend to use language as an instrument of analysis and synthesis in abstract problem solving and for "decontextualization." This important term refers to using language without dependence upon shared perceptions or action, permitting one to conceive of information as independent of the speaker's point of view and to communicate with those outside one's daily experience regardless of their affiliation or location. In observing these class-related differences in language usage among children, Bruner comments, "I do not know, save by everyday observation, whether the difference is greater still among adults, but my impression is that the difference in decontextualization is greater between an English barrister and a dock worker than it is between their children" (p. 149).

A necessary inference from Bruner's findings is that, if indeed some adult cultures discourage development of the self-awareness essential for decentration, decontextualization, and a sense of identity in their children, these same deprivations and their consequent constraints must, *ipso facto,* pertain in adulthood. Moreover, there is reason to believe that this condition pertains not only to most people in some places but to some people in most places.

Another interpretation of the development of cognitive structures is that of Adorno's "negative dialectics" (Buck-Morss, 1987). According to Adorno, development involves achieving cognitive instability, a disequilibrium between the structures of consciousness and those of reality. The critical method as defined by Adorno creates a disequilibrium in thinking by stressing the ambivalence underlying the assumed identity of word and thing. This approach emphasizes that the way a thing is conceptualized is not truly natural but is a historical product of a particular social structure. Adorno's emphasis is compatible with transformation theory, which sees the transformative learning process as a conscious and intentional one that begins with a dilemma and moves forward as distorted assumptions in meaning structures become transformed through critical reflection.

The existence of a precognitive perceptual consciousness in infancy is suggested by Merleau-Ponty. According to his theory, the child is egocentrally involved with his or her body and feelings, constituting a fundamental awareness of being in the world that Merleau-Ponty takes to be the basis for self-reflectivity. Greene (1975, pp. 307–308) observes:

If Merleau-Ponty is right and the search for rationality is indeed grounded in a primary or perceptual consciousness, the individual may be fundamentally aware that the structures of 'reality' are contingent upon the perspective taken and that most achieved orders are therefore precarious . . . . The stage sets are always likely to collapse . . . . Disorder, in other words, is continuously breaking in; meaninglessness is recurrently overcoming landscapes which once were demarcated . . . . Learning is a mode of orientation — or reorientation — in a place suddenly become unfamiliar.

Greene's observation is quite compatible with that of Heron (1988, p. 42), who attributes human skill in "bracketing" — holding certain of our beliefs in abeyance in order to allow ourselves to assess an experience from outside our usual frame of reference — to the monitoring effect of prelinguistic presentational construal upon our efforts at propositional construal, through what I have identified as intuition. Heron's distinction between presentational and propositional construal is important to transformation theory (see Chapter One).

Sociologists have recognized that the achievement of interactive competence, the ability to take part in increasingly complex action systems, is central to identity formation (Döbert, Habermas, and Nunner-Winkler, 1987). From a cognitive point of view, this is understood as an aspect of the gradual diminution of childish egocentricity by stages of role taking. Selman (in Döbert, Habermas, and Nunner-Winkler, 1987, p. 290) differentiates three stages of role taking. First, the child learns that others see the same situation from different perspectives and thus comes to differentiate points of view as well as interpretations, including motives, thoughts, intentions, and feelings. The child can deal with these differing perceptions only one at a time. In a second stage, the child learns to understand its own intentions and behavior from the perspective of others, thus making possible reciprocal perspectives. In the third stage, those interacting can not only take the role of the other but also learn from the viewpoint of a third person how their own perspectives are reciprocally involved with those of the other. For the process of socialization, this is a major breakthrough because it now becomes possible for the child to objectify reciprocal expectations from the viewpoint of a disinterested group member, a short step away from coming to recognize that action within roles is also regulated by the expectations of the "generalized other." Our capacity to take (hypothesize) the perspective of another toward ourselves, to see both our own perspective and that of the other from the point of view of a neutral observer, and then to return to our own viewpoint permits reflective as well as spontaneous interpersonal relations.

With the advent of formal operations in adolescence, we also become able to differentiate the normative context of values that have become institutionalized into motives for action and to differentiate between what we say and the normative context of our utterances during dialogue. As was pointed out in Chapter Three, rational argumentation — dialogic reasoning — is necessary for hypothetical thought because establishing the truth of a hypothesis requires the giving of reasons. Reflexive distancing may involve either guiding ourselves by hypotheses about the hypotheses lying behind the actions of others or by thematizing and systematically examining problematic validity claims. Hypothetical thought also permits us to hypothesize concerning another's options. Learning to treat propositions hypothetically is what formal operational thought means. However, it is another matter to transfer hypothetical thinking from propositions to action norms, and this is what is required to make the transition from role acting to discourse. Transformation theory holds that being able to transfer hypothetical thinking to the propositions upon which our norms are predicated is a distinctively adult process.

Perspective Transformation in Adult Development

This section reviews treatment of the process of perspective transformation in the literature of adult development. It will examine different interpretations of the process or stages of adult development, discuss Basseches's view of adult development as the emergence of dialectical thinking, explain why perspective transformation can be regarded as the central process in adult development, describe the role of perspective transformation in life decisions, and, finally, show the relevance to transformation theory of certain studies of cognitive function in aging.

The Process of Adult Development. There is little consensus among theorists regarding what constitutes developmental progress. For some, such as Erikson, Gould, and Levinson, this refers to a new posture or reconfiguration of the self in response to age-related realities in the life cycle. For others, such as Valiant, it is a substitution of ego defenses attuned to mature reality for the immature defenses that proved functional in childhood. Favell (1982), Kagan (1980), and Kuhn (1983) have questioned whether human cognitive development advances in a stagelike manner at all (Blanchard-Fields, 1989, p. 92). They feel that there may be predictable, orderly sequences of experience in adulthood rather than inclusive, shared internal or external structures. Others see the concept of developmental stages as capitalist ideology (Lichtman, 1987), and still others suggest that changes in behavior that appear to be developmental are only new responses to changing contexts, responses that always had been available but never had been needed before. Broughton holds that efforts to place individuals on the rungs of particular developmental ladders assume that reasoning is relatively separate from particular tasks. He claims that this questionable assertion leads to efforts to establish fixed cognitive structures that disregard both history and the role of the individual's praxis (Blanchard-Fields, 1989, p. 128).

Many sociologists, especially ethnomethodologists, reject the notion of socialization as an inexorable unfolding that leads toward maturity. Fiske and Perlin have failed to find widely shared psychosocial or psychological stages (Bee, 1987, pp. 73–76). They point out that the social world of the child, or anyone designated as being at a lower stage of development, involves a culture entirely meaningful in its own terms. In their view, change results from cultural contact rather than development to a higher stage. Children or others found at a relatively undeveloped stage of development are treated simply as strangers to the culture (Musgrove, 1977, p. 5).

Gould (1978) comments that the commonality among stage theories is that a new set of facts (*i.e.*, a stage) evokes a change in behavior patterns and this can provoke confusion and conflict that, as we have seen, may be the result of distorted epistemic, sociolinguistic, or psychological presuppositions involving inhibitions, defenses, or character patterns.

As indicated earlier, transformation theory suggests a form of developmental progression in adulthood that does not follow clearly defined steps or stages, although the studies by Kitchener and King of stage development toward reflective judgment (see Chapter Five) do suggest different levels of readiness of adults to learn to accept rational discourse as a model of problem solving. These levels are significantly linked to both age and education.

The phases of transformative learning are not invariant stages of development. They may best be understood by Sloan's (1986) concept of phases of meaning becoming clarified. Although slippery and subject to diversions and self-deception, the transformative learning process is irreversible once completed; that is, once our understanding is clarified and we have committed ourselves fully to taking the action it suggests, we do not regress to levels of less understanding. Reaching this point of full understanding and commitment can be extremely difficult, however, and many people do regress before they reach this point.

Development of Dialectical Thinking. Michael Basseches approaches adult development in terms of the emergence of modes of thinking associated with the dialectical intellectual tradition. He holds that dialectical thinking is an important element in cognitive maturity, which may be achieved in the late adolescent and adult years. As we will see, Basseches's definition of dialectical thinking includes perspective transformation.

Basseches (1984, p. 22) defines dialectic as "developmental transformation (*i.e.*, developmental movement through forms) which occurs via constitutive and interactive relationships." Forms refer to cognitive structures — what we have called meaning schemes and perspectives. Dialectical thinking refers to a mode of cognitive functioning organized by (a) a set of assumptions about the pervasiveness of change and (b) ways of conceptualizing change as the emergence of contradictions within a system, leading to the formulation of a new, more inclusive system. Dialectical thought "results in the creative activity of thinking *determining* the use of structures, rather than leaving thought *determined* by demands for stasis that structures impose" (p. 57).

Basseches identified twenty-four "schemata" or "movements of thought" from a review of the literature that he believes are components of dialectical thinking. These are organized by "the underlying model of dialectic," which I interpret to mean the inferential logic of transformative learning.

Basseches's schemata may describe steps in a dialectical analysis of phenomena, ways of introducing the dialectical perspective into the process of inquiry, or ways of maintaining dialectical movement within one's own thought. In considering transformation we have a particular interest in the latter function. Basseches designates his schemata as either motion oriented, form oriented, relationship oriented, or meta-formal. Meta-formal schemata are particularly relevant to transformative learning. They presuppose the ability to understand particular phenomena in the context of larger organizing forms (here meaning perspectives) and describe ways of relating these forms or perspectives to each other.

Basseches describes nine meta-formal schemata (pp. 76–155; my comments are bracketed):

1. Location (or description of the process of emergence) of contradictions or sources of disequilibrium within a system (form) or between a system (form) and external forces or elements which are antithetical to the system's (form's) structure [identifying the disorienting dilemma]
2. Understanding the resolution of disequilibrium or contradiction in terms of a notion of transformation in developmental direction [recognition that moving toward an alternative perspective is movement toward a more inclusive, differentiating, and integrated way of interpreting reality]

3. Relating value to (a) movement in the developmental direction, and/or (b) stability through developmental movement
   [making a value judgment to move forward in the process
   of reflective critique and action. This can also pertain to
   the conative dimension of taking reflective action — of willing oneself to act upon a reflective insight.]
4. Evaluative comparison of forms (systems) [comparative
   analysis of the justifications for differing perspectives]
5. Attention to problems of coordinating systems (forms) in
   relation [relating the new meaning perspective to one's
   larger universe of meaning perspectives, that is, one's "lifeworld"]
6. Description of open self-transforming systems [seeing the
   learning process as being open to the assessment of new
   perspectives that can change the way one sees reality]
7. Description of qualitative change as a result of quantitative change within a form [for example, inductive identification of a new meaning perspective by examining several
   examples of how others who share that perspective interpret reality differently from oneself]
8. Criticism of formalism based on the interdependence of
   forms and contents [making a critique of an old meaning
   perspective in terms of disjunctures between theory and
   practice]
9. Multiplication of perspectives as a concreteness-preserving
   approach to inclusiveness [comparative assessment of all
   available perspectives, relating theory to practice and ab-
   stractions to concrete situations].

   Basseches also identifies criteria for comparing forms
(meaning perspectives):

1. Their levels of equilibrium (inclusiveness, differentiation,
   and integration)
2. Their potential for contribution to development
3. Their susceptibility of coordination with other forms, making them stable through developmental change
4. Their practical value

5.   Their conformity to a "masterform" [superordinate mean-
     ing perspective]. (p. 134)

Perspective Transformation as Development. An essential point
made in many studies, including my own (Mezirow, 1978), is
that transformation can lead developmentally toward a more
inclusive, differentiated, permeable, and integrated perspective
and that, insofar as it is possible, we all naturally move toward
such an orientation. *This is what development means in adulthood.*
It should be clear that a strong case can be made for calling
perspective transformation the central process of adult development.

   Many developmental psychologists have contributed ideas
directly related to understanding the importance of perspective
transformation in development. For example, Perry (1970)
found that youth eventually accepts the inherent relativity of
multiple intellectual perspectives, thereby discovering that reality
is ordered not from a single perspective but from several. Arlin
(1975) found evidence to show that critically reflective "problem finding" or problem posing is a distinctively adult stage of
cognitive development. Richards and Commons (Commons,
Richards, and Armon, 1984) postulated an ultimate postformal stage called "cross-paradigmatic operations," in which an
adult acquires the capacity to relate perspectives that appear
to be independent of one another. Broughton (1977) reported
that "theoretical self-consciousness" emerges only in adulthood.
Kitchener and King identified the developmental steps leading
toward adult reflective judgment that we described in Chapter
Five (Mines and Kitchener, 1986). Basseches (1984), as we have
just seen, analyzed the uniqueness of dialectical thinking in adulthood. All these analyses and findings are highly compatible with
transformation theory. However, it is the work of Gisela Labouvie-Vief (1984) that has most explicitly identified the central role
of perspective transformation in adult development.

   Labouvie-Vief sees development as a two-phase process.
The first phase takes place between birth and adolescence. It
consists of the "decoding of certain biological automatisms and
the bilateral encoding of cultural automatisms" (p. 169). This

process provides structures of preliminary stability and a sense of autonomy.

The second phase of development, initiated after adolescence, compels the individual to reexamine these structures and confront the cultural-symbolic assumptions behind them. "This confrontation initiates a fuller decoding of the cultural environment, and a progressive differentiation from the regulations imposed by the culture," Labouvie-Vief explains (p. 169). As a result of this phase, the person reinterprets his or her early sense of autonomy as a mere living out of social expectations. Autonomy becomes not merely the rejection of interpersonal dependence but the product of examining the relational constraints on one's thought and actions. "Reliances on the self, interplay of motoric, symbolic and abstract forms, breaking up well-trodden paths of thought and conscious utilization of such multimode organization to *reculer pour mieux sauter* . . . all appear to mark the achievement of autonomy" (p. 173). Labouvie-Vief notes that this new mode of organization, which emphasizes breaking rather than perpetuating paradigms, has been emphasized by researchers such as Riegel, who was concerned with dialectical thought in life span psychology, and by others such as Gruber and Koestler, who were concerned with scientific creativity.

Psychologists have found that the transition into the autonomy crisis—and perspective transformation—occurs between thirty-five and fifty-five years, and its duration may extend from five to twenty years. Many individuals fail to negotiate this crisis successfully and enter adulthood with rigid and highly defended thought patterns (p. 179).

The test of a developmentally progressive perspective is not only that it is more inclusive, discriminating, and integrative of experience but also that it is permeable (open) to alternative perspectives so that inclusivity, discrimination, and integration continually increase.

Moving to a more developmentally progressive meaning perspective involves making a decision at each phase of the transformative learning process.

Perspective Transformation in Life Decisions. Tod Sloan has challenged humanistic psychologists who would have us believe that psychological growth is attributable to "natural" forces. His unique study of the narratives of adults making significant life decisions provides persuasive evidence that, on the contrary, such growth results from experience in self-reflection and interaction. He notes, "The person left to rely on natural, inner growth processes will often take the turn toward addiction, masochism, or suicide in the midst of transition periods" (1986, p. 107).

Sloan points out that each phase in Brammer and Abrego's (1981) stages of a life transition represents an aspect of decision making as well as a way of coping. These phases include (1) shock and immobilization, (2) denial, (3) depression, (4) letting go; (5) testing options, (6) searching for meaning, and (7) integration. These are remarkably similar to the phases of perspective transformation that we identified in our college reentry study (Mezirow, 1975).

Sloan found that the decision-making process continues beyond the conscious experience of having made a decision. The meaning of the decision depends as much on its consequences as on the considerations leading up to it. An initial decision to change can block out an area to be filled in later by other decisions that, in effect, specify the intentions underlying the initial decision. As Sloan puts it, "The first phase only announces, 'I'll go for this!' or 'No more of that!' The transition phase serves to find answers to the question, 'Now what?'" (p. 108). Some of the intentions to make a transformational change are revealed only after the initial point of commitment.

Sloan interprets the Brammer-Abrego stages of transition as *stages of meaning becoming clarified* within the decision-making process. The first step, shock and immobilization, may refer less to feelings leading to a decision than to those of being surprised afterward by what one has just committed oneself to. These feelings may include elation, despair, or a mixture of both. Denial results from the suppression of potential conflict over losses. Depression could be understood as a consequence of this denial and/or of the fear that important relationships will be disrupted and that some problems will not be alleviated by the change. "Letting go" pertains to "a type of mourning over projects or aspects of relationships which had to be left behind or curtailed" (p. 109). "Testing options" involves a search for substitutes to provide common ground in which the learner may impulsively enter into new relationships or haphazardly begin new projects. (Some learners, however, refrain from making new involvements in order to avoid making old mistakes again or because of fear of the unfamiliar.)

The "search for meaning" involves constructing an explanation of the circumstances that brought about a change in light of its complex aftermath. These interpretations usually are very limited and are often compensations to "rebuild self-esteem, side-step guilt, punish oneself for losses or rationalize the inevitable" (p. 109). The final stage of the transition process, "integration," involves a combination of planning, imaginative self-projection, and commitment to a new life-style. This new "life structure" illuminates issues that brought about the decision to change. Sloan notes different "compositional styles" that show in this final stage. Some people make a clean break with the past after a transformation, for example, while others try to maintain or reestablish old patterns of connection by, say, immediately seeking affiliations with churches or civic organizations similar to those left behind after moving to a new city. Overcompensating is another style. Overcompensators might, for instance, place too little emphasis on money when it had previously been of major importance or move from being bored to being exhausted. Still another style is to reinstate projects or relationships abandoned in the course of the transformation.

In spite of differences in their styles, all those who have completed a process of transformative learning experience a feeling of rebirth, of a new beginning. Unfortunately, this feeling may not last. "The image of what lies ahead remains glowing in idealized form on the foundation of experiences in the distant past. This fresh start at the threshold of a new life sphere is not unlike an infatuation. It will typically fade as it is battered by actuality," Sloan notes (p. 112). Somewhere Stephen Singular has written of women who have experienced perspective transformations and have succeeded in their careers only to discover that "beyond the rainbow there awaits another set of chains." This disillusionment may, however, result eventually in another perspective transformation, and so on in a process that potentially continues throughout an adult's life.

Perspective Transformation in Aging. A model of cognition in aging that is compatible with transformation theory has been suggested by Labouvie-Vief and Blanchard-Fields (1982). Their research, critique of mainstream studies, and review of an impressive body of supporting research suggest that apparent regression and deficits in cognitive abilities reported in the aging may, in fact, be artifacts of youth-centered models and research methods that fail to recognize that older adults may exhibit a mode of cognitive functioning qualitatively different from that of youth. Mature adults' stability may be mistaken for rigidity, for example.

This difference in cognitive function, which may be the product of progressive perspective transformations occurring during middle adulthood, consists of greater awareness of the social context or dimensions of a problem, greater focus on an analysis of premises, greater awareness of psychological factors and individual and social goals in analyzing task situations, and greater integration of logic and feelings. Older adults' "mode of encoding shifts to dimensions of gist, social evaluation, and explicit self-reference," the authors say (p. 204). The result is a more mature level of cognitive differentiation, involving a mode of reasoning that the authors characterize as autonomous, socially oriented, and dialectical. Aging does not always involve these progressive transformations, but it may be appropriately understood as "a *potentially* adaptive process" (p. 206).

Labouvie-Vief summarizes the differences in cognition between younger and older adults that she has found:

> Young adults . . . focus on logical and semantic surface relationships of propositions. They isolate units of information as if they referred to abstract entities and do not explore psychological complexity latent in these propositions. Tasks are accepted at face value, performance is motivated out of compliance with authority, and the search is for "cor-

rect" solutions. Older adults, in contrast, evaluate task structures within systematic matrices and vis-à-vis social and personal goals. Superficially, older adults resemble children in the latter activity but, unlike children, are aware of the psychological contradictions creating logical ambiguity. [1984, p. 178]

We noted in Chapter One that there appear to be several kinds of memory. Neurologists (for example, Tulvig, 1989) have found evidence for distinguishing between episodic and semantic memory. Episodic memory refers to remembering and recollecting personal episodes, semantic memory to knowing and recalling impersonal facts. Psychologists also have identified implicit memory for skills that one exercises automatically, such as riding a bike. As indicated earlier, there is no evidence of decline in semantic and implicit memory with age. Declines in episodic memory observed in the 70s appear due to situational variables (such as retirement, in which one may not exercise mental facilities as much as before) rather than to aging itself. Psychologists believe that the elderly use semantic memory for distant memories and rely upon a failing episodic memory to remember recent events. Elderly people learn the same way they did when they were younger, but they may not remember where or when they learned a particular thing as well as they could formerly (Goleman, 1990).

Theoretical Overviews of Perspective Transformation

This section and the two that follow analyze the process of perspective transformation as it has been discussed by a variety of researchers. The sections will describe both the components or phases of the process and its dynamics (how the components are sequenced and interact over time). This section describes studies that consider perspective transformation from several different theoretical viewpoints.

As we have indicated, transformation theory is not a stage theory, but it emphasizes the importance of the movement toward reflectivity in adulthood as a function of intentionality and sees it advanced through increased ability and experience, which may be significantly influenced by educational interventions. Transformative learning involves an enhanced level of awareness of the context of one's beliefs and feelings, a critique of their assumptions and particularly premises, an assessment of alternative perspectives, a decision to negate an old perspective in favor of a new one or to make a synthesis of old and new, an ability to take action based upon the new perspective, and a desire to fit the new perspective into the broader context of one's life. Perspective transformation involves (a) an empowered sense of self, (b) more critical understanding of how one's social relationships and culture have shaped one's beliefs and feelings, and (c) more functional strategies and resources for taking action. Taking an action is an integral dimension of transformative learning.

Lifeworlds: A Phenomenological View. Phenomenologists use the concept of *lifeworld* (see Chapter One) to refer to what has been identified here as the prevailing paradigms or collectively held sociolinguistic meaning perspectives in a traditional village society. Danny Wildemeersch and Walter Leirman (1988) apply the lifeworld concept to transformative learning. They attribute the following components to the lifeworld: routinelike actions that enable people to execute everyday activities in an unquestioning way, tacit aspirations compatible with these actions, culturally accepted means of implementation resulting from the actions and aspirations, and dominant social goals and cultural values that legitimate the actions and aspirations.

There are three stages in the development of transformation: the self-evident lifeworld, the threatened lifeworld, and the transformed lifeworld. Each is characterized by its own unique dialogue.

A "narrative dialogue," which tells a story or describes an action, characterizes interpersonal communication and ensures the self-evident character of the lifeworld by affirming and reaffirming our subjective and objective social reality, making our actions seem true and normal. The way we define our personal reality and the prevailing cultural definitions related to the social structure are complementary. This dialogue thus is characteristic of the self-evident lifeworld.

The threatened lifeworld involves what is described in transformation theory as a dilemma, especially the type of dilemma associated with life transitions. A situation arises in which contradictions related to the anxiety-producing dilemma — what writers about transformation theory refer to as "manifest situational contradictions" — become apparent. These writers suggest that at this stage a type of conversation that they call "transactional dialogue," a rational analysis of the evidence and arguments pertaining to alternative viewpoints, is needed. Wildemeersch and Leirman say that whether the learner falls back on old, accepted aspirations and actions or goes forward to explore new perspectives and initiatives "depends on contextual factors, autobiographic antecedents, gender, race and class differences or educational elements" as well as "sociological aspects related to the educational process" (p. 22). They do not elaborate on this provocative observation.

In the transformed lifeworld a third kind of dialogue is apparent, a "discursive dialogue" (what we have called critical discourse) that involves "a conscious exploration of the relationship between one's own problematic situation and similar problems related to other places and other themes" (p. 23). A person in this final stage of development perceives individual problems and conflicts as structural in nature — that is, is capable of reflection. As we saw in Chapter Four, reflection implies the capacity to identify and interpret different perspectives from a theoretical point of view. This final stage in the transformation process is characterized as having a rational and a motivational dimension. Wildemeersch and Leirman refer to "competence motivation": the learner is motivated to move forward through the stages of transformation by a sense of personal competence, acquired from prior experiences, that allows him or her to overcome feelings of dependence and lack of power and sustains developmental efforts. Success leads to a new action pattern that is directed by reflection and based upon transactional and discursive dialogue. Changes in actions or aspirations may be partial. After this final stage, learners resort to a new type of "self-evidence" that allows them to function normally in everyday, routine situations.

Transformational Logic and Orthogenesis. Mention was made in Chapter One of the work of James Loder (1981), who has asserted that there is a universal transformative logic, a "grammar of the knowing event" (pp. 26–27), that informs learning involving *conflict* between what is known and what must be understood. In the language of transformation theory, conflict is the result of a disorienting dilemma. This is followed by an *interlude for scanning* of indeterminate duration. The third step is a *constructive act of imagination,* an intuitive insight by which the elements of the ruptured situation are transformed and the learner arrives at a new perception, perspective, or worldview. This is followed by *release and openness* and a fifth step involving *interpretation* of the imaginative solution into the original context by spelling out connections and seeking a consensus.

The learner's natural intention to complete the act of knowing, of making meaning (line of action) provides continuity in this process. Loder sees intention as a condition of being in tension and stretching oneself toward completion from the past, through the present, and toward the future (p. 35).

Loder holds that transformational logic provides the pattern that governs the process of transition between stages of human development. We spend most of our time in the transition phases of the developmental process. He describes the concept of orthogenesis, "the tendency of a living organism, personality, society or symbol system to unfold in a given direction with relative disregard for the constraints of the environment" (p. 129), as a process found by researchers in biology to be dominant in the development of every cell, tissue, and organism. Loder holds that orthogenesis follows a transformational logic.

Applied to developmental stages — whether moral, ethical, epistemic, intellectual, pertaining to reflective judgment, or pertaining to ego — orthogenesis involves a comprehensive general equilibrium. Loder describes orthogenetic stages as beginning with *differentiation,* in which environmental demands and emerging organic potential call for higher levels of integration and of ability to manage complexity. This stage is followed by a period of *specification,* in which the organism or personality develops processes of specialization and maturation. For example, a newborn infant develops such processes as grasping, sucking, and hand-eye coordination, each of which follows its own schedule of development. All these processes come together in the next developmental stage, *integration.* Each new integration generates two results: "(1) it makes possible a much more efficient use of energy; for example, energy need not be continually dissipated in the search for trustworthy patterns of behavior but instead [can] be invested in new explorations, and (2) it generates its own reinforcement; that is, the efficiency of the more well-integrated behavioral pattern automatically gains the rewards of adaptational success" (p. 130).

Orthogenesis (and its formulation as transformative logic), then, controls the process of moving within and between developmental stages. Loder concludes, "It is the pattern of new life by which we make disordered things make sense; it is the dynamic order by which we construct fixed or stable orders; it is the process by which we compose content" (p. 131).

As we have seen, transformation theory asserts that transformative learning involves processes of scanning, construal, imaginative insight, and interpretation — all directed by a line of action and selectively preconditioned by our meaning perspectives — but adds the transforming processes of reflection and validity testing. The orthogenetic influence accounts for our persistent movement toward making and transforming the meaning of our experience and our extreme inability to tolerate areas of meaninglessness.

The views of Wildemeersch and Leirman, who use the language of phenomenology to focus attention on the differences in dialogue in the self-evident lifeworld, the threatened lifeworld, and the transformed lifeworld, provide a sociological interpretation of the process of transformation. Loder, by contrast, has analyzed the process of transformation in terms of internalized actions. These positions provide valuable and compatible perspectives on the process of transformative learning.

Precritical, Critical, and Postcritical Learning Postures. Phil Mullins, who has studied students in religious studies classes, suggests the possibility of a "postcritical" learning posture following precritical and critical ones (1988). Precritical learners, according to Mullins, are apprehensive that seemingly settled issues may be found to be unsettled after all and thus see new ideas as potential threats rather than opportunities. They view traditions other than their own as exotic and misguided and find foreign belief systems titillating or shocking but are really part of the "human" world. They think about religious phenomena only from an intensely personal perspective. Such learners tend to think concretely rather than abstractly, to read books without thinking of the books' particular social, political, historical, or technological contexts, and to have difficulty understanding theoretical notions such as comparison of different points of view or religions.

Learners with a critical posture "have internalized the basic assumptions and thought patterns associated with literate cultures" (p. 7). Their commitment to write and read nurtures the development of qualities of abstraction, interiority, and individuality. They no longer take words for granted as spoken events in which meaning arises spontaneously in discourse but instead see them as visual signs to be carefully interpreted. They come to see questioning and doubt as indispensable to finding truth. These learners think of religion as a social phenomenon that may be studied with a detached eye. They read texts critically by relating them to the social world, and they see meaning as a particular function of history (p. 9).

In the postcritical posture, the learner "recovers the personal sensibility that dominates precritical thinking." Learners in this stage accept belief as the ground of common life. To them, "belief is both an individual and communal fact which is an inevitable and an acceptable life foundation for creatures like the human being with sophisticated symbolic powers. Postcritical students not only recognize this philosophical insight but recognize also that the insight reflexively includes within it applicability to their own quest for self-understanding. That is, their own activities are recognized as belief-guided endeavors seeking further understanding" (p. 9).

Mullins's formulations are an interesting counterpart to Freire's levels of consciousness and to the model of the development of critical judgment presented by Kitchener and King (see Chapter Five). There is no inherent contradiction in these different descriptions of the movement from a prereflective posture to a postreflective posture in very different cultural settings.

Discernment in Transformation: A Jungian View. Robert Boyd and J. Gordon Myers (1988) draw upon Jung's theories to suggest a different dimension of personal transformation. They focus on the prelinguistic and extrarational sources of meaning, the ones referred to in Chapter One as responsible for presentational construal. This theoretical perspective pictures the self as made up of such components as *ego, archetypes* (instincts and primordial patterns located in the collective unconscious), the *shadow* (personality configurations or identities other than those we have chosen to develop, which may be accessed through dreams, intruding thoughts, meditation, and sometimes imagination), *anima* and *animus* (the feminine component in men and the masculine component in women, important in many personal transformations that involve a recognition of the part they play in one's life), and the *persona* (the public personality, with which the ego must avoid identifying so that the ego can make a conscious decision to employ or not to employ it).

Boyd and Myers point out that transformation is not solely rational. A complement to rational learning is the process of *discernment,* which involves the development of what I would call "presentational awareness." Discernment leads to a contemplative insight, "a personal illumination gained by putting things together and seeing them in their relational wholeness" (p. 224), and a union between ourselves and our world. Discernment is made up of three activities: *receptivity* or openness to the symbols, images, and other influences of the shadow, anima, animus, persona, and archetypal configurations; *recognition,* awareness that an experience is authentic, that is, vitally connected to our own inner history as persons; and *grieving,* "a kind of 'talking back' to the extrarational message demanding . . . attention at this time" (p. 277). Grieving, in turn, has four phases: numbness and panic, pining and protest, disorganization and despair, and restabilization and reintegration.

According to these authors, the essential questions for transformative education concern whether the learner is learning to develop (1) dialogues between the ego and the other components of the self, (2) awareness and understanding of the way in which cultural symbols impact upon his or her life, and (3) awareness and understanding of symbols and the processes of symbolization. Boyd and Myers suggest that the essential virtues for the transformative educator are seasoned guidance, which can help the learner create an inner dialogue, and compassionate criticism, which can help the learner question his or her present way of viewing reality and enter the process of discernment.

The Jungian formulation, as interpreted by these authors, represents an alternative approach to that presented in this book for explaining psychological distortions in meaning perspective. However, it complements the viewpoint of the book by placing an important emphasis on the significance of presentational awareness and the centrality of the self in transformative learning.

Outlines of the Transformation Process

My own research (Mezirow, 1978) and that of others has shown that, although the transformation of *meaning schemes* (specific beliefs, attitudes, and emotional reactions) through reflection is an everyday occurrence, it does not necessarily involve self-reflection. We often merely correct our interpretations. On the other hand, the transformation of a *meaning perspective,* which occurs less frequently, is more likely to involve our sense of self and always involves critical reflection upon the distorted premises sustaining our structure of expection. Perspective transformation is the process of becoming critically aware of how and why our assumptions have come to constrain the way we perceive, understand, and feel about our world; changing these structures of habitual expectation to make possible a more inclusive, discriminating, and integrative perspective; and, finally, making choices or otherwise acting upon these new understandings.

Perspective transformation can occur either through an accretion of transformed meaning schemes resulting from a series of dilemmas or in response to an externally imposed epochal dilemma such as a death, illness, separation or divorce, children leaving home, being passed over for promotion or gaining a promotion, failing an important examination, or retirement. A disorienting dilemma that begins the process of transformation also can result from an eye-opening discussion, book, poem, or painting or from efforts to understand a different culture with customs that contradict our own previously accepted presuppositions. Any major challenge to an established perspective can result in a transformation. These challenges are painful; they often call into question deeply held personal values and threaten our very sense of self.

The Phases of Transformation. My national study of women who were returning to college after a hiatus to participate in specialized reentry programs (Mezirow, 1975) suggests that the process of personal transformation involves ten phases. In this study, my co-workers and I conducted structured interviews with eighty-three women in twelve programs in New York, New Jersey, California, and Washington, with fifty alumnae of the programs, and with the professionals operating these programs and similar ones on twenty-four additional campuses. We delineated the concept of perspective transformation inductively from this fieldwork. The phases of perspective transformation appeared to be as follows:

1. A disorienting dilemma
2. Self-examination with feelings of guilt or shame
3. A critical assessment of epistemic, sociocultural, or psychic assumptions
4. Recognition that one's discontent and the process of transformation are shared and that others have negotiated a similar change
5. Exploration of options for new roles, relationships, and actions
6. Planning of a course of action

7. Acquisition of knowledge and skills for implementing one's plans
8. Provisional trying of new roles
9. Building of competence and self-confidence in new roles and relationships; and
10. A reintegration into one's life on the basis of conditions dictated by one's new perspective.

These phases were subsequently confirmed in research by Joyce Morgan (1987), who studied thirty displaced homemakers who had become separated or divorced or had suffered the death of a spouse and were involved in a college program especially designed for them. Morgan reports the stages of the particular transition of this group as "shock and devastation, pain and rejection, immobilization and depression, gaining confidence, exploring options, decision making and establishment of independence" (p. 204).

This group of women often turned to religion for solace after experiencing the guilt and shame of critical self-reflection. However, they ultimately came to rely on themselves as well. Morgan notes:

> For most of the women who had experienced a perspective transformation, the following major belief shifts occurred: defining their personal identity as separate from roles and relationships, taking responsbility for themselves, recognizing negative effects of total dependence, recognizing that there are options for ways of thinking and acting and that one has choices to make, recognizing the benefits of being alone, viewing a relationship with a man as a nice extra rather than as an essential for well-being, viewing divorce as acceptable, understanding that having a relationship or being a wife and mother does not preclude having a career. [p. 230]

Williams (1986) undertook an empirical study to determine how well perspective transformation could explain the process that led to the development of abusive behavior toward one's spouse and whether it might assist in understanding and facilitating change in that behavior. Williams studied twenty-five self-selected men who had abused their wives and were admitted into a twelve-week educational program designed to recognize and facilitate the process of perspective transformation. Pre- and post-measures included intake and exit interviews and five self-report instruments administered immediately before and after the program and twelve weeks later to measure outcomes perceived to be related to perspective transformation: Rosenberg's Self-Esteem Scale, Conflict Tactics Scales, Rotter's Locus of Control Scale, the Index of Role Preferences, and an Index of Spouse Abuse. A therapist and three researchers independently rated the taped exit interview of each person completing the program on a seven-point scale of low to high perspective transformation, with criteria based upon the ten phases suggested in my reentry study.

Correlations among raters were high. Most of the phases identified in the earlier study also were found in this population, and the perspective transformation ratings were found to be of greater value than the other measures in providing insight into the changes among the subjects interviewed. The educational program designed to foster perspective transformation lowered the use of abusive behavior in the subjects, and "those who had undergone a perspective transformation were the ones who made the greatest change in lowering their use of physically abusive behavior . . . . A change in meaning perspective did relate significantly to change in behavior" (pp. 214–15). Williams concludes that perspective transformation "is a viable theory for explaining the processes of change in abusive behavior . . . and in designing a treatment program to facilitate change" (p. 210).

Perspective transformation that occurred as a result of ill health was studied by Ella Katherine Hunter (1980). She found a pattern of change that allowed the following phases: (1) an interest in health foods, (2) denial of serious problems that were approaching crisis proportions, (3) recognition of the existence of a critical life crisis, (4) readiness to take major action in order to handle the crisis, (5) a period of critical change, (6) a time of life satisfaction, and (7) spiritual development. The most active and rapid period of change was seen as a response to a severely threatening situation that had been denied until its potential for damage was overwhelming. Participants were forced to undergo the pain and adversity of change in order to cope with unresolved difficulties. Ultimately they succeeded in overcoming the imminent crisis and became satisfied with the change they had made.

The studies by Mezirow, Morgan, Williams, and Hunter all attest to the difficulties that perspective transformations involve for the learner and the typically difficult negotiation, compromise, stalling, backsliding, self-deception, and failure that one observes in transformative learning. In the reentry study we identified two points at which such behavior was common. One is at the beginning, when the learner is exposing to critical analysis his or her established ideas, values, and sense of order, as well as the feelings that he or she has about these assumptions. The other is the point at which a commitment to reflective action logically should follow insight but is so threatening or demanding that the learner is immobilized. This is the point in the transformative learning process at which the conative plays a specific role. It is not enough to understand intellectually the need to change the way one acts; one requires emotional strength and an act of will in order to move forward. Backsliding in the process of transformation may be explained by the learner acquiring an insight that results in a transformation in meaning scheme that may contribute over time toward a change in meaning perspective but at the moment comes into conflict with the established meaning perspective and is overwhelmed by it. The learner then becomes unable to act upon his or her new insight. The power of the threat presented by actions inspired by a new meaning perspective depends upon the nature of the threat, how pressing the disorienting dilemma was that initiated the process, and how effectively the learner has personalized and integrated into his or her experience what has been learned about the epistemic, sociocultural, or psychic forces that affect his or her way of understanding.

The conflict between meaning scheme and perspective can result in self-deception and neurosis (Shapiro, 1989, p. 194). The self-deception that can impede progress in perspective transformation was illustrated dramatically in our reentry study by Roberta, a woman of thirty-eight:

> Soon after embarking on a re-entry program "to find a direction to go in terms of college or a job," [Roberta] became intensely involved in a consciousness-raising group organized by an instructor. "We just went crazy and the things that came out of people who had it locked away were so painful that we all rather cried with whoever it was that was opening up." Despite the intense and empathetic nature of the experience, however, Roberta failed to personalize what she had learned about sex stereotypes and the common problems of women. Although she acquired the vocabulary and undoubtedly a measure of understanding, she was unable to integrate these insights into her experience. Instead, she misinterpreted what she learned to rationalize her inability to take action. Roberta tried volunteering but quit; she started a college course but dropped out. Her husband's business failed, but, despite earlier experience as a secretary, she could not bring herself to take a job. Roberta justified her inaction on the basis of what she felt she had learned, that "one should not do what others expect of them, only what one wants to do"—even if this is nothing. [Mezirow, 1978, pp. 16–17]

A Model of Transformation. Jane Taylor (1989) developed a six-step model of the process of transformative learning and applied it to analysis of a case study. The following is an outline of her model:

Phase I   Generation of Consciousness
      Step 1:   Encountering trigger events
      Step 2:   Confronting reality

Phase II Transformation of Consciousness
    Step 3: Reaching the transition point
        (a) Decision to shift vision of reality
        (b) Dramatic leap or shift that "just happens" in a way not consciously planned
    Step 4: Shift or leap of transcendence
Phase III Integration of consciousness
    Step 5: Personal commitment
    Step 6: Grounding and development

Taylor observes that trigger events may be life-shattering occurrences such as natural disasters, or they may be personal upheavals, troubling contradictions between meaning systems, external social events, or cumulative internal changes. The initial confrontation of a dilemma may be self-induced (as when a writer becomes involved in the act of writing or when learning results in works of art or invention), induced by life circumstances, or induced by other people such as an educator or a therapist.

The phase that Taylor calls "generation of consciousness" can take several forms. It can result from an unexpected and original world vision, like the Copernican Revolution. It can result from appropriating a perspective promoted by a powerful or charismatic leader, as in early socialization or entry into a religious or political cult. It can result from assimilating a ready-made reality, as in secondary socialization into a profession or discipline. It can result from appropriation of a meaning perspective created in a special environment such as a culture circle, a consciousness-raising group, or a class. Finally, it can result from appropriation of a "bridge-paradigm" in a secure "practice laboratory" environment such as that of T-groups, which can mediate between old perspectives and the application of new ones in everyday situations.

Step 4, "a shift or leap of transcendence," means an awareness that a new perspective transcends an old one. This often involves sudden insight, but it also can occur as a gradual revelatory awareness. This transformative experience, which is variously described as a leap of faith, creative leap, contextual shift, metamorphosis, reconstruction, reframing, or perceptual alternation, results in heightened awareness; personal power; capacity for action, reflection, or decision; and developmental progress or emancipation.

Step 5, "personal commitment," involves a decision to commit to the new perspective: an act of intention, purpose, and will. Step 6, "grounding and development," refers to a confirmation, application, implementation, and extension of the new perspective that involves the development of new skills, understandings, and behaviors. Taylor found personal and group support to be most essential at this stage.

Transformation in Special Settings

A number of researchers have studied the process of perspective transformation in particular settings. These settings include religious communities, workplaces, and several kinds of special classes. Although differences were noted, the transformation process showed basic similarities in all settings.

Transformation in Response to Marginality. Although profound changes in a person's life are not required for a perspective transformation — accretions of changes in meaning schemes can also produce transformation — the study of transformations associated with major life crises has proven methodologically more feasible than the study of those resulting from more gradual changes. In one such study, Frank Musgrove, an English sociologist, undertook seven ethnographic case studies of profound change in adult life to examine the processes of adult resocialization (1977). Musgrove's focus was on the modification of consciousness in adulthood through the experience of marginality, so he studied groups of people who had moved into unusual, extreme, or abnormal life roles. He compared the experiences of men and women who had become blind in adult life, those who had contracted incurable physical disabilities and had been institutionalized, self-employed artists, recent entrants to the Anglican ministry and to a Sufi commune, Hare Krishna devotees, and professed adult homosexuals. All these roles involved marginality, which Musgrove defines phenomenologically as "change from a former position which was accepted as self-evident and normal, which was taken for granted, and presented itself as not in need of further analysis. Change to a marginal position brings into question three basic ingredients of reality: time, typicality, and preconstituted (recipe) knowledge. Marginal situations, at least when first encountered, make time, types, and recipes problematical" (p. 7).

Musgrove builds upon concepts of marginality developed by anthropologists Mary Douglas (1966) and Victor Turner (1974) and especially upon the work of the sociologist of knowledge, Peter Berger (Berger and Luckmann, 1966). Both Douglas and Turner studied liminality, the threshold state, among tribal people. They define liminal people as those who are outside the mainstream of social life and elude the established classifications of a particular society. Because marginal or liminal people threaten the world of everyday life by not fitting these classifications, Berger suggests that marginality is terrifying, but he points out that it also can be liberating and transforming. He writes, "Both in practice and in theoretical thought, human life gains the greatest part of its richness from . . . any experience of stepping outside the taken-for-granted reality of everyday life, any openness to the mystery that surrounds us on all sides" (quoted in Musgrove, 1977, p. 11).

Berger sees modern adults as "conversion-prone"—poised for transformation—and Musgrove set out to test this idea. He found that even such a dramatic change as going blind in adulthood, becoming stricken by multiple sclerosis and institutionalized, leaving work in a mill to become an artist, changing from engineering to the priesthood, accepting one's homosexuality, or entering a commune of Eastern mystics did not in itself result in a major transformation of identity. In other words, significant or even dramatic changes in behavior did not necessarily mean corresponding changes in values and meanings, nor did significant changes in values and meanings necessarily result in correspondingly significant changes in behavior. "Finding new recipe knowledge," Musgrove writes, "does not necessarily sustain a new reality: it supports and even strengthens the old. . . .

New typifications and categories can be minimized and isolated, accommodated to old structures of meaning, leaving former definitions of the self and the world substantially intact" (pp. 14–15).

Changes were greatest in those entering the communes (Sufi and Hare Krishna) and in the homosexuals; those who turned deliberately to a new life, placing themselves outside of mainstream society and hoping to change it rather than to adapt to it, were the most likely to change themselves as well. The film *Born on the Fourth of July* depicts the truth of this finding. Its hero, Ron Kovac, paralyzed from the waist down in the Vietnam War, is wrenchingly unable to adjust to the banality of his own traditional values and those of his family and community. Only after aimless rebellion and desperation does he undergo a perspective transformation and find new meaning in life by becoming an antiwar activist.

Musgrove found that transformations as a response to marginality occurred more frequently in early adult life. He suggests that people are more open to new modes of experience in their early adult years than they are later. He also found that significant change can occur incrementally over many years.

Another interesting finding of Musgrove's study challenges the assumed importance of significant others in personal change and reaffirms the overwhelming importance of the "historical (or untransformed) self." While others were found to be important in testing a marginal person's new reality, their support did not play a major strategic role in promoting transformations, and the inmate culture of institutions was found to have a mere "trivial influence" on perspective transformation. "'Transformations of perspective' do not, as one such theorist suggests, follow so readily from the 'displacement of significant others,'" Musgrove writes (p. 221).

Musgrove believes that marginality in this context is best understood as a stage or phase in a social process in which those who experienced transformations emerged from a period of social uncertainty and ambiguity similar to Turner's "liminality." In the postliminal stage, such people may either turn back toward or turn away from society's center. Musgrove found that the likelihood of turning away seemed to be related to age, but the likelihood of turning back did not.

Musgrove urges that the efforts of adult education focus on people in their twenties and early thirties and that these efforts be essentially in the direction of moral education, "in the sense of affording time, opportunity, and preferably a range of real-life experiences for exploration of the moral universe and one's conception of self" (p. 227). However, transformation theory holds that the abilities to move from a pre- to a postrational orientation, to become critically reflective, and to participate more fully and freely in rational discourse exist throughout adult life.

Transformation as a Transcendent Experience. Perspective transformation often involves profound changes in self, changes with cognitive, emotional, somatic, and unconscious dimensions. Ross Keane (1985) made an insightful phenomenological analysis of his own transformation and those of five other men committed to a religious life-style. His findings refine and reinforce the pattern of perspective transformation that has emerged from other studies. They are important enough to warrant extended description.

The transformative learning experience described by Keane involved four phases. It began with *disorientation,* or a disorienting dilemma, an "inner disequilibrium in which the harmony of the self is disturbed yet the problem is neither understood nor satisfactorily named." Disorientation started a doubting process in which old meaning perspectives were perceived as inadequate in the face of heightened awareness of inconsistencies within the self. Keane found disorientation to be associated with a period in which the pressures of life had eased or in which those studied transited from their normal activities to full-time study. Disorientation could come gradually or, if the learner missed the accumulating signs of unease, disorientation could "explode into awareness," accompanied by emotional turmoil, disturbing dreams, and physical pain as well as cognitive confusion.

The second phase in the transformation process was a *search for meaning and peace.* This involved a search for identity, a seeking of personal integration. Keane identified three processes in this phase:

The first process is: Developing autonomy in searching. Doubters develop autonomy and self direction as they: move from reliance on a limited number of sources of knowledge and assistance and seek assistance from a variety of sources; move from uncritical acceptance of advice and knowledge and take a more critical stance; move from viewing helpers as sources of instant answers and begin viewing them as resources in finding one's own answers; move from assuming that existing boundaries and circumstances are non-negotiable and start to test boundaries and question assumed non-negotiable realities.

The second learning process is: Trusting the harmony of the total self. Doubters become empowered by this process as they learn to move from a reliance on others' sense of truth and start to trust their own inner sense of rightness and truth; move from an oblivious or disregarding stance toward fleeting physical or emotional changes and become aware and trusting of the messages they contain; move from insensitivity to feelings and become sensitive and able to interpret the messages contained in contrasts and variations in feeling; move from insensitivity to the messages contained in recurrent and persistent symbols towards a more open and trusting awareness of the unconscious revealing itself in this way.

The third learning process is: Learning how to learn more effectively. Doubters are empowered by this process when they: move from stumbling around in the multidimensionality of change and start looking for patterns of behavior; move from a desperate, indiscriminate grasping of every possible form of assistance which suits their learning style; move from a fearful clinging to the security of the known and let go and start risking and experimenting with new behaviors; move from pas-

sive acceptance of personality handicaps and learning deficits and actively develop their functions and
abilities; move from viewing resistance and avoidance behaviors as insurmountable obstacles and
start seeing them as challenges, opportunities for
self-knowledge and invitations to change. [pp. 188–
189]

The second phase of the transformative process, the search
for meaning and personal integration, was facilitated when the
learner found a satisfactory name to describe the disorienting
experience. This could alleviate initial fears and a sense of helplessness. Incorrect naming, however, could be seriously mis-
leading. The process of organizing the self involved a synthesis
between valued aspects of the old perspective and insights of
the new. At the same time, the learner needed to gain both emotional and cognitive freedom from old realities. This meant that
the learner had to sweat out a waiting period of the nonrational —
intuitive, spiritual, emotional — in order to become congruent
with the rational once again.

The third phase of the transformation process was one
of self-acceptance, the experience of insight that recognizes and
accepts a truth about the self that previously has been unac-
knowledged at the rational level. This turning point was pre-
ceded by helplessness, depression, despair, and self-doubt. The
process of achieving self-acceptance was difficult but could be
assisted. It was more likely to occur when the learner discov-
ered a meaning perspective that assisted in organizing his or
her experiences, actively searched out patterns of behavior and
habits of perception, revisited the past to confront assumptions
about self, attended to "the subconscious, to projections, to
dreams, to the spiritual and intuitive, to messages from symbols and physical states, to the dialectic between feeling and
knowing, to feedback from others and the use of imagery" (p.
191), and secured helping relationships that involved empathic
and nonjudgmental listening and "invitational" questioning that
pointed out underlying assumptions.

The fourth phase in the transformative learning process

was integration. This phase involved the reordering of meaning schemes and the exploration of new definitions of the possible. It was a process of ambivalence and ambiguity, reflection and feedback, and it led to the ability to transcend polarities, reconceptualize contradictions, and view reality more dialectically and less in terms of absolutes and polarized opposites such as self and role or actual and espoused theories. Procedures that facilitated this stage included "reading on both sides of an issue, reflection on patterns of emotional responses to familiar situations, journaling, dialogue with significant others, imaging and times of prayer and retreat" (p. 193).

Not all learning transformations involve such profound self-redefinition, of course. When they do, however, Keane found that they foster movement toward a stronger, more compassionate, more complex, and better integrated self. Keane's orientation is that of a religious person, with a focus on the self, autonomy, and personal development. Nonetheless, he clearly is describing the same process of perspective transformation delineated by others cited in this chapter.

Transformation in the Workplace. Perspective transformation in the workplace and the question of whether critical reflection can change an organization was studied by Ann Brooks (1989), who also attempted to determine the ways that organizations affect the development of critically reflective employees. The organization she studied was a service corporation that employed about 70,000 people. The corporation was attempting to cope with major changes mandated by government deregulation.

The belief guiding Brooks's study was that "a work force capable of reflecting on the assumptions that are behind dysfunctional attitudes and behavior is best suited not only to respond to the challenges of a changing environment but to contribute to and actualize the company's strategy in a way that meets contextual challenges" (p. 12). Her interviews with twenty-nine managers, nominated as critically reflective by their peers, identified three types of critical reflection: reflection-in-action, reflection on ethical issues, and strategic planning.

Critical reflectivity was encouraged or developed by additional responsibility and participation, certain educational experiences, and openness on the part of management. Critically reflective learning was found to involve empathically taking another person's or group's perspective and listening to intuition—what Brooks calls "first-order thinking" (p. 147). "Second-order thinking" included perspective taking, monitoring thought processes, gathering information, and using analytical processes. Monitoring involved maintaining honesty, dealing with real issues, trying not to categorize people, avoiding approaching a problem emotionally, and looking for opportunities in any changing situation. Critically reflective participants reported using the following analytic strategies: making pieces fit, searching for a unifying principle, looking for implications, and identifying discrepancies (p. 154). The ability to be critically reflective was traced to a pattern of questioning and critique within the family and to personal transformations such as intercultural encounters, personal illness, divorce, and failure at work.

The adult learners in Brooks's study described five insights gained through perspective transformation: "I am the originator of my own destiny," "Survival requires an affirmation of living," "Openness results in more successful interpersonal relationships," "I must have the courage of my convictions," and "There are more realities than one" (p. 159). Critically reflective employees tended to look inward for direction and values rather than toward the company. Brooks found, however, that whether or not critical reflection led to taking social or political action depended upon the factor of risk in the situation. Companies can bottle up the critical reflection of employees by making critique of assumptions too costly.

Critical reflection in the context of an organization focuses upon implementation of policy and strategy, Brooks found. If companies bar critically reflective employees' access to policy and strategy, they prevent implementation that could help in changing the organization to respond more appropriately to changing situations.

The study of perspective transformation in such natural settings as the workplace or the family environment is much needed. Brooks points the way for this kind of research.

Other Studies. A study of twenty volunteers working within the Methodist Church was conducted by Trudie Preciphs (1989) to determine how they came to change their beliefs and actions in relation to positions taken by national church leadership. Preciphs studied the relative magnitude of change in perspective experienced by each volunteer on social issues, the content of his or her beliefs and values, the action orientation of change, and changes in the ways the volunteer reflected on his or her reality, that is, in critical reflective thinking. Through a training program involving formal and informal learning situations, sixteen volunteers became critically reflective and changed their position on one or more of the issues addressed by the agency in such areas as homosexuality, cross-cultural awareness, and inclusive language about God and humanity. Susan, a representative volunteer, said that the training program "helped me to look at how we function and the roles we play out and how myths and stereotypes had shaped me and others. Up to then I had never looked at that, and to hear that, it made me take a look at myself and the traps I had been falling into" (p. 134).

Informal learning experiences in the program involved dialogue, storytelling, sharing significant experiences, and linking personal struggle or pain with social issues. Formal learning involved storytelling, workshops, seminars, presentations, sensitivity sessions, using dialogue for sharing experiences, community building, training on issues, and linkage of personal struggles with social issues. In this intimate context of religious service, emotional encounter, and community building, transformative learning appeared to flourish. However, the volunteers in this national program encountered stress and resistance when they took their new perspectives on social issues back to their local groups. The national program nonetheless provided many of the volunteers with the strength to take stands on social issues that were at odds with the conventional viewpoints in their home communities.

Linda Marie Young (1988) studied learning by twenty mothers participating in a series of postpartum classes. Among other objectives, she attempted to determine whether this learning could be understood by using my explanation of the processes and functions of learning. The subjects categorized their learning experiences according to operational definitions developed by Young that identified what I have described as instrumental learning, dialogic (communicative) learning, and self-reflective learning. At the beginning of the program, learnings were about equally distributed among these types. After the training, about half the learning reported was categorized as instrumental, and the other half was equally divided between dialogic and self-reflective learning. Infant-oriented learnings tended to be classified as instrumental and mother-oriented learnings as self-reflective. Mothers particularly valued sharing common feelings, concerns, and self-examination. The subjects also classified what they learned according to whether it modified what they already knew (learning within meaning schemes), added information in a parallel but new structure (learning new meaning schemes), or changed their way of looking at things (transformative learning). Learning initially was equally divided among these processes. By the end of the training, however, about half the learnings involved new meaning schemes, and the other half was divided between learning within meaning schemes and meaning transformation. The study establishes the importance of dialogic and self-reflective learning in postpartum classes.

In an analysis of critically self-reflective learning in Alcoholics Anonymous, Peter Hough (1990) found support groups such as AA to be powerful expediters of transformative learning. If one is driven by an addiction or dysfunctional behavior to seek help, the critically self-reflective mode is greatly enhanced by making a personal commitment to live by an explicit set of principles such as AA's "Steps of Rational Recovery" ("I admit I have become chemically dependent, and the consequences of that dependency are unacceptable," "I surrender all ideas of perfection for myself and others, and my first goal is to learn to accept myself as I am: a fallible yet very worthwhile human being," and others), by a mentor-protege relationship, and by being able to distance oneself and explore the dysfunctionality of an old meaning perspective through a self-revelatory group in which members share their common experience. Hough notes the importance of making simple the language of critical self-reflection and transformative learning so that learners of diverse backgrounds can identify their own learning experience. Terms such as *self, assumption, reflectivity, premise, perception, belief, value,* and *identity* need examples and definitions that are clear and easy to understand. Self-directed learning in other types of self-help groups has been researched by Hammerman (1989).

Nancy Dudley (1987) studied the process of paradigm shift (perspective transformation) in five men and five women "from the view of humans as separate from and dominant over nature to an ecological world view which recognizes our embeddedness in nature" (p. 1). She found evidence of the evolutionary nature of this transformative change; that is, change was gradual, followed a steplike or spiral pattern, moved steadily in the same direction, and was purposeful. Dudley characterized the process as following these overlapping themes: separation from routine patterns (a "frame-break"), transcendence over ordinary patterns, mindful and willing participation, validation, integration (acting upon one's new paradigm) as opposed to a pull to familiar patterns, and sensitivity to a universe of pattern and meaning (pp. 221–222). Dudley's analysis is compatible with the findings reported in the studies previously cited here.

Molly Daniels (1990) studied ideas about critical reflection and its facilitation and perceptions of the influence of institutional culture on transformative learning among seventeen faculty members and administrators in a unit of a nontraditional university that placed major emphasis on developing critical reflection. She found philosophical differences between faculty with "humanistic" and those with "radical" philosophies (Elias and Merriam, 1980), involving, respectively, a Rogerian nurturance and a Freirian problem-posing orientation. She also noted discrepancies between faculty members' perceptions and those of administrators concerning the effects of institutional culture.

A model linking lifelong learning with transpersonal psychology was developed by Jill Newman Henry (1988) in an unpublished study entitled "Development and Learning for Transformation." Among the many books devoted to exploring the nature of personal transformation that have come to my attention are those of Sherman (1987) and Berardo (1982) on mid-life transitions; Fingarette (1963), Gould (1978), and Shainberg (1973) on psychoanalytic process; Boud and Griffin (1987) on developmental personal learning; Schlossberg (1984) on counseling; Schön (1983) on learning to become a professional; Peck (1987) on spiritual development; Martin (1988) on women returning to school; Goodman (1979) on confrontations with social forces; Bridges (1980) and O'Neill and O'Neill (1978) on managing life transitions; and Ferguson (1980) on transformation as a movement.

Collective Transformations

Perspective transformations occur not only in isolated individuals but also in people involved in groups and social movements. This section will describe the socially interactive nature of the process of perspective transformation, including the way the process occurs in consciousness raising and in social movements. It will also identify major impediments to critically reflective discourse in groups.

Perspective transformation is a social process often involving points of view expressed by others that we initially find discordant, distasteful, and threatening but later come to recognize as indispensable to dealing with our experience. We look to others to communicate alternative perspectives that may explain our dilemmas. When we find a promising perspective, we do not merely appropriate it but, by making an imaginative interpretation of it, construe it to make it our own. The resulting perspective never will be exactly the same as that originally expressed by the other, just as the full range of meaning that we attach to words or concepts always will vary to some extent from the connotations attributed to the same words or concepts by others.

The social process of perspective transformation further involves testing our new perspective on friends, peers, and mentors. Their reinforcement can be vitally important in making transformation possible. We validate the new perspective through rational discourse. We also have to work out the changed relationships with others that result from our new perspective.

Consciousness Raising. We are familiar with the power of consciousness-raising groups in the women's movement to effect personal transformations on a large scale. This learning process has been perceptively analyzed by Mechthild Hart (in Mezirow and Associates, 1990). Hart writes that consciousness raising "ignites around the theme of oppression, presupposes a certain view about knowledge and knowing that empowers rather than extinguishes the individual knower, and . . . calls for a relationship between theory and practice that starts with a however vaguely felt or articulated acknowledgement of power and ends in a systematic understanding of the nature and complexity of the entire power-bound social reality. To 'raise consciousness' means to arrive at such an awareness and to anchor the process of becoming aware in individual reality rather than in analyses and theories that were produced elsewhere" (p. 35).

Hart lists the significant elements of consciousness raising as "acknowledgement and analysis of oppression, acceptance of the importance of personal experience as the original content for critical reflection, planned homogeneity of the learning group and direct reflection of the critique of the mechanisms of power in a structure of equality among all the participants of these groups" (p. 24). To begin with, he explains, it is essential that the learning group see itself as oppressed and relatively powerless in relation to others who benefit from the existing allocation of influence and power. There also must be time for retroactive premise reflection, so the potentially transformative learning experience should be conducted separately from task-oriented group activity.

Consciousness-raising groups and feminist educators struggle against the kind of objectivism that assumes the marginality or irrelevance of personal knowledge, a prejudice highly valued in the worlds of scientists, lawyers, and academics. At the same time, the groups resist learners' urge to locate authenticity only in immediately felt experience. Hart sees subjectivity as requiring a self-consciousness that is akin to thinking theoretically about personal experience: for consciousness raising, she says, "a theoretical distance from personal experience has to be gained" (p. 30). Personal experience is to be recognized as organized by forces and structures located outside individual experience. It should be used both as the "content" for analysis and self-reflection and as a departure point for gaining socially validated knowledge.

Homogeneity among group members in terms of experience and background assumptions is an important condition for consciousness raising. When group members come from different sexes, races, or classes, it is often much more difficult to reach the mutual sense of trust necessary to permit intimate self-disclosure, to generate a fund of vital information, and to develop a shared interest in liberation.

It is especially important that there be no major differences in social power among group members. Privileged members of a consciousness-raising group must learn difficult lessons in how to become "actively and supportively silent" (p. 24). The group must move toward increased reciprocity and equality among its members. Consciousness-raising groups characteristically were leaderless (that is, without a designated leader), accepted norms of dialogue that assured that everyone was heard, and provided for support and abstention from criticism of other group members. Group members validated each other as women and created new forms of interaction and relationship among themselves.

Hart describes Allen's four phases of consciousness-raising groups — "opening up," "sharing," "analyzing," and "abstracting" — as involving significant moments in the process rather than successive or invariant stages. Opening up refers to those moments in which feelings are expressed and experiences are recounted. Sharing refers to phases in which similarities in experience are identified. "The non-individual, testimonial character of these experiences moves to the center of attention" (pp. 32–33), and deliberate efforts are made to overcome competitive habits of speech and interaction.

Often groups go around the circle and let all members talk about their experiences before comments are made; some groups tell members to talk only about their own experience and not refer to what others have said. In a "second round," people may consciously reflect on their previous contribution in light of others' comments, noting how the remarks of others have helped them understand their own experience as being similar or different. This activity includes disclosure, analysis (asking questions about how the society functions), and abstraction (relating the concepts and analysis undertaken to a discussion about abstract theory).

Social Movements. Becoming critically self-reflective can be powerfully facilitated by a relevant social movement. Over the past twenty years most adults in the United States have arrived at a new perspective about Afro-Americans, civil rights, the Vietnam War, the environment, and/or women's rights in the context of a social movement. Our personal dilemmas often are precipitated or reinforced by what we hear and see and read. If a social movement supports an alternative meaning perspective that affords relief from the stress generated by our dilemma, we will be more likely to be receptive to it. Identifying with a social movement provides perhaps the most powerful reinforcement of a new way of seeing our own dilemma.

Social movements, in turn, gain great power when people identify with them as part of a personal perspective transformation. For example, the social activist adult education programs of the Highlander Center near Knoxville, Tennessee, were a major influence in fostering the civil rights movement in the United States (Horton, 1990). The adult literacy education programs established in China, Cuba, and Nicaragua following the revolutions in those countries proved to be among the most effective in the world.

Mathias Finger (1989a and b) describes a new paradigm for social action emerging out of new social movements in Europe, including the "Green" movement, new peace movements, and spiritual or religious movements collectively known as "New Age" movements. Finger contrasts these with "old" movements, including labor, feminist, human rights, and Third World movements for economic, social, and political emancipation. He characterizes these old movements as organized efforts to use education to achieve such social goals of the Enlightenment and modernity as justice, liberty, equality, and emancipation. These collective goals have been put before the goals of the individual.

Finger contrasts the concept of education as a means toward political emancipation with the view in the new movements, in which transformative education is valued for itself. These movements feel that the old approach to modernity has failed. They believe that the aim of education should not be to achieve social goals but rather to induce a process of personal transformation that inevitably will influence social, cultural, and political life. Social and cultural transformations happen only to individuals. Transformation in the way one lives and thinks therefore becomes the ultimate criterion for evaluating adult education.

The new movements both provide an environment and serve as a catalyst for fostering personal transformations, define the future topics of adult transformation, link social transformation with personal transformation, and help people understand that transformations are based upon personal emotional commitments to "learning our way out" of specific dilemmas associated with social concerns. People involved in these movements believe that the motive for transformation comes from deeply moral, even religious, motives; transformations are not simply cognitive in nature. "Adult transformation is . . . mainly informal, local and communitarian, based on concern, commitment and experience, rooted in and contributing to the development of a local culture," Finger says (p. 18). The purpose of the new movements is to reestablish in a new mode the link between the person and society. According to Finger, the new movements feature *experiential learning, learning through consternation* (learning experiences that arouse one's emotions), *holistic learning* (learning a way of life), and *identity learning* (learning that personal identity cannot be separated from the way one lives and one's social commitments) (p. 21). Marilyn Ferguson's popular book, *The Aquarian Conspiracy* (1980), describes several similar group movements that involve personal transformations.

Communicative communities continually recreate and elaborate social reality by actively producing meanings through their interpretations of the world. Social movements may be understood as active creators of new forms and meanings of social reality by reality testing through emancipatory discourse. Protest, dissent, and opposition to oppressive social arrangements may be precursors of these new social realities.

Impediments to Critically Reflective Discourse in Groups. A substantial body of literature describes impediments to critically reflective or rational discourse in groups. Overreliance on authority and structure, fear of confronting conflict, and the inherent paradox of individuality and effective group participation are familiar issues. Irving Janis (1983) coined the word "groupthink" to refer to a mode of thought that he found to be characteristic of deep involvement in a cohesive group in which the desire for unanimity precludes a realistic assessment of alternative courses of action. His case studies for analyzing this phenomenon included such political fiascos as the Bay of Pigs, Pearl Harbor, the Cuban Missile Crisis, the escalation of the Vietnam War, and the Watergate cover-up.

Janis showed that the quality of decision making deteriorates as conformity pressures come to dominate a group's deliberations. Pressures toward conformity include self-censorship, the illusion of unanimity, direct pressure on dissenters, and self-appointed "mindguards" (group members who protect the leader from thoughts that they believe would impair the leader's confidence in the soundness of his or her decisions). The message of all these pressures is to avoid divisiveness and "rally round the leader." Janis notes: "The more amicability and *esprit de corps* among members of a policy-making in-group, the greater is the danger that independent critical thinking will be replaced by groupthink, which is likely to result in irrational and dehumanizing actions directed against out-groups," (p. 13).

Major conditions for groupthink include group cohesiveness, homogeneity in social background and ideology, group deliberations insulated from critical assessments by others who are informed or expert, lack of a tradition of impartial leadership (which precludes open inquiry and critical thinking), and absence of norms by which to maintain procedural methods for prescribing decision-making tasks such as search and appraisal.

Groups are more likely to resort to groupthink (1) when they deliberate under conditions of high stress from an external threat with little hope of a better solution than one posed by the leader and (2) when low self-esteem has been induced temporarily by recent failures, excessive difficulty in decision making, or lack of apparent alternatives except those that violate the group's ethical standards (p. 244).

Although groups with traditions and established procedures that facilitate critical inquiry probably are capable of making better decisions than single individuals, groupthink has been found to result in such distortions as an incomplete survey of alternatives or objectives, failure to examine risks of preferred choice or failure to reappraise initially rejected alternatives, poor information search, selective bias in processing information at hand, and failure to work out contingency plans (p. 75). Janis's ideas are borne out by the work of Ernest May (1973), who found that failures in major foreign policy decisions in Washington often have occurred because of reliance on questionable historical parallels, analogies, or precedents made without input by historians, who might have helped the group making the decisions see their assumptions about history more critically.

Rational discourse in groups also can be impeded when group members' enthusiasm causes their perspectives to become impermeable to alternative points of view; that is, the members become "true believers." This is especially likely to happen if members' relationship to the group is organic rather than contractual (Mezirow, 1978). An organic relationship is one predicated upon complete identification with the group. Many conversions involve such relationships. For example, some women who enter a consciousness-raising group abandon further reflective critique of their relationship with the group and instead give the group their unconditional allegiance.

When a *developmental* perspective transformation involves a relationship to a social movement or other new reference group, however, the relationship is contractual rather than organic. Contractual solidarity is based upon a clear understanding that what each party offers will be subject to continuing critical reassessment and that as conditions change, the relationship will change as well (Singer, 1965). In contractual solidarity there are no "true believers" or zealots who abandon reflective critique and critical dialogue in favor of blind deference to group codes, norms, authority, or ideology.

Summary

This chapter examined a broad spectrum of research related to transformation theory. It discussed the development of adult thinking skills (including critical reflection), the role of perspective transformation in adult development, several theoretical overviews of perspective transformation (including phenomenological, orthogenetic, and Jungian views), outlines of the transformation process, transformation in special settings (including "marginal" circumstances, religious environments, and the workplace), and transformations in group settings (including consciousness-raising groups and social movements). The chapter presented the following key propositions:

1. There are two dimensions to transformative learning, the transformation of meaning schemes and the transformation of meaning perspectives. The transformation of meaning schemes is integral to the process of reflection. As we assess our assumptions about the content or process of problem solving and find them unjustified, we create new ones or transform our old assumptions and hence our interpretations of experience. This is the dynamics of everyday reflective learning. When occasionally we are forced to assess or reassess the basic premises we have taken for granted and find them unjustified, perspective transformation, followed by major life changes, may result.

2. Development involves two phases: preadolescents decode biological and encode cultural automatisms, and adults reexamine these cultural structures and the assumptions behind them to achieve developmentally more progressive meaning perspectives.

3. Cultures vary in developing the self-awareness necessary for decentration, decontextualization, and development of identity, all of which are necessary for one to understand or "take" the perspective of another or understand how one's own perspective interacts with another's in the eyes of a third party. These qualities, as well as the ability to think abstractly (and thus distance oneself from one's own beliefs and ideas), are associated with education, particularly reading and writing.

4. Development in adulthood refers to movement toward

more developmentally progressive meaning perspectives. A developmentally progressive meaning perspective is more inclusive, discriminating, integrative, and permeable (open) than less developed ones. The transformations likely to produce developmentally advanced meaning perspectives usually appear to occur after the age of thirty.

5. Older adults often move to a more mature level of cognitive differentiation that involves greater awareness of context (especially awareness of psychological factors and individual and collective goals), more analysis of premises, and integration of logic and feelings. These qualitative changes are often misunderstood by youth-oriented developmental models and research methods, which attribute changes in older adults to loss of cognitive function due to aging.

6. Our need to make and transform meaning appears to be orthogenetic in nature—that is, to imitate inevitable patterns of biological development. Each transformation of a meaning scheme or perspective makes more efficient use of energy and generates its own reinforcement because the resulting behavioral pattern is better integrated and more open to new ideas, which provides for greater adaptational efficiency.

7. Critically reflective thinkers move from abstract critique to critical self-reflection, thereby "recovering the personal" and a stronger sense of self-understanding. Discernment is a complement to critical reflection. It involves enhancing presentational awareness and clarifying the influences of the prelinguistic on the way one feels, understands, and acts.

8. Perspective transformation involves a sequence of learning activities that begins with a disorienting dilemma and concludes with a changed self-concept that enables a reintegration into one's life context on the basis of conditions dictated by a new perspective. The sequence of transformative learning activities is not made up of invariable developmental steps; rather, the activities should be understood as sequential moments of "meaning becoming clarified."

9. Indications of movement through a transformation include seeking assistance from a wider variety of sources of knowledge; taking a more critical stance; looking at helpers as resources

for finding one's own answers rather than as authorities who will provide the answers; testing boundaries and assumptions; actively looking for patterns of behavior and avoidance in oneself; greater awareness of emotions, physical states, intuition, and dream symbolism; and searching for forms of assistance compatible with one's learning style.

10. Marginal situations tend to make the taken for granted become problematic, which can lead to transformative learning. The likelihood of transformation is greater if the marginal situation was entered voluntarily.

11. Perspective transformation is a social process: others precipitate the disorienting dilemma, provide us with alternative perspectives, provide support for change, participate in validating changed perspectives through rational discourse, and require new relationships to be worked out within the context of a new perspective. There is evidence, however, that "significant others" may not always be central to perspective transformation.

12. Employers can encourage or discourage perspective transformations among employees. Employees who have become critically reflective can help employers develop creative strategies for dealing with change.

13. Effective consciousness raising in a group involves acknowledgment of oppression, critical reflection on personal experience, the legitimation of personal knowledge, homogeneity of the group, and reflection on the mechanisms of power and equality among group members.

14. Social movements can significantly facilitate critical self-reflection. They can precipitate or reinforce dilemmas and legitimate alternate meaning perspectives. Identifying with a cause larger than oneself is perhaps the most powerful motivator to learn. In turn, people who have undergone perspective transformations can bring great power to social movements.

15. The transformation process and rational dialogue in groups will be hindered if group members possess an unquestioning, "organic" loyalty to the group rather than a "contractual" or provisional loyalty or if members indulge in "group-

think" in order to protect a leader from conflict or to present an appearance of unanimity.

16. New social movements challenge the assumption that education should be used as a means to accomplish particular social goals. They redefine the purpose of education as personal transformation, which they see as the only way to assure cultural transformation and a better society.

7

✑ Fostering Transformative Adult Learning

Sixty-five years ago Eduard Lindeman, the most influential leader among those who established adult education as a professional field in the United States, defined his ideal of adult education as "a cooperative venture in non-authoritarian, informal learning, the chief purpose of which is to discover the meaning of experience; a quest of the mind which digs down to the roots of the preconceptions which formulate our conduct; a technique of learning for adults which makes education coterminous with life and hence elevates living itself to the level of adventurous experiment. . . . Rather than studying 'subjects,' the learner begins with his or her own immediate problems impeding self-fulfillment. The teacher moves from acting as an authority figure to become . . . the guide, the pointer-out, who also participates in learning in proportion to the vitality and relevance of his facts and experiences" (Brookfield, 1987a, p. 4).

Transformation theory provides a foundation for ideals like Lindeman's by explaining the learning dynamics that are involved when we dig down to the roots of our assumptions and preconceptions and, as a result, change the way we construe the meaning of experience. Philosopher Maxine Greene describes meaningful learning as involving a process of disclosure, reconstruction, and generation. She says that the learner's central concern is with "ordering his own life-world when dislocations occur," that is, when the learner experiences "moments when the recipes he has inherited for solving problems no longer seem to work" (1975, p. 307). In modern life these dislocations are endemic. What Greene calls dislocations are transformation theory's "disorienting dilemmas." As we have seen in earlier chapters, the failure of recipe learning often leads to premise reflection and perspective transformation.

In Chapter Four we saw that reflection on the content, and even more on the process, of problem solving is the mechanism by which transformations in meaning schemes occur or new schemes are created as we encounter new data that do not fit our preconceived notions. We also noted how the nature of our meaning schemes becomes modified as we incorporate new data that do fit them. When we encounter disorienting dilemmas and even our most intense efforts to extricate ourselves through content or process reflection fail, we often turn to reflection on the premises behind our actions. Premise reflection may result in our redefining our problem and acting upon our transformed insights. This process of perspective transformation is a generic form of adult learning. It has been associated with a variety of concepts and experiences, including adult development, critical reflectivity, creativity, artistic expression, psychoanalytic therapy, conscientization, dialectical thinking, consciousness raising, philosophical analysis, some forms of religious conversion, and Eastern mysticism.

Emancipatory education is about more than becoming aware of one's awareness. Its goal is to help learners move from a simple awareness of their experiencing to an awareness of the *conditions* of their experiencing (*how* they are perceiving, thinking, judging, feeling, acting—a reflection on process) and beyond this to an awareness of the *reasons why* they experience as they do and to action based upon these insights. Taking action itself involves the significant and distinctive process of instrumental learning, which can become decisive for successful transformative learning. The job of adult educators is to help learners look critically at their beliefs and behaviors, not only as these appear at the moment but in the context of their history (purpose) and consequences in the learners' lives.

Toward a Philosophy of Adult Education

Transformation theory is a theory of adult learning. As such, it attempts to describe and analyze how adults learn to make meaning of their experience. A philosophy of adult education predicated upon this understanding of the nature of adult learning is a prescription for the educational interventions that are appropriate to help adults learn.

Establishment of Ideal Learning Conditions. In Chapter Three, following Habermas, I made the claim that we all depend upon consensual validation to establish the meaning of our assertions, especially in the communicative domain of learning, and that an ideal set of conditions for participation in critical discourse is implicit in the very nature of human communication. These same conditions are fundamental to a philosophy of adult education because they are also the ideal conditions for adult learning. They are essential components in the validating process of rational discourse through which we move toward meaning perspectives that are more developmentally advanced, that is, more inclusive, discriminating, permeable, and integrative of experience. Under these ideal conditions, participants in discourse

- Have accurate and complete information
- Are free from coercion and self-deception
- Have the ability to weigh evidence and evaluate arguments
- Have the ability to be critically reflective
- Are open to alternative perspectives
- Have equality of opportunity to participate, and
- Will accept an informed, objective, and rational consensus as a legitimate test of validity.

If the cardinal goal of adult education is to help learners learn what they want to learn and at the same time acquire more developmentally advanced meaning perspectives, it follows that these ideal conditions of adult learning become the criteria for evaluating educational programs; they constitute an educator's "bottom line." "Ideal" is used here not as an unattainable goal of perfection but as a judgment of value. The ideal is present in every action, as a judgment of better and worse. Not only educational practices but economic, political, and social practices and institutions as well may be judged according to the degree to which they foster or impede the realization of these ideal conditions of participation in adult learning for all.

Free, full adult participation in critical discourse and resulting action clearly requires freedom, democratic participation, equality, reciprocity, and prior education through which one has learned to assess evidence effectively, make and understand relevant arguments, develop critical judgment, and engage in critical reflection. Such participation also implies a reasonable minimal level of safety, mental and physical health, shelter, and employment opportunity, as well as acceptance of others with different perspectives and social cooperation. Values such as freedom, democracy, justice, equality, and social cooperation may be cherished so universally at least partly because they represent the essential conditions under which human beings can make sense or meaning of their experience.

Andragogy. Andragogy is the professional perspective of adult educators. It has been defined as an organized and sustained effort to assist adults to learn in a way that enhances their capability to function as self-directed learners. A study by Suanmali (1981) documented nearly unanimous agreement among 174 members of the Commission of Professors of Adult Education that an adult educator, as a practitioner of andragogy, must fulfill the following goals set forth by Mezirow (1981, p. 42).

1. Progressively decrease the learner's dependency on the educator.
2. Help the learner understand how to use learning resources, especially the experience of others, including the educator, and how to engage in reciprocal learning relationships.

3. Assist the learner to define his/her learning needs, both in terms of immediate awareness and in terms of understanding the cultural and psychological assumptions influencing his/her perceptions of needs.
4. Assist the learner to assume increasing responsibility for defining learning objectives, planning his/her own learning program, and evaluating progress.
5. Help the learner organize what is to be learned in relationship to his/her current personal problems, concerns, and levels of understanding.
6. Foster learner decision making, select relevant learning experiences that require choosing, expand the learner's range of options, and facilitate the learner's taking the perspectives of others who have alternative ways of understanding.
7. Encourage the use of criteria for judging that are increasingly inclusive and differentiating in awareness, self-reflexive, and integrative of experience.
8. Foster a self-corrective, reflexive approach to learning— to typifying and labeling, to perspective taking and choosing, and to habits of learning and learning relationships.
9. Facilitate posing and solving of problems, including problems associated with the implementation of individual and collective action, and recognition of the relationship between personal problems and public issues.
10. Reinforce the self-concept of the learner as a learner and doer by providing for progressive mastery and for a supportive climate with feedback to encourage provisional efforts to change and to take risks; by avoiding competitive judgment of performance; and by appropriate use of mutual support groups.
11. Emphasize experiential, participative, and projective instructional methods and use modeling and learning contracts where appropriate.
12. Make the moral distinction between helping the learner understand his/her full range of choices and ways to improve the quality of choosing and encouraging the learner to make a specific choice.

These practice injunctions clearly bear a close relationship to transformation theory. Helping adults elaborate, create, and transform their meaning schemes (beliefs, feelings, interpretations, decisions) through reflection on their content, the process by which they were learned, and their premises (social context, history, and consequences) is what andragogy is about.

New data — information and interpretations of subject "content" — are filtered not only through existing meaning schemes but also through meaning perspectives, which often distort the way one learns. This is why the educator must not simply focus on the materials to be learned or their "presentation skills" if significant learning is intended. When learners suffer from tunnel vision, when they encounter troublesome issues, when they have difficulty in learning or lack motivation, they must be helped to become aware of the relationship of new data to what they already know — their relevant meaning schemes — and to understand why they see the new data as they do. This means that the educator must actively encourage reflective discourse through which learners can examine the justification for their meaning schemes and perspectives as well as focusing on the new data presented.

Ethical Considerations

Encouraging learners to challenge and transform meaning perspectives raises serious ethical questions. For example, is it unethical for an educator to:

- Intentionally precipitate transformative learning without making sure that the learner fully understands that such transformation may result?
- Facilitate a perspective transformation when its consequences may include dangerous or hopeless actions?
- Decide which among a learner's beliefs should become questioned or problematized?
- Present his or her own perspective, which may be unduly influential with the learner?
- Refuse to help a learner plan to take action because the edu-

cator's personal convictions are in conflict with those of the learner?

- Make educational interventions when psychic distortions appear to impede a learner's progress if the educator is not trained as a psychotherapist?

I believe that all of these things, if done properly, are ethical. This section will explain the reasons for this belief.

Initiating and Facilitating Transformation. Given the nature of adult learning as a transformative process of examining assumptions to test their validity, no ethical question can be raised about either precipitating or facilitating this process. A learner can express only interests or needs defined within his or her current meaning perspective, a perspective that the learner may, upon critical examination, find distorting or dysfunctional. The adult educator must accept the learner's initial learning priorities, but the educator is not ethically bound to confine the learner to the learner's initial limitations or constraints in perspective.

Perspective transformation is a mode of adult learning that neither learner nor educator is able to anticipate or evoke upon demand. Because this mode serves a crucial adaptive function by helping the learner resolve a dilemma by differentiating and integrating experience more inclusively, there is no real question about whether the learner should value a new perspective over an old one. The learner may have difficulty in accepting and acting upon this new degree of clarity because it conflicts with an established meaning perspective or because of self-deception, lack of knowledge of how to act upon the new perspective, or situational factors that preclude action. Neither these possibilities nor the fact that the learner may come to an unanticipated redefinition of his need or action priorities as a result of an educational experience are valid ethical arguments against an educator fostering critical reflection or transformative learning.

The educator may anticipate overwhelming difficulties and dangers that a learner will face if he or she is encouraged to become critically reflective in the process of transformative learning and moves to take action on these insights. This also is no argument against emancipatory education. The learner should not be denied a full understanding of his or her situation, feelings, and resources, even if it is impractical to act upon that understanding. It is always acceptable to postpone acting until the timing is more favorable or to limit one's actions to what is feasible under the circumstances. The educator's objective should be only that the learner learn freely and decide, on the basis of the best information available, whether or not to act and, if so, how and when.

The essence of adult education is to help learners construe experience in a way that allows them to understand more clearly the reasons for their problems and the action options open to them so that they can improve the quality of their decision making. Deciding which among a learner's beliefs should be problematized has its ethical counterpart in an educator's selecting the subject content and approaches that are most appropriate to address a learner's needs and will best facilitate learning in a traditional classroom. The learner's response indicates the correctness of the educator's decision making.

Handling Value Conflicts Between Educator and Learners. Helping a learner bring formerly unquestioned assumptions and premises into critical awareness in order to understand how he or she has come to possess certain conceptual categories, rules, tactics, and criteria and then to judge their validity enhances the learner's crucial sense of control over his or her life. Doing such a thing certainly falls within the generally accepted role of an educator. To help a learner become aware of and assess alternative meaning perspectives for viewing a problem is not to tell the learner what to do but only to present different sets of rules, tactics, and criteria for judging.

There is no such thing as a value-free educational experience; to avoid the question of values is to opt for perpetuating the unexamined values of the status quo. Since most educators are committed to helping learners change and believe that such change should lead to making the world a better place, they cannot be expected to hide their own ways of seeing and interpreting. Advancing one's own perspective as one of several alternative

points of view from which a learner may gain insight is per-
fectly ethical, even though the status of the educator may tend
to influence the learner inadvertently. What should be unacceptable is a deliberate effort to "sell" one's point of view or to
manipulate learners into agreeing with it or acting upon it. An
educator is expected to be particularly aware of this potential
subversion and to lean over backward to avoid it. This problem seems to me no different for adult educators who are fostering critical reflection than for educators in any other setting.
We assume that educators know the difference between education and indoctrination, and we should keep in mind that adult
learners usually do, too.

Transformation theory holds that planning and taking
action—that is, making a decision—is an integral phase of the
transformation process. But what if adult educators find that
their values are in opposition to those of their learners? Are they
obligated to help the learners plan and take actions with which
they, the educators, disagree? I once posed this problem to Myles
Horton of the Highlander Center. "Certainly not," he responded.
"Educators should work only with those with whom they can
have a feeling of solidarity."

Horton was talking about social action educators working in a nonformal program setting. Other adult educators with
programs open to the public may find themselves working with
learners whose social or political viewpoints clash with their own.
As long as there is agreement that everyone's interpretations
will be open to reflective discourse, there is no reason for an
educator to have reservations about working with such learners.
However, if the learners decide upon a course of action as a
result of reflective discourse that the educator cannot ethically
accept, the educator is quite correct to withdraw from further
educational intervention. On the other hand, if action formulated by learners is acceptable to the educator, the educator can
and should (to the extent that circumstances permit) help the
learners plan tactics and develop the skills required to carry out
the action.

Dealing with Psychological Problems. Because transformative
learning and emancipatory education must address distortions

in psychological as well as epistemic and sociolinguistic meaning perspectives, are adult educators engaging in psychotherapy if they help a learner discover and grapple with those distortions? Here it is necessary to make a careful distinction between adults who are having commonly encountered difficulties in dealing with familiar life transitions and those who have extreme neurotic, psychotic, or sociopathic disorders and require psychotherapy. Adult educators need to be taught how to make these distinctions.

Therapy in medicine, from which psychoanalytic therapy derives, means treatment of disease. Those who choose to participate in psychotherapy enter the therapeutic relationship as patients or clients. Adult educators, of course, normally are not qualified to treat psychological disease. However, there is no reason why they cannot act as counselors or instructors to help essentially healthy learners deal with life transitions. Such activity unquestionably requires psychological understanding and sensitivity, but it is not therapy.

Counseling in an educational setting is an accepted practice, and there are many advantages to helping adult learners deal with psychological assumptions in such a setting. The focus of the interaction in this setting is on accomplishing a specific task-related objective, such as returning to college or the job market, making new friends, or trying out a new life-style. The status accorded to those who study in an academic setting may help to allay learners' anxiety or give them a feeling of legitimacy as they examine personal problems. Furthermore, educational settings usually are relatively safe places in which to try out new roles and ideas. The norms in such settings protect learners from personal attack or humiliation, and competition among learners generally is discouraged in adult education programs. Especially in programs that focus on life transitions, learners can find others going through similar experiences and identify with these people as role models.

Educators can provide the emotional support and theoretical insight into transformative learning that is necessary to help learners correct the most common psychological distortions in meaning perspective. Graduate programs should prepare all adult educators to work with people who are encountering common problems in negotiating life transitions, times when adults are most ready for examination of assumptions and major perspective transformations. The advent of such new resources as the "Therapeutic Learning Program" (Gould, 1990), which incorporates many of the benefits of clinical insight into a computer program for adult learners involved in difficult life transitions, presents promising new possibilities for educators who are trying to help such learners.

Education for Social Action

Some theorists have complained that transformation theory, as I have attempted to formulate it, fails to recognize the importance of power in distorting educational and dialogic relationships, lacks a social critique for identifying specific forces that impede adult learning and development, focuses disproportionately on personal transformation, and does not regard collective social action as the essential objective of all transformative learning and emancipatory adult education (Collard and Law, 1989; Griffin, 1988; Tennant, 1988; Hart, 1990a; Clark and Wilson, 1990).

I have relied on Habermas's social critique to provide the social theoretical context for transformation theory. I also believe that when adult learners become critically reflective of social norms and cultural codes as they examine the sociolinguistic distortions in their prior learning, they are making a similar critique. Critique is an inherent function of adult learning.

The role of the adult educator is to encourage such a critique and at the same time keep it as rational as possible. The educator is an empathic provocateur and role model, a collaborative learner who is critically self-reflective and encourages others to consider alternative perspectives, and a guide who sets and enforces the norms governing rational discourse and encourages the solidarity and group support that is necessary when learners become threatened because comfortably established beliefs and values have been challenged. The educator helps learners link self-insights with social norms and thereby realize that their dilemmas are shared. He or she also helps learners understand the process of adult learning in which they are participating.

The educator helps the learners see and come to grips with the discrepancies between their avowed beliefs and their actions (Mezirow and Associates, 1990).

Educating through Discourse. There is no question that the ideal conditions of adult learning are seldom, if ever, fully attained or that participants in critical discourse, including the educator, differ in their power to get others to do as they wish. Because educators can anticipate the intrusion of unequal status and thus of potential influence among those involved in discursive communities, they can, and should, plan intentionally to counter the effects of this intrusion on critical discourse in educational settings. They do this by setting and enforcing norms of participation in these communities that embody the ideal conditions of learning insofar as possible, including rules regarding equal opportunity to participate, role reciprocity, "bracketing" biases, focusing on issues, hearing alternative arguments, examining assumptions, and seeking consensus. Implicit in any learning community is a mutual sense of solidarity among participants that entails acceptance of and identification with the values of the community. Adult educators are careful not only to interact with learners within this set of norms but to model doing so. (Even social action educators such as Horton and Freire carefully differentiate between assuming a leadership role in social action situations and helping to prepare learners to assume such a role.) In this way they can use their power as educators to create communities of critical discourse that are what Maxine Greene (1986) refers to as "spheres of freedom," authentic spaces in which the "dialectic of freedom" may be achieved.

In doing their best to control forces that permit power to be used to coerce or distort communications, educators are following the ideal behind the process of jury selection. Those believed to have the power to influence jurors unduly are routinely excused from serving on juries, as when formal rules preclude lawyers, psychologists, psychiatrists, and social workers from serving or informal determinations by lawyers reject potential jurors who are university professors or other authority figures that the lawyers believe may be disproportionately influential.

Social Goals versus Personal Development. Adult learning transforms meaning perspectives, not society. The aspect of transformative learning that relates most closely to education for social action is action resulting from transformations in sociolinguistic meaning perspectives. Such action ultimately can change society, but whether or not perspective transformation results in participation in specific collective social actions depends upon a number of situational, psychological, and knowledge variables. Adult education should help adults move toward more developmentally advanced meaning perspectives. However, there is little agreement among adult educators as to whether this goal should be subordinated to social goals—liberty, justice, equality, emancipation, and so on—or whether, as Finger (1989a and b) claims (see Chapter Six), the approach of using education to foster political goals has proven inadequate, and the way to assure cultural transformation is to encourage personal transformation.

Transformation learning theory, as interpreted here, sees this as a false dichotomy. Freedom, equality, democracy, literacy, and emancipation are not to be understood as handmaidens of modernization or national development but rather as necessary conditions for making meaning of experience that are implicit in the nature of human communication and learning. Rather than seeking these abstract political goals directly, education facilitates the process of learning, which ideally depends for its implementation upon the realization of these political conditions.

In short, education is the handmaiden of learning, not of politics; but significant learning, involving personal transformations, is a social process with significant implications for social action. When adults learn to correct the distorted sociolinguistic assumptions that have constrained the adoption of more developmentally advanced meaning perspectives, learning to take social action—often collective social action—becomes an integral part of transformative learning. Education thus can help learners construe personal meaning rationally and derive political goals that inspire the emotional commitment that motivates action. Adults can learn what freedom, equality, democracy, and emancipation mean in microcosm as they strive toward the realization of these ideals in communities of rational discourse, and they can act politically to create interpersonal relationships, organizations, and societies in which others can discover the meaning of these values as well.

Action is an integral and indispensable component of transformative learning. Perspective transformation involving sociolinguistic distortions ideally should involve a recognition that what was initially thought to be a private dilemma is shared by others and may be a public issue. For example, in consciousness raising, women come to recognize that what they thought was their personal problem is in fact a widely shared problem of sex stereotyping and that social action to change institutionalized practices based upon such stereotypes is essential. Sociolinguistic distortions often result in unquestioned, institutionalized social practices that can be changed only through collective political action. Personal transformation involving sociolinguistic distortions can happen only when a perspective of social change is involved, and social change, in turn, depends upon personal transformation.

Adult Education and Social Action. Social action means different things to different people. It can refer to involvement with others in assessing the validity of a collective frame of reference. It can also refer to the process of bringing about changes in relationships (for example, between a woman who has had a consciousness-raising experience and her husband, resulting in a revision in traditional roles), changes in organizations (managers replacing old perspectives that emphasize command and control with new perspectives that involve guidance for employee decision making and social democracy in the workplace), or changes in systems (collective social action to change political, economic, educational, bureaucratic, or other systems). Changing systems is a difficult and often threatening political undertaking that normally involves an extended time period of sustained involvement. Taking action as a result of critical reflection may be impeded by lack of information, situational constraints, psychological blocks, or the absence of required skills.

Kieffer (1981), who studied the transition of lower-income and working-class people who had recently acquired "participatory

competence" through involvement in grass roots citizen organizations, arrived at a concept of "empowerment" that had the
following three features: (1) a more potent and efficacious sense
of self, (2) more critical understanding of social and political
relations, and (3) more functional strategies and resources for
social and political action. Empowerment, by this definition,
could be an outcome of perspective transformation.

Social action educator Tom Lovett (Lovett, Clark, and
Kilmurray, 1983, p. 109) reminds us, however, that transformative education alone is insufficient for effective social action:
"The liberation of more and more people's efforts is not the problem, since efforts are wasted without a macro-economic strategy
that can coordinate them successfully, which is precisely what
is lacking." In other words, according to Lovett, significant social
transformation means making changes in the economic system,
and this requires a strategy and opportunities that go beyond
local activism. That may be so. Transformation theory—and
adult educators—can promise only to help in the first step of
political change, emancipatory education that leads to personal
transformation, and to share the belief that viable strategies for
public change will evolve out of this. Social activist educators
can help learners learn to analyze their common problems
through participatory research and the tactics of collective social action. The social action educator's role is limited to fostering
critical awareness and insight into the history and consequences
of accepted social norms, cultural codes, ideologies, and institutionalized practices that oppress learners; to helping learners
discover options for action and to anticipate the consequences
of these options by becoming familiar with previous efforts to
bring about change; to building solidarity with others similarly
oppressed; and to helping learners develop the confidence and
the ability to work with others to take collective action, to interpret feedback on their efforts, to deal with adversity, and to
learn direct-action tactics for dealing with the system.

Lovett (p. 145) cautions that social action education also
must reaffirm the importance of teaching subject matter content and "at the very least some old-fashioned instruction, set
into an ordered curriculum, which includes basic information

and skills required to execute necessary management tasks." Instrumental learning is a vital part of preparation for social action. The importance of learning new information and skills of taking social actions is a crucial dimension for perspective transformation from an ethical point of view. Educators must beware of placing learners in a vacuum by making them aware of the need for collective source change without helping them acquire the information and skills needed to implement it.

Finally, it should be noted that although social action is crucial, it cannot be the only goal of adult learning and education. Just as there are diverse forms of social action, so there are diverse forms of perspective transformation — sociolinguistic, epistemic, and psychological — and each has its own form of praxis. Transformative learning experiences that result in epistemic or psychological changes may only very indirectly lead to change in a specific social practice or institutionalized ideology, or they may not lead to collective action at all. To recognize the importance of epistemic and psychic distortions is not to unduly "psychologize" adult learning or to diminish the importance of sociolinguistic distortions and the need for social action.

The Role of Adult Educators in Social Action. Social action educators are specialists within adult education who are concerned with community development. Although not every adult educator can be a social action educator, leaving the traditional educational setting to join learners in their communities and help them take collective social action based upon insights acquired through transformative learning, all adult educators can become activists in fighting to overcome social practices and institutional constraints that keep adults from realizing their most fundamental human right — to make meaning of their experience. All adult educators have the responsibility to do the following:

1. Actively foster learners' critical reflection upon their assumptions, not only concerning the content and process of problem solving, but also concerning the premises behind their sociolinguistic, epistemic, and psychological beliefs.

2.   Establish communities of rational discourse in classrooms, workshops, conferences, and action settings, with norms consistent with the ideal conditions of learning, within which beliefs may be questioned and consensually validated.
3.   Help learners learn how to take appropriate action resulting from transformative learning to the extent feasible.

In addition, adult educators who administer programs for the public have a professional responsibility to do the following:

1.   Make sure that instructors understand and are committed to their basic responsibilities (see preceding).
2.   Allocate available program resources to extend educational opportunities for critical discourse to those most in need of them.
3.   Offer educational opportunities for critical discourse that address current public issues.

All adult educators have a responsibility to participate actively in public initiatives in support of political, economic, and social changes that assist all adult learners to overcome constraints that hinder their full, free participation in rational dialogue.

Transformative Learning and the Design of Adult Education Programs

The four processes of learning—by extending meaning schemes, creating new ones, transforming old ones, and transforming perspectives—always occur in the context of the learner's line of action, reflecting his or her intention, purpose, and feelings. As we saw in Chapter Three, the process involved in fulfilling the purpose of instrumental learning is considerably different from that involved in fulfilling the purpose of communicative learning. It follows that programs of adult education designed to help learners fulfill each purpose also should be different. The need for different approaches, however, has seldom been recognized.

Education designed to facilitate instrumental learning is the most familiar kind, a fact that reflects American convictions concerning the power of the methods of problem solving codified by the natural sciences. Indeed, many people think that this kind of education (and learning) is the only kind. The typical program generated by this orientation defines educational objectives in terms of specific behaviors that are to be acquired in order to accomplish a certain task, as determined previously by a process of "task analysis." Determination of the difference between present performance level and that required by the task constitutes a "needs assessment."

An educational program of this type usually is composed of a fixed sequence of exercises reduced to their component elements ("modules"), each more difficult than the last. Every exercise proceeds through the pattern of explanation, demonstration, practice, test, and feedback. Often the program is implemented through "learning laboratories" or "learning centers" that feature computer software or other preprogrammed material.

Each learner is slotted into the program at a level of proficiency determined by pretesting and proceeds at his or her own pace. This is called "individualized instruction." The learner's achievement is evaluated, often at the end of each exercise, by comparing levels of skills or "competencies" demonstrated before and after the educational experience and/or by measuring the degree to which anticipated learning outcomes are achieved. As an example, adult literacy is seen from this perspective as a matter of matching meanings to words, learning the syllables, and combining words into sentences and sentences into paragraphs. Literacy programs using this approach emphasize a present-recite/test-correct mode (Mezirow, 1975). "Functional literacy" has come to mean interpreting literacy learning as instrumental learning.

This technicist approach to education spawns such familiar terms and concepts as "education for behavior change," behavioral objectives, needs assessments, competency-based education, task analysis, skill training, anticipated learning outcomes, management by objectives, "accountability," criterion-referenced evaluation, and empirical-analytical research. The approach may or may not be appropriate and useful in the domain of instrumental learning, depending upon the specific situation. Its main drawback is that it tends to limit the act of task-oriented learning arbitrarily to instrumental learning. As we have noted in Chapter Three, task-oriented learning often involves significant elements of communicative learning as well. Most adult learning involves values, feelings, ideals, moral decision making, self-concept, or other concepts defined by social norms. Such learning must address "ill-defined problems," as distinct from puzzles that have correct solutions (Kitchener and King, 1990), and thus must involve communicative learning.

When educators have attempted to foster communicative learning using the kind of program designed for instrumental learning, they usually have failed. Unfortunately, applying educational approaches designed for instrumental learning to all learning is endemic in the field of adult education. The most common form this has taken is the attempt to broaden the definition of behavioral skills to encompass all learning, including learning the meaning of what is communicated and learning about oneself. The assumption seems to be that these things are learned in much the same way as any other behavioral skill except that practice occasionally requires the use of hypothetical reality contexts such as role playing, which are unnecessary in learning to operate a lathe or perform other manual tasks. In fact, however, the facilitation of communicative learning requires an entirely different kind of educational approach.

Adult education's primary objective is to help those whom society deems fully responsible for their acts to become more reflective in posing and solving problems, to become more critically self-reflective, to participate more fully and freely in rational discourse and action, and to move developmentally toward more reliable perspectives. Educators in this domain are concerned primarily with fostering the ability to participate democratically in critical discourse, through which learners assess the validity of assertions made and implied as people communicate with each other. A program designed to encourage communicative learning, therefore, should have as its goal the establishment of the ideal conditions for rational discourse and adult learning listed earlier in this chapter. Such a program should assist learners to do the following:

- Decontextualize
- Become more aware of the history, contexts (norms, codes, reaction patterns, perceptual filters), and consequences of their beliefs
- Become more reflective and critical in their assessment of both the content and the process of problem solving and of their own ways of participating in this process
- "Bracket" preconceived ideas and openly examine evidence and assess arguments
- Make better inferences, more appropriate generalizations, and more logically coherent arguments
- Be more open to the perspectives of others
- Rely less on psychological defense mechanisms and be more willing to accept the authority of provisional consensual validation of expressed ideas.

Transformative or emancipatory learning involves all this, but in addition it focuses upon a critique of premises that need reassessment in order to correct inadequately developed or distorted epistemic, sociolinguistic, or psychological preconceptions. It opens language to both redefinition through reflection and the accretion of new layers of meaning continuously as we seek to be understood and to understand others in dialogue. Freire (1970b) has shown how teaching literacy in the context of transformative learning can foster powerful motivation to learn.

From the viewpoint of transformation theory, needs assessment and evaluation become two moments in reflective dialogue. The former determines what in the learner's experience is to become problematized, and the latter determines the extent to which the initial statement of priority of needs has been revised as a result of transformative learning and examines the gains that have been made in context awareness, reflectivity, openness to the perspectives of others, democratic participation in reflective discourse, and the taking of more effective reflective action.

The rest of this section will offer suggestions for the design of adult education programs intended to foster communicative and transformative learning. It will consider needs assessment, student readiness for transformational learning, instructional methods, and evaluation.

Assessment of Needs and Interests. Needs assessment must be seen as the process of helping adults think through the reasons for their initially expressed needs. Adults often are not fully aware of their best interests. What they say they want may be inconsistent with their actions. A group may act in a way that clearly reflects wants or needs of which no single member is aware. Both individuals and groups may be unaware of their needs or may not have an interest in satisfying certain needs at a particular time or under particular circumstances.

Desires become interests through the exercise of reason: we make a reasoned judgment that a desire ought to be satisfied. The ultimate criterion for this judgment is some ideal of our self-concept, of the "good life," or of how we want to live. For example, we may come to recognize certain of our behaviors as inconsistent with the way we want to be as healthy, autonomous, and responsible adults and thus decide that we have an interest in changing those behaviors. Geuss (1981, pp. 46-49) extends this concept by reminding us that an alcoholic may be said to have an interest in giving up alcohol even though the alcoholic does not recognize that he or she has such an interest. We can make this interpretation because we know that health is central to almost anyone's concept of the good life, and excessive use of alcohol cannot be integrated into that life.

Real interests are those we would form if we had more perfect knowledge and freedom: that is, if we were able to participate more fully in an ideal discourse. Our real interests — like those of the alcoholic — may be hidden from us by physical, ideological, or psychological distortion or coercion, by deprivation, or by unquestioned social norms or other assumptions. A serf in the Middle Ages seldom questioned the assumptions that supported his serfdom. Before the women's movement, women seldom questioned the social expectations embedded in stereotypical sex roles. The oppressed commonly internalize the values of their oppressors. Sociologist C. Wright Mills (1961, p. 194) observed that when "we take the simple democratic view that what men are interested in is all that concerns us, then we are accepting the values that have been inculcated, often deliberately by vested interests. These values are often the only ones men have had a chance to develop. They are unconsciously acquired habits rather than choices."

If we recognize that there is another set of interests that we would prefer to have if the circumstances under which we live were more advantageous — that is, involving more knowledge and greater freedom — these are our real interests (pp. 49–54). Thus, if a woman who has always accepted the traditional women's role uncritically is vaguely aware that her present interests may be less authentic (less consistent with her self-concept or concept of the good life) than the interests of her more emancipated friends, their interests are her real interests. Her real interests are those that she herself would share if she were freed from a belief system based upon sex stereotypes; she would know what she wanted if she knew what she could want.

Clearly, simplistic conceptions pertaining to needs assessment in adult education programs must be modified. It is unfair to expect a learner to do more initially than indicate immediate desires or interests without regard for the inadequacy, distortion, or self-defeating nature of the meaning perspective within which these have been defined. Once the learner has recognized his or her real interests, the educator can help the learner articulate and interpret them in relation to anticipated learning outcomes.

The educator starts out accepting learners' expressed needs and interests and develops programs to accommodate them. In the process of helping learners understand their needs, the educator helps them explore the reasons for these needs, which reside in assumptions or premises of the learners' beliefs.

Readiness for Transformative Learning. Learners enter an educational experience at different levels of readiness for transformative learning. In our study of reentry women (Mezirow,

1978, pp. 12–15) we found conventional learners, who remained fully assimilated within the traditional cultural perspective; threshold learners, whose participation in the educational program was prompted by a disorienting dilemma; emancipated learners, who had never fully accepted the prescribed roles traditionally assigned to them and had already engaged deeply in self-examination; and transformation learners, who realized how the culture and their own attitudes conspired to define and limit their self-concept, life-style, and options through prescribed, stereotypic roles. The transformation learners came to realize that many of what they had thought were personal problems were shared by other women and in fact were public issues.

In Chapter Six I reported on the phases of the transformation process, as deduced from our reentry study. Any group of adult learners is likely to include some who are already involved in different phases of this process. Creating a dialogic community with such diversity is possible but difficult. (The task is made easier when learners are self-selected and are actively looking for ways to deal with similar disorienting dilemmas.) However, the diversity helps to assure that there will be more than one learner in any given phase, so that the chance of forward movement is enhanced for everyone. There is some evidence to suggest that those just one phase ahead can be more influential in fostering transformative changes than those more advanced. Modeling is extremely useful in bringing about major transformative changes.

In some cases the educator may face the task of trying to precipitate transformative learning in a group made up entirely of conventional learners. For example, Freire (1970b) has demonstrated the possibilities of using education to bring about transformative learning among illiterate and semiliterate people, and Hart (1990a) has analyzed the learning process within consciousness-raising groups in the women's movement (see Chapter Six). When trying to induce transformative learning in conventional learners, an educator must bring them to define and elaborate all the factors that sustain their unquestioned meaning perspectives.

Instructional Methods. A companion volume to this book, *Fostering Critical Reflection in Adulthood: A Guide to Transformative and Emancipatory Learning* (Mezirow and Associates, 1990), presents a collection by seventeen authors of program approaches and specific techniques designed to help learners become critically reflective of their meaning perspectives. Settings analyzed include the workplace, women's consciousness-raising groups, collective social action groups, and workshops and classes. Specific educational approaches suggested include ideology analysis, critical incidents, life histories, journal writing, literature, media analysis, a therapeutic learning computer program, and analysis of epistemic habits of expectation. Such techniques as repertory grids, metaphor analysis, conceptual mapping, and a new mode of action-reason-thematic analysis also are described.

With a little help, one can identify the assumptions behind one's own viewpoint on anything. For example, one of the best ways of helping anyone learn to read is to help the learner identify key words, phrases, or sentences that pertain to his or her own beliefs and the assumptions supporting them. Graduate students in adult education can analyze assumptions underlying their beliefs regarding adult learning and the role of the adult educator by asking questions such as the following:

- What are the assumptions underlying the proscription that we evaluate only anticipated learning outcomes, thereby defining learning in terms of acquiring prescribed competencies or in terms of behavioral objectives?
- What are the assumptions when one describes adult learning as "self-directed"?
- What are the assumptions underlying your definition of your most recent significant learning experience?

Evaluation. If a goal of education is to foster transformative learning, dogmatic insistence that learning outcomes be specified in advance of the educational experience in terms of observable changes in behavior or "competencies" that are used as benchmarks against which to measure learning gains will result in a reductive distortion and serve merely as a device of indoctrination. In our study of women entering college after a long hiatus, we found that standardized tests failed to measure changes in locus of control, personal competence, or self-concept within educational programs concerned with fostering transformative learning (Mezirow, 1978).

How then might evaluation be designed to take transformative learning into account? In describing our study, we stated that "the most productive points of departure for the systematic assessment of perspective transformation and related changes in transitional adults are their expectations, goals and degree of sophistication with respect to problem awareness" (Mezirow, 1978, p. 51). One way to perform an evaluation of these matters is to focus upon changes in reflection — the extent to which the learner has reflected on the content and process of problem solving, both in the context of thoughtful action and in retroactive reflection, and the quality of this reflection. The educator also should attend to resulting changes in meaning schemes and their consequences in action. When the learner is confronted with a disorienting dilemma, the educator can focus on the extent and quality of the learner's premise reflection and the resulting perspective transformation and reflective action.

As indicated earlier, other evidence of change should focus on progressive growth in decontextualization; greater openness to the perspectives of others; greater awareness of the sources and consequences of norms, codes, reaction patterns, and perceptual filters that make up the context of daily life; increased quality of participation in and willingness to submit to the mediating authority of reflective discourse; and changes in long-established patterns of expectations and behaviors.

One approach to evaluation in transformative learning programs would be to develop hypothetical dilemmas, ask learners to respond to them before and after the program, and then have learners indicate why they responded as they did. Each administration of the dilemmas could be followed by group discourse aimed at achieving agreement on issues raised. Reasons given could be rated independently by several raters, and learners also could be rated for changes in the quality of their participation in group discourse. Other types of "projective" evaluation techniques might also work, as might rating of changes evidenced in learning journals, repertory grids, metaphor analyses, conceptual mapping, critical incidents, analysis of media, assessments of reflective judgment, and other approaches to fostering critical reflection in adulthood (Mezirow and Associates, 1990).

Research on Transformative Learning

The problem facing the researcher who wishes to study transformative learning is finding a way to gain access to the meaning schemes and perspectives of the subjects of the research. Observation merely reveals behavior, and subjects who answer questions often are unable to articulate their understandings and intentions or to use words that have the same meaning for both themselves and the researcher. All too often respondents present their "espoused theories"—what they think they believe—rather than their "theories-in-use," or what their actions suggest that they believe (Candy, 1989).

Some of the research methods used in an attempt to overcome these problems include participant observation, life histories, case study, critical incident technique, repertory grids, Q Sort, open-ended interviews, learning journals, metaphor analysis, conceptual mapping, reflective judgment interviews, and the action-reason-thematic technique (Mezirow, 1990). Researchers look for similarities and differences in perception, thought, judgment, feelings, and action, preferably in real life rather than in contrived situations. Additional subjects often are selected on the basis of their relevance for testing further the validity of emerging patterns; in grounded theory research, this is referred to as theoretical sampling. For example, if the "constrained" vision of society described in Chapter Five were being mapped, a researcher would select subjects who share it in order to contrast it with a different perspective.

Roger Gould's work provides an example of how useful research on transformative learning can be. Gould conducted videotaped workshops over several months for adults having trouble negotiating life transitions. From this activity, combined with his broad experience as a psychotherapist, he was able to determine common patterns of problems encountered, dysfunctional reactions that impeded change, defense mechanisms, traumatic childhood experiences with parents that precipitated problems, and resulting erroneous assumptions and premises that inhibit appropriate action. Gould's analysis was so inclusive and discriminating that he was able to turn his findings into a computer program that appears to fulfill many of the functions of short-term therapy (Gould, 1990).

Research in transformative learning focuses upon the process of rationality — of how reflective thought, discourse, and action come into being and what their consequences are. It confines itself largely to limited rather than universal claims. Judgments made by the researcher depend upon examples from the experiences of the researcher and others rather than upon representative samples of universally agreed-upon categories, as in positivist research. Examples are analyzed, but no analysis is final or complete; new data, new contexts, and new perspectives make every judgment or belief provisional. This type of inquiry, like the learning processes being studied, takes the form of questioning claims, examining evidence, assessing arguments, and examining possible interpretations through discourse rather than arriving at a single final certainty through hypothesis testing and deductive logic.

Adult education researchers have pioneered in the development of participatory or action research that blurs the distinction between learning and research (Gaventa and Horton, 1989b). In this kind of study, the subjects do the research themselves. The process involves: (1) actively participating in developing a plan of action, (2) taking action, (3) observing what happens, and (4) critically reflecting on the results as a basis for (5) further planning, action, and reflection, and so on through a succession of cycles. Drawing upon the ideas of Habermas, Carr and Kemmis (1983) introduced the critical reflection dimension into this research paradigm. In their proposal, participatory action research would, in effect, integrate the concept of using critical discourse for the validation of learning as a phase in a collective action process. The ideal conditions described earlier for adult learning and rational discourse also would apply as criteria for such action research.

A vivid example of action research was produced a few years ago by the Highlander Center for Education and Research near Knoxville, Tennessee. The center trained people with limited education from fifty poor Appalachian communities in six states to dig into public records in their region (Gaventa and Horton, 1989a). The startling results showed that a few large mining companies owned most of the land but were paying little or no taxes on much of it, resulting in little public money for schools, housing, and social services. Two-thirds of the mine owners in the study were found to have paid under twenty-five cents an acre in property taxes! Those involved in this participatory research subsequently planned and took collective social action to make public officials aware of the situation and rectify it. This resulted in new statewide grass roots organizations, the mobilization of public opinion, and court rulings that produced major changes.

Conclusion

Not all learning is transformative. We can learn simply by adding knowledge to our meaning schemes or learning new meaning schemes with which to make interpretations about our experience. Adult education, as the intentional effort to help adults learn, is clearly charged with responsibility for this kind of learning, and it can be a crucially important experience for the learner.

Transformative learning involves reflectively transforming the beliefs, attitudes, opinions, and emotional reactions that constitute our meaning schemes or transforming our meaning perspectives (sets of related meaning schemes). The relationship between educator and adult learner in this kind of learning is like that of a mentor trying to help a friend decide how to deal with a significant life problem that the friend may not yet have clearly identified as the source of his or her dilemma. The educator helps the learner focus upon and examine the assumptions—epistemological, social, and psychological—that underlie beliefs, feelings, and actions; assess the consequences of these assumptions; identify and explore alternative sets of assumptions; and test the validity of assumptions through effective participation in reflective dialogue. Professional adult educators have this cardinal function in addition to the roles they play as content specialists, group process facilitators, academic counselors, trainers, social workers, social activists, or administrators of educational programs.

We professional adult educators have a commitment to help learners become more imaginative, intuitive, and critically reflective of assumptions; to become more rational through effective participation in critical discourse; and to acquire meaning perspectives that are more inclusive, integrative, discriminating, and open to alternative points of view. By doing this we may help others, and perhaps ourselves, move toward a fuller and more dependable understanding of the meaning of our mutual experience.

Summary

This chapter has presented the basic goals that I believe should be incorporated in a philosophy of adult education. These include helping learners to be self-guided, self-reflective, and rational and helping to establish communities of discourse in which these qualities are honored and fostered. The chapter also examined ethical considerations involved in helping adults achieve transformative learning, including issues related to value conflicts and psychological problems. It discussed the relationship among transformative learning, adult education, and social action. Finally, it considered ways to incorporate techniques that encourage transformative learning into such aspects of adult education programs as needs assessment, instructional methods, and evaluation, as well as into research on adult learning.

Propositions about adult education presented in this chapter include the following:

1. The goal of adult education is to help adult learners become more critically reflective, participate more fully and

freely in rational discourse and action, and advance developmentally by moving toward meaning perspectives that are more inclusive, discriminating, permeable, and integrative of experience.

2. The central responsibility of the adult educator who wishes to encourage transformative learning is to foster learners' reflection upon their own beliefs or meaning schemes through a critical examination of the history, context, and consequences of their assumptions and premises. A collateral responsibility is to create communities of discourse with norms that are consistent with the ideal conditions of learning.

3. The ideal conditions for participating in critical discourse also constitute the ideal conditions for adult learning.

4. Initiation and facilitation of transformative learning by an educator are ethical, even though neither the educator nor the learner can predict the outcomes of the process and even though actions resulting from the process may be dangerous or may be impossible to take at a given time.

5. Education for transformative learning is ethical as long as the educator does not attempt to force or manipulate learners into accepting his or her own perspective but instead encourages learners to choose freely from among the widest range of relevant viewpoints. However, an educator is not bound to help learners carry out actions that conflict with the educator's own code of ethics even if the learners decided upon those actions after rational discourse.

6. Adult educators should have sufficient psychological knowledge and sensitivity to be able to help healthy learners deal with common psychic distortions in meaning perspective that impede negotiation of difficult life transitions. Educators should be able to distinguish between these learners and those whose mental problems require professional psychotherapeutic treatment.

7. All transformative learning involves taking action to implement insights derived from critical reflection. When distortions addressed by transformative learning are sociocultural, social action becomes an integral part of the process of transformative learning. Social action may involve production of

changes in relationships, organizations, or political, economic, or cultural systems. Changing systems involves collective political action, which is often a long and difficult process.

8. Freedom, democracy, equality, justice, and social cooperation are among the necessary conditions for optimal participation in critical discourse. Adult educators should actively support both educational and social initiatives that advance these values. They also should assist learners to understand what is involved in taking collective social or political action. Although education for collective social action is an area of specialization within adult education, every adult educator should have basic knowledge of this process.

9. The learning process and educational interventions — needs assessment and setting of objectives, determination of readiness for learning, program or curriculum development, instruction, and evaluation — are inherently different depending on whether the intent of the learner involves instrumental or communicative learning. Although both domains of learning play a part in most learning experiences, emphasis on one or the other calls for interventions appropriate to that domain. Educational approaches appropriate for instrumental learning often have been misapplied to communicative learning.

10. A learner's real interests are those that the learner would prefer if he or she had more knowledge, greater freedom, and less distorted meaning perspectives. The authenticity of a learner's interests is measured by their congruence with the learner's self-concept or concept of the good life. Assessment of learner "needs" should be broadened to include their real interests.

11. Evaluation of gains made as a result of transformative learning should attempt to map the learner's initial meaning perspective and compare it with his or her later meaning perspective. Differences analyzed should include changes in interests, goals, awareness of problems, awareness of contexts, critical reflectivity and action, openness to alternative perspectives, ability to participate freely and fully in rational discourse, and willingness to accept consensual validation as a mode of problem solving in communicative learning.

✍ References

Angeles, P. A. *A Dictionary of Philosophy.* London: Harper & Row, 1981.

Arlin, P. "Cognitive Development in Adulthood: A Fifth Stage?" *Developmental Psychology,* 1975, *2,* 602–606.

Barer-Stein, T. "Learning as a Process of Experiencing the Unfamiliar." *Studies in the Education of Adults,* 1987, *19,* 87–108.

Basseches, M. *Dialectical Thinking and Adult Development.* Norwood, N.J.: Ablex, 1984.

Bateson, G. *Steps to an Ecology of Mind.* New York: Basic Books, 1972.

Bee, H. L. *The Journey of Adulthood.* New York: Macmillan, 1987.

Berardo, F. M. (ed.). *Middle and Late Life Transitions: The Annals of the American Academy of Political and Social Science,* 1982, *464.*

Berger, P., and Luckmann, T. *The Social Construction of Reality.* New York: Doubleday, 1966.

Berkson, W., and Wettersten, J. *Learning from Error: Karl Popper's Psychology of Learning.* La Salle, Ill.: Open Court, 1984.

Bernstein, R. J. (ed.). *Habermas and Modernity.* Cambridge, Mass.: MIT Press, 1985.

Blanchard-Fields, F. "Postformal Reasoning in a Socioemotional Context." In M. Commons and others (eds.), *Adult Development.* New York: Praeger, 1989.

Blumer, H. *Symbolic Interactionism: Perspective and Method.* Englewood Cliffs. N.J.: Prentice-Hall, 1969.

227

Boud, D., and Griffin, V. *Appreciating Adults' Learning: From the Learner's Perspective.* London: Kogan Page, 1987.

Boud, D., Keough, R., and Walker, D. (eds.), *Reflection: Turning Experience into Learning.* London: Kogan Page, 1985.

Bowers, C. A. *The Promise of Theory: Education and the Politics of Cultural Change.* New York: Longman, 1984.

Boyd, R. D. "Facilitating Personal Transformation in Small Groups." *Small Group Behavior,* 1989, *20,* 459–474.

Boyd, R. D., Kondrat, M. E., and Rannells, J. S. "The Developmental Stages of the Anima and Animus in Small Groups II." *Group Analysis,* 1989, *22,* 149–59.

Boyd, R. D., and Myers, J. G. "Transformative Education." *International Journal of Lifelong Education,* 1988, *7,* 261–284.

Brammer, L. M., and Abrego, P. J. "Intervention Strategies for Coping with Transitions." *The Counseling Psychologist,* 1981, *9,* 19–36.

Bridges, W. *Transitions: Making Sense of Life's Changes.* Reading, Mass.: Addison-Wesley, 1980.

Brookfield, S. *Understanding and Facilitating Adult Learning.* San Francisco: Jossey-Bass, 1986.

Brookfield, S. *Developing Critical Thinkers.* San Francisco: Jossey-Bass, 1987a.

Brookfield, S. *Learning Democracy.* London: Croom Helm, 1987b.

Brooks, A. K. "Critically Reflective Learning Within a Corporate Context." Unpublished doctoral dissertation, Teachers College, Columbia University, 1989.

Broughton, J. "'Beyond Formal Operations': Theoretical Thought in Adolescence." *Teachers College Record,* 1977, *79,* 89–97.

Bruner, J. "On Perceptual Readiness." *Psychological Review,* 1957, *64,* 123–152.

Bruner, J. *The Relevance of Education.* New York: Norton, 1973.

Bruner, J. *Actual Minds, Possible Worlds.* Cambridge, Mass.: Harvard University Press, 1986.

Buck-Morss, S. "Piaget, Adorno and Dialectical Operations." In J. Broughton (ed.), *Critical Theories of Psychological Development.* New York: Plenum Press, 1987.

Candy, P. C. "Constructivism and the Study of Self-Direction in Adult Learning." *Studies in the Education of Adults,* 1989, *21,* 95–116.

Carr, W., and Kemmis, S. *Becoming Critical: Knowing Through Action Research.* Victoria, Australia: Deakin University, 1983.

Cell, E. *Learning to Learn from Experience.* Albany: State University of New York, 1984.

Clark, M. C., and Wilson, A. L. "Through the Paradigm: An Analysis of Mezirow's Theory of Adult Learning." Paper prepared for presentation at the Adult Education Research Conference, Athens, Ga., May 1990.

Collard, S., and Law, M. "The Limits of Perspective Transformation: A Critique of Mezirow's Theory." *Adult Education Quarterly,* 1989, *39,* 99–107.

Commons, R., Richards, F. A., and Armon, C. (eds.). *Beyond Formal Operations in Late Adolescent and Adult Cognitive Development.* New York: Praeger, 1984.

Daloz, L. A. "The Story of Gladys Who Refused to Grow: A Morality Tale for Mentors." *Lifelong Learning,* 1988, *2,* 4–7.

Daniels, M. E. "Disjunctures in Theory and Practice for the Critically Reflective Practitioners in an Environment for Minority Adult Students." Unpublished doctoral dissertation, Teachers College, Columbia University, 1990.

Danto, A. C. *Encounters and Reflections.* New York: Farrar, Straus & Giroux, 1990.

Dewey, J. *How We Think.* Chicago: Regnery, 1933.

Döbert, R., Habermas, J., and Nunner-Winkler, G. "The Development of the Self." In J. Boughton (ed.), *Critical Theories of Psychological Development.* New York: Plenum Press, 1987.

Douglas, M. *Purity and Danger: An Analysis of the Concepts of Pollution and Taboo.* New York: Pantheon Books, 1966.

Douglas, M. *Purity and Danger.* Harmondworth, England: Penguin Books, 1974.

Dudley, N. Q. "The Experience of Changing to a New World View: A Phenomenological Study of the Emergent Paradigm Shift." Unpublished doctoral dissertation, University of Victoria, 1987.

Elias, J. L., and Merriam, S. *Philosophical Foundations of Adult Education.* Huntington, N.Y.: Krieger, 1980.

Evans, A., Evans, R., and Kennedy, W. *Pedogogies for the Non-Poor.* Maryknoll, N.Y.: Orbis, 1987.

Favell, J. "On Cognitive Development." *Child Development,* 1982, *53,* 1–10.

Ferguson, M. *The Aquarian Conspiracy; Personal and Social Transformation in the 1980s.* Los Angeles: Tarcher, 1980.

Fingarette, H. *The Self in Transformation.* New York: Harper, 1963.

Finger, M. *Apprendre une issue; l'education des adults à l'age de la transformation de perspective [Adult Education in an Age of Perspective].* Lausanne, Switzerland: Editions L.E.P. Loisirs et Pedagogie S.A., 1989a.

Finger, M. "New Social Movements and Their Implications for Adult Education." *Adult Education Quarterly,* 1989b, *40,* 15–22.

Fiske, S., and Taylor, S. *Social Cognition.* New York: Random House, 1984.

Foucault, M. *The Archeology of Knowledge.* New York: Pantheon, 1972.

Freire, P. *Cultural Action for Freedom.* Monograph Series No. 1. Cambridge, Mass.: Harvard Education Review and Center for the Study of Development and Social Change, 1970a.

Freire, P. *Pedagogy of the Oppressed.* New York: Herder and Herder, 1970b.

Gagne, R. M. *The Conditions of Learning.* (Rev. ed.) New York: Holt, Rinehart & Winston, 1972.

Galanter, E., and Gerstenhaaber, M. "On Thought: The Extrinsic Theory." *Psychological Review,* 1956, *63,* 218–227.

Gaventa, J., and Horton, B. D. "A Citizens' Research Project in Appalachia, USA." In *Highlander Research and Education Center: An Approach to Education Presented Through a Collection of Writings.* New Market, Tenn.: Highlander Center, 1989a.

Gaventa, J., and Horton, B. D. "Participatory Research in North America." In *Highlander Research and Education Center: An Approach to Education Presented Through a Collection of Writings.* New Market, Tenn.: Highlander Center, 1989b.

Geertz, C. *The Interpretation of Cultures.* New York: Basic Books, 1973.

Geuss, R. *The Idea of a Critical Theory: Habermas and the Frankfurt School.* Cambridge: Cambridge University, 1981.

Gidden, A. *New Rules of Sociological Method.* New York: Basic Books, 1976.

Glaser, B., and Strauss, A. *The Discovery of Grounded Theory.* Chicago: Aldine, 1967.

Goffman, E. *Frame Analysis.* New York: Harper & Row, 1974.

Goleman, D. "Insights into Self Deception." *New York Times Magazine,* May 12, 1985a, p. 42.

Goleman, D. *Vital Lies, Simple Truths: The Psychology of Self Deception.* New York: Simon & Schuster, 1985b.

Goleman, D. "Studies Offer Fresh Clues to Memory." *New York Times,* March 27, 1990.

Goodman, E. *Turning Points: How People Change Through Crisis and Commitment.* Garden City, N.Y.: Doubleday, 1979.

Gould, R. L. *Transformation: Growth and Change in Adult Life.* New York: Simon & Schuster, 1978.

Gould, R. L. "Adulthood." In H. Kaplan and B. Sadock (eds.), *Comprehensive Textbook of Psychiatry.* (5th ed.) Baltimore: Williams & Wilkins, 1989.

Gould, R. L. "The Therapeutic Learning Program." In J. Mezirow and Associates (eds.), *Fostering Critical Reflection in Adulthood: A Guide to Transformative and Emancipatory Learning.* San Francisco: Jossey-Bass, 1990.

Gouldner, A. W. *The Dialectic of Ideology: The Origins, Grammar and Future of Ideology.* New York: Seabury Press, 1976.

Graesser, A. C., and Clark, L. F., *Structures and Procedures of Implicit Knowledge.* Norwood, N.J.: Ablex, 1985.

Gramsci, A. *Prison Notebooks.* New York: International Publishers, 1971.

Greene, M. *The Teacher as Stranger.* Belmont, Calif.: Wadsworth, 1973.

Greene, M. "Curriculum and Consciousness." In W. Pinar (ed.), *Curriculum Theorizing.* Berkeley: McCutchan, 1975.

Greene, M. "In Search of a Critical Pedagogy." *Harvard Education Review,* 1986, *56,* 427–441.

Grendlin, E. T. "Befindlichkeit: Heidegger and the Philosophy of Psychology." *Review of Existential Psychology and Psychiatry,* 1978-79, *16,* 43–71.

Griffin, C., "Critical Thinking and Critical Theory in Adult Education." In *Transatlantic Dialogue: A Research Exchange.* England: University of Leeds, 1988.

Habermas, J. *Knowledge and Human Interests*. Boston: Beacon Press, 1971.

Habermas, J. *The Theory of Communicative Action*. Vol. 1: *Reason and the Rationalization of Society*. Vol. 2: *Lifeworld and System: A Critique of Functionalist Reason*. (Trans. Thomas McCarthy.) Boston: Beacon Press, 1984, 1987.

Halpern, D. F. *Thought and Knowledge: An Introduction to Critical Thinking*. Hillsdale, N.J.: L. Erlbaum, 1984.

Hammerman, M. L. "Commonalities of Self-Directed Learning and Learning in Self-Help Groups." Unpublished doctoral dissertation, Northern Illinois University, 1989.

Hanson, N. R. "Reduction: Scientists Are Not Confined to the H-D Method." In L. Krimerman (ed.), *Nature and Scope of Social Science*. New York: Appleton-Century-Crofts, 1981.

Hart, M. "Consciousness Raising." In Jack Mezirow and Associates (eds.), *Fostering Critical Reflection in Adulthood: A Guide to Transformative and Emancipatory Learning*. San Francisco: Jossey-Bass, 1990a.

Hart, M. "Critical Theory and Beyond: Further Perspectives on Emancipatory Education." *Adult Education Quarterly*, 1990b, *40*, 125–138.

Hattiangadi, J. N. *How Is Language Possible?* La Salle, Ill.: Open Court, 1987.

Heaney, T., and Horton, A. "Reflective Engagement for Social Change." In J. Mezirow and Associates (eds.), *Fostering Critical Reflection in Adulthood: A Guide to Transformative and Emancipatory Learning*. San Francisco: Jossey-Bass, 1990.

Henry, J. N. "Development and Learning for Transformation: A Model Linking Lifelong Learning and Transpersonal Psychology." Unpublished doctoral dissertation, University of Georgia, 1988.

Heron, J. "Validity in Cooperative Inquiry." In P. Reason (ed.), *Human Inquiry in Action: Developments in New Paradigm Research*. London: Sage, 1988.

Horton, M., with J. and H. Kohl. *The Long Haul: An Autobiography*. New York: Doubleday, 1990.

Hough, P. T. "An Investigation of Critical Self-Reflective Learning Among Members of Alcoholics Anonymous." Unpublished doctoral dissertation, Teachers College, Columbia University, 1990.

Hultsch, D., and Pentz, C. "Research in Adult Learning and Memory: Retrospect and Prospect." *Contemporary Educational Psychology*, 1980, *5*, 298–320.

Hunter, E. K. "Perspective Transformation in Health Practices: A Study in Adult Learning and Fundamental Life Change." Unpublished doctoral dissertation, University of California, Los Angeles, 1980.

Janis, I. L. *Groupthink: Psychological Studies of Policy Decisions and Fiascoes.* (2nd ed., rev.) Boston: Houghton Mifflin, 1983.

Jarvis, P. *Adult Learning in the Social Context.* London: Croom Helm, 1987.

Johnson-Laird, P. "How Is Meaning Mentally Represented?" In U. Eco, M. Santambrogio, and P. Violi (eds.), *Meaning and Mental Representations.* Bloomington: Indiana University Press, 1988.

Kagan, J. "Perspectives on Continuity." In G. Brim and J. Kagan (eds.), *Constancy and Change in Human Development.* Cambridge, Mass.: Harvard University Press, 1980.

Keane, R. "The Experience of Doubt and Associated Learning in Religious Men." Unpublished doctoral dissertation, University of Toronto, 1985.

Kelly, G. A. *The Psychology of Personal Constructs.* (Vols. 1 and 2) New York: Norton, 1963.

Kieffer, C. H. "The Emergence of Empowerment: The Development of Participatory Competence Among Individuals in Citizen Organizations." Unpublished doctoral dissertation, University of Michigan, 1981.

Kisiel, T. "Paradigms." In G. Eloistad (ed.), *Contemporary Philosophy: A New Survey.* The Hague: Martinus Nijhoff, 1982.

Kitchener, K. S. "Educational Goals and Reflective Thinking." *The Educational Forum*, Fall, 1983.

Kitchener, K. S., and King, P. "The Reflective Judgment Model: Transforming Assumptions About Knowing." In J. Mezirow and Associates (eds.), *Fostering Critical Reflection in Adulthood: A Guide to Transformative and Emancipatory Learning.* San Francisco: Jossey-Bass, 1990.

Klein, D. B. *The Concept of Consciousness: A Survey.* Lincoln: University of Nebraska, 1984.

Knowles, M. *Self-Directed Learning: A Guide for Learners and Teachers.* New York: Cambridge Books, 1975.

Knox, A. B. *Adult Development and Learning.* San Francisco: Jossey-Bass, 1977.

Kolb, D. A. *Experiential Learning: Experience as a Source of Learning and Development.* Englewood Cliffs, N.J.: Prentice-Hall, 1984.

Kuhn, D. "On the Dual Executive and Its Significance in Developmental Psychology." In D. Kuhn and I. A. Meacham (eds.), *On the Development of Developmental Psychology.* Basel: Karger, 1983.

Kuhn, T. S. *The Structure of Scientific Revolutions.* Chicago: University of Chicago Press, 1962.

Labouvie-Vief, G. "Logic and Self-Regulation from Youth to Maturity: A Model." In M. Commons, F. A. Richards, and C. Armon (eds.), *Beyond Formal Operations: Late Adolescent and Adult Cognitive Development.* New York: Praeger, 1984.

Labouvie-Vief, G., and Blanchard-Fields, F. "Cognitive Ageing and Psychological Growth." *Ageing and Society,* Vol. 2, Part 2. Cambridge: Cambridge University Press, 1982.

Lakoff, G. "Cognitive Semantics." In U. Eco, M. Santambrogio, and P. Violi (eds.), *Meaning and Mental Representations.* Bloomington: Indiana University Press, 1988.

Lakoff, G., and Johnson, M. *Metaphors We Live By.* Chicago: University of Chicago Press, 1980.

Langer, E. J. *Mindfulness.* Reading, Mass.: Addison-Wesley, 1989.

Lichtman, R. "The Illusion of Maturation in an Age of Decline." In J. Broughton (ed.), *Critical Theories of Psychological Development.* New York: Plenum Press, 1987.

Loder, J. I. *The Transforming Moment: Understanding Convictional Experiences.* San Francisco: Harper & Row, 1981.

Long, H. B. *Adult Learning: Research and Practice.* New York: Cambridge Books, 1983.

Lovett, T., Clark, C., and Kilmurray, A. *Adult Education and Community Action.* London: Croom Helm, 1983.

McCarthy, T. "On Misunderstanding 'Understanding.'" *Theory and Decision,* 1973, *3,* 351–370.

Marsick, V. (ed.), *Learning in the Workplace.* London: Croom Helm, 1987.

Martin, J. E. *Second Chance; Women Returning to Study.* New York: Viking Penguin, 1988.

May, E. R. *"Lessons" of the Past: The Use and Misuse of History in American Foreign Policy.* London: Oxford University Press, 1973.

May, R. "Gregory Bateson and Humanistic Psychology." *Journal of Humanistic Psychology,* 1976, *16,* 33–51.

Mezirow, J. *Education for Perspective Transformation: Women's Reentry Programs in Community Colleges.* New York: Center for Adult Education, Teachers College, Columbia University, 1975.

Mezirow, J. "Perspective Transformation." *Adult Education,* 1978, *28,* 100–110.

Mezirow, J. "A Critical Theory of Adult Learning and Education." *Adult Education,* 1981, *32,* 3–24.

Mezirow, J., and Associates. *Fostering Critical Reflection in Adulthood: A Guide to Transformative and Emancipatory Learning.* San Francisco: Jossey-Bass, 1990.

Mills, C. W. *The Sociological Imagination.* New York: Grove Press, 1961.

Mines, R. A., and Kitchener, K. S. *Adult Cognitive Development: Methods and Models.* New York: Praeger, 1986.

Morgan, J. H. "Displaced Homemaker Programs: The Transition from Homemaker to Independent Person." Unpublished doctoral dissertation, Teachers College, Columbia University, 1987.

Mullins, P. "Cognitive Development in the Introductory Course: The Pedagogue's Typological Imagination." *Teaching Learning Issues,* 1988, *62.*

Musgrove, F. *Margins of the Mind.* London: Methuen, 1977.

Nisbet, R., and Ross, L. *Human Inference: Strategies and Shortcomings of Social Judgment.* Englewood Cliffs, N.J.: Prentice-Hall, 1980.

O'Neill, N., and O'Neill, G. *Shifting Gears.* New York: Avon, 1978.

Parsons, A. S. "The Conventions of the Senses: The Linguistic and Phenomenological Contributions to a Theory of Culture." *Human Studies,* 1988, *2,* 3–41.

Peck, M. S. *The Different Drum: Community Making and Peace.* New York: Simon & Schuster, 1987.

Perry, W. G. *Forms of Intellectual and Ethical Development in the College Years: A Scheme.* New York: Holt, Rinehart & Winston, 1970.

Piaget, J. *Six Psychological Studies.* New York: Random House, 1967.

Polanyi, M. *The Tacit Dimension.* Garden City, N.Y.: Doubleday, 1967.

Preciphs, T. K. "Understanding Adult Learning for Social Action in a Volunteer Setting." Unpublished doctoral dissertation, Teachers College, Columbia University, 1989.

Reddy, M. J. "The Conduit Metaphor—A Case of Frame Conflict in Our Language About Language." In A. Ortoni (ed.), *Metaphor and Thought.* Cambridge: Cambridge University Press, 1979.

Rogers, M. "The Topic of Power." *Human Studies,* 1982, *5,* 183–194.

Rosenfield, I. *The Invention of Memory: New View of the Brain.* New York: Basic Books, 1988.

Roth, I. "Challenging Habits of Expectation." In J. Mezirow and Associates, *Fostering Critical Reflection in Adulthood.* San Francisco: Jossey-Bass, 1990.

Schlossberg, N. K. *Counseling Adults in Transition.* New York: Springer, 1984.

Schön, D. A. "Generative Metaphor: A Perspective on Problem-Setting in Social Policy." In A. Ortony (ed.), *Metaphor and Thought.* Cambridge: Cambridge University Press, 1979.

Schön, D. A. *The Reflective Practitioner: How Professionals Think in Action.* New York: Basic Books, 1983.

Shainberg, D. *"The Transforming Self": New Dimensions in Psychoanalytic Process.* New York: Intercontinental Medical Book Corp., 1973.

Shapiro, D. *Psychotherapy of Neurotic Character.* New York: Basic Books, 1989.

Shapiro, M. J. *Language and Political Understanding.* New Haven: Yale University Press, 1981.

Sherman, E. *Meaning in Mid-life Transitions.* Albany: State University of New York Press, 1987.

Singer, E. "Identity vs. Identification: A Thorny Psychological Issue." *Review of Existential Psychology and Psychiatry,* 1965, *5,* 160–175.

Sinnott, W. E. "Meanings of 'Paradigm' as Ways of Understanding Adult Education: An Interpretative Excursion Through the Literature." Unpublished study, St. Francis Xavier University, Antigonish, Nova Scotia, 1986.

Skinner, B. F. "B. F. Skinner Insists It's Just Mind Over Matter," *New York Times,* Sept. 13, 1987.

Sloan, T. S. *Deciding: Self-Deception in Life Choices.* New York: Methuen, 1986.

Sowell, T. *A Conflict of Visions.* New York: Morrow, 1986.

Suanmali, C. "The Core Concepts of Andragogy." Unpublished doctoral dissertation, Teachers College, Columbia University, 1981.

Sztompka, P. *System and Function.* New York: Academic Press, 1974.

Taylor, J. A. *Transformative Learning: Becoming Aware of Possible Worlds.* Unpublished Master of Arts thesis, University of British Columbia, 1989.

Tennant, M. *Psychology and Adult Learning.* London: Routledge, 1988.

Tulvig, E. "Remembering and Knowing the Past." *American Scientist,* 1989, *77,* 361–367.

Turner, V. W. *The Ritual Process.* Harmondsworth, England: Penguin Books, 1974.

Wertsch, J. (ed). *The Concept of Activity in Soviet Psychology.* Armonk, N.Y.: M. E. Sharpe, 1979.

Wildemeersch, D., and Leirman, W. "The Facilitation of the Life-World Transformation." *Adult Education Quarterly,* 1988, *39,* 19–30.

Williams, G. H. "Perspective Transformation as an Adult Learning Theory to Explain and Facilitate Change in Male Spouse Abusers." Unpublished doctoral dissertation, Northern Illinois University, 1986.

Winter, R. *Learning from Experience: Principles and Practices in Action Research.* London: Falmer Press, 1989.

Wittgenstein, L. *Philosophical Investigations.* (3rd ed.) (Trans. G. E. M. Anscombe.) New York: Macmillan, 1958.

Wolff, J. "Hermeneutics and the Critique of Ideology." *The Sociological Review*, 1975, *23*, 811–828.

Young, L. M. "Postpartum Programs: Mothers' Concerns, Learnings and Perceived Effects." Unpublished doctoral dissertation, University of Toronto, 1988.

Yussen, S. R. (ed.). *The Growth of Reflection in Children.* Orlando, Fla.: Academic Press, 1985.

Zaner, R. M. *The Context of Self.* Athens: Ohio University Press, 1981.

✎ Index

A

Abrego, P. J., 157–158
Action: communicative, 65–66, 69–72, 75; critical self-reflective, 110; habitual, 106, 114; non-reflective, 106–108; and praxis, 12; reflective, 108–110; social, 209–212; thoughtful, 106, 107; and transformative learning, 209
Action research, 222–223
Adult development: and dialectical thinking, 152–155; and learning, 7; and perspective transformation, 150–160; process, 151–152. *See also* Development
Adult education: and andragogy, 199–201; ethical considerations, 201–206; ideal learning conditions, 198–199; philosophy, 198–201; and social action, 209–211; social goals vs. personal development, 208–209; and transformation, 202–203. *See also* Education
Adult education programs: communicative learning, 214–215; evaluation, 219–221; needs/interests assessment, 216–217
Adult learning: forms, 93–94; multidimensionality, 89; nature,

89–96; and presuppositions, 5; and self-deception, 19. *See also* Adult learning theory; Learning
Adult learning theory: associative bond, 8; Bateson's, 89–91; Cell's, 91–93; contextual, 9–10; and Habermas, 64–69; and information processing model, 8–9; Kolb's experiential, 103; Popper's, 38–41; and reflection, 103–104; transformative, 4–7. *See also* Learning; Learning theory
Aging, 159–160
Andragogy, 199–201
Angeles, P. A., 119
Argumentation, 68
Arlin, P., 155
Armon, C., 155
Associative bond theory, 8
Assumptions, 133. *See also* Presuppositions
Availability heuristic, 120

B

Barer-Stein, T., 83–84
Basseches, M., 110, 152–154, 155
Bateson, G., 47, 48, 89–91, 93
Becker, E., 51
Bee, H. L., 151
Berardo, F. M., 185
Berger, P., 58, 131, 175

239

240

Berkson, W., 39, 41, 93
Bernstein, R. J., 66
Blanchard-Fields, F., 151, 159
Blumer, H., 14
Boud, D., 101, 185
Bowers, C. A., 1–2, 3, 57, 69
Boyd, R. D., 14, 16, 143, 166, 167
Bracketing, 149
Brammer, L. M., 157–158
Bridges, W., 185
Brookfield, S., 105, 196
Brooks, A. K., 180–181
Broughton, J., 108, 155
Bruner, J., 112, 146–148
Buck-Morss, S., 148

C

Candy, P. C., 221
Carr, W., 222
Cell, E., 56, 89, 91–93, 103, 104
Clark, C., 210
Clark, L. F., 48, 111
Clark, M. C., 206
Cognitive style dimensions, 128–129
Collard, S., 206
Commission of Professions of Adult
Education, 199
Commons, R., 155
Communication: defined, 75–76;
and metaphors, 82
Communicative action: defined, 75;
dynamics, 69–72; and learning,
70–71; and lifeworld, 69–70; and
social interaction, 71–72; and va-
lidity testing, 65–66
Communicative competence, 68–69
Communicative learning: and con-
sensual validation, 75–77; vs. instrumental learning, 79–80; and
learning through metaphors,
80–82; and metaphorical-
abductive logic, 85–85; and rationality, 78–79; research, 85–86;
and unknown, 82
Competence motivation, 162
Comprehension: and analysis,
25–26; extrinsic theory, 23–24;
and meaning construal, 24–25;
and rationality, 25–26; and sym-

bolic models, 20–23; and trans-
formative logic, 26–27
Conation, 14
Conscientization, 136–137
Consciousness: defined, 22; levels,
135–137; precognitive perceptual,
148
Consciousness raising: elements,
186; and group homogeneity,
187; group phases, 187; and ob-
jectivity, 186–187
Consensual validation, 76–77
Constrained/unconstrained visions of
society, 137
Constructs, 52. See also Personal constructs
Content reflection, 107
Contextual theories, 9–10
Critical inquiry, 101–102
Critical reflection: and decentration,
147; and early development,
145–150; and emancipatory
learning, 87–88; group, 190–191;
and social movements, 188; in
workplace, 180–181. See also
Reflection
Cultural grammars, 18
Culture: constrained/unconstrained
visions, 137–138; and language,
57–59, 147; and self-
consciousness, 147; of silence,
136; and symbolic models, 23;
and transformative thought, 3

D

Daloz, L., 129–130
Daniels, M., 184
Danto, A., 99
Darwin, C., 28
Decentration, 147–148
Development: conceptual, 146–147;
and culture, 147; intellectual,
146; and orthogenesis, 163–164;
and perspective transformation,
155–156. See also Adult development
Dewey, J., 10, 37, 73, 100–102,
104, 123, 127
Dialectic-presuppositional logic, 110
Dialectical thinking: Basseches's

reflection, 111; and psychological problems, 204–206; and rationality, 67–69; as rebirth, 158–159; readiness, 217–218; research, 221–223; sociolinguistic context, 64–69; Taylor's model, 172–174; and validity testing, 65–67. *See also* Adult education; Perspective transformation
Transformative logic, 26–27, 163–164
Transsituational learning, 92
Tulvig, E., 30, 160
Turner, V., 175

U

Unknown: and communicative learning, 82–84; and imagination, 83; model for experiencing (Barer-Stein), 83–84

V

Validity: claims, 68; criteria, 66
Validity testing: and consensual vali-

dation, 76; and communicative learning, 76; and Habermas, 65–67; and rational discourse, 77; and reflection, 101; and transformative learning, 65–67

W

Walker, D., 101
Wertsch, J., 13, 19
Wettersten, J., 39, 41, 93
Wildemeersch, D., 161–162, 164
Williams, G. H., 169
Wilson, A. L., 206
Wittgenstein, L., 54, 56
Wolff, J., 83

Y

Young, L. M., 182
Yussen, S. R., 112, 114, 116

Z

Zaner, R. M., 16